Contents

List of Illustrative Material

CHECKLISTS

FIGURES

PRACTICAL ACTIVITIES

TABLES

Acknowledgements

Many people have made helpful comments and suggestions in the course of preparing this book. We would like to thank all our colleagues, in particular, Kate Ashcroft, Simon Catling, Nick Clough, Richard Eke, Tony Ghaye, John Isaac, John Lee, Pam Sammons, Hugh Starkey and Rob Withers. We would also like to thank our editors, Juliet Wight-Boycott and Sandra Margolies, and two helpful but anonymous readers. Our students (particularly Jemma Rowe, Lyndsey Reeves and Mandy Reid) are to be thanked for trying out many of the activities contained in the book. Last, but not least, we gratefully acknowledge the support of our families, Ros, Ben, Amy, Ben and Joe.

Finally, we also thank the following authors and publishers for permission to reproduce previously published materials:

Robin J. Alexander for Table 6.2, from *Primary Teaching* (1984), London: Holt, Rinehart & Winston.

Barry Fraser and Darrell Fisher for the short form of 'My Class Inventory', from their *Assessment of Classroom Psychological Environment: Workshop Manual* (1983), Bentley: Western Australian Institute of Technology.

Croom Helm Ltd and Patrick Easen for material from his *Making School-Centred INSET Work* (1983), London: Croom Helm.

The Royal Society and the Institute of Mathematics and Its Applications for their policy document *Girls and Mathematics* (1986).

Hodder & Stoughton Ltd for material from I. A. Rodger and J. A. S. Richardson, *Self-Evaluation for Primary Schools* (1985).

Inner London Education Authority, for the 'Me at School' form designed by members of the Junior School Project team based at the Research and Statistics Branch.

Tony Ghaye for Figure 10.1, redrawn from 'Discovering Classroom Underlife', a paper presented to the 1984 Classroom Action Research Conference, Cambridge Institute of Education.

Preface

This book has been designed to support both teachers who wish to enquire into their own practice and students who are on enquiry-based courses using a 'reflective teacher' model. The book makes considerable use of self-evaluation and action–research approaches which represent particular ways of conceptualizing the relationship between theory and practice. Both of these approaches have become more prominent in professional development in recent years and are already well established on courses in Australia, the United States, Europe and in other parts of the world. In the current British context, they can be seen as an alternative to the application of externally devised procedures for 'teacher appraisal'.

We hope that as new teacher-education courses are designed and old ones restructured, the model may also provide an opportunity for introducing a new and collaborative relationship between 'education' and 'professional' staff within teacher-education institutions.

We also hope that the approach has its own integrity in terms of encouraging the development of both socially aware and professionally competent teachers. Such teachers would not only be able to adapt flexibly to future social and educational circumstances, but also feel able to contribute to bringing about changes.

Finally, we note that the notion of 'reflective teaching' implies that readers will interact with the ideas put forward in this book—will reflect on, revise and perhaps reject those ideas as they 'make them their own'. We hope that our readers will constantly question and refine educational issues, and we would be very interested to receive comments, criticisms and suggestions.

Andrew Pollard, Bristol Polytechnic
Sarah Tann, Oxford Polytechnic
January 1987

Introduction

The main aim of this book is to support student teachers and teachers who wish to reflect upon their teaching in a systematic fashion. We hope that this process will lead them to share their experiences in positive ways with their colleagues. Such reflection and sharing could help to account for achievements, to analyse anxieties and to identify areas for future development.

The book is designed as a handbook which can be easily dipped into and from which ideas can be taken and developed. Selected issues, particular procedures and related activities, are set out so that analysis and practical suggestions are readily accessible. Each chapter also contains a section of 'Notes for Further Reading', annotated lists of particular books which we would recommend to readers to extend their study of certain issues and procedures and to provide greater detail than a book of this nature can possibly manage.

However, this book is intended to be more than a practical guide to self-evaluation of classroom practice. We have set the analysis and activities within a theoretical framework which attempts to link classroom practice and educational theory with current educational, political and social debates. Thus, this book offers a broad context—the context of the 'extended professional'—within which to reflect upon teaching.

When we initially approached the writing of this book, we fully recognized that all forms of action inevitably involve people in making judgements based on values and commitments—and this is certainly true for teachers. We therefore wanted to produce a framework which recognized the necessity of professional judgements by individual teachers and yet was also informed by a set of value-commitments that would command widespread support in moral and ethical terms.

We considered many of the documents which have flowed from the DES and HMI in recent years, reflecting wide-ranging concerns about the quality of educational provision. However, at a more fundamental level, we felt a particular need to emphasize the links between education, human rights and democracy. In this respect one can learn a great deal from looking at the Universal Declaration on Human Rights and the European Convention on Human Rights, which were both developed in the post-war years. More recently, there has been a specific educational Recommendation from the Council of Europe's Committee of Ministers, entitled 'Teaching and Learning about Human Rights in School' (Council of Europe 1985), to which Great Britain is a signatory. It is worth citing some parts of this document here.

There are two statements on the curriculum:

> The understanding and experience of human rights is an important element of the preparation of all young people for life in a democratic and pluralistic society. It is a part of social and political education, and it involves intercultural and international understanding.
>
> (1.1)

Concepts associated with human rights can, and should, be acquired from an early stage. For example, the non-violent resolution of conflict and respect for other people can already be experienced within the life of a pre-school or primary class.

(1.2)

In terms of both knowledge to be acquired and the climate within schools in which such work should take place, it is stated:

The study of human rights in schools should lead to an understanding of, and sympathy for, the concepts of justice, equality, freedom, peace, dignity, rights and democracy. Such understanding should be both cognitive and based on experience and feelings. Schools should thus provide opportunities for pupils to experience affective involvement in human rights and to express their feelings through drama, art, music, creative writing and audio-visual media.

(3.3)

Democracy is best learned in a democratic setting where participation is encouraged, where views can be expressed openly and discussed, where there is freedom of expression for pupils and teachers, and where there is fairness and justice. An appropriate climate is, therefore, an essential complement to effective learning about human rights.

(4.1)

For teacher education, the task is also spelt out clearly:

The initial training of teachers should prepare them for their future contribution to teaching about human rights in their schools. For example, future teachers should:

(i) be encouraged to take an interest in national and world affairs;
(ii) be taught to identify and combat all forms of discrimination in schools and society and be encouraged to confront and overcome their own prejudices.

(5.1)

These are challenging ideas, but ones which have to be faced if we are to provide the best possible quality of education for all the children in our society. The work of a professional educator thus involves a heavy degree of social responsibility. We hope that this book will help its readers to reflect on these concerns, as well as to improve their 'practice' more generally.

This book has three parts. Part 1 is entitled 'Becoming a Reflective Teacher'. It offers a theoretical rationale for the approach (Chapter 1) and provides an analysis of the relationship between individuals, education and society (Chapter 2). It concludes with a review and examination of ways of investigating classrooms (Chapter 3).

Part 2, 'Being a Reflective Teacher', represents the classroom-focused, practical core of the book. Each chapter is devoted to a particular aspect of the teaching–learning process. Each has the same structure: a significant issue is discussed, practical activities for classroom investigation are presented, follow-up points are suggested and guidance for further reading is given.

The issues selected in Part 2 are ones which are basic to classroom life—examining ourselves, our values, aims and commitments (Chapter 4); classroom relationships (Chapter 5); planning what to teach, choosing curriculum aims and objectives (Chapter 6); how to organize a classroom (Chapter 7); classroom management (Chapter 8); communication skills (Chapter 9); and learning processes, social consequences and classroom policies (Chapter 10).

Part 3 looks 'Beyond Classroom Reflection' to consider reflective teaching and innovation in schools as a whole (Chapter 11). In this part, the place and responsibilities of reflective primary-school teachers in society (Chapter 12) are also reconsidered.

Part 1

Becoming a Reflective Teacher

Chapter 1

Reflective Teaching

INTRODUCTION

1 THE NEED FOR REFLECTIVE TEACHING

2 THE MEANING OF REFLECTIVE TEACHING

2.1 Reflective teaching implies an active concern with aims and consequences, as well as with means and technical efficiency.

2.2 Reflective teaching combines enquiry and implementation skills with attitudes of openmindedness, responsibility and wholeheartedness.

2.3 Reflective teaching is applied in a cyclical or spiralling process in which teachers continually monitor, evaluate and revise their own practice.

2.4 Reflective teaching is based on teacher judgement, informed partly by self-reflection and partly by insights from educational disciplines.

INTRODUCTION

The complicated nature of educational issues and practical classroom teaching ensures that a teacher's work is never finished. When practicalities, personal ideals and wider educational concerns are considered together, the job of reconciling the numerous demands and possible conflicts often seems to be overwhelming. As an infant teacher explained to us recently:

> I love my work, but it's a constant struggle to keep it all going. If I focus on one thing, I have to neglect another. For instance, if I talk to a group or to a particular child, then I have to keep an eye on what the others are doing; if I hear someone read, then I can't help with maths problems or be in a position to extend other children's language when opportunities arise; if I put out clay, then I haven't got room for painting; if I get a lot of creative writing going, then I can't also concentrate on maths; if I go to evening courses, then I can't prepare as well for the next day; if I spend time with my family, then I worry about my class; but if I rush around collecting materials or something, then I feel guilty for neglecting the family. It's not easy . . . but I wouldn't do any thing else.

Such dilemmas are frequently expressed, not only by experienced teachers, but even more by student teachers.

This book is intended to provide a practical guide to some ways of reflecting on and resolving such issues. It suggests that a combination of the practitioner's professional judgement and the use of social scientific methods can help in tackling such dilemmas. The book is based on the belief that collaboration is necessary between teachers and other educationalists so that theory and practice develop from and with each other. We would argue that the separation of academic and practical spheres of activity, which has existed for many years, has been wasteful and has resulted in many lost opportunities to improve the quality of educational provision and practice.

Furthermore, we believe that there has been a tendency to separate both theory and practice from questions of values, aims and commitments. A consequence of this can sometimes be that, as teachers, we may not always consider the assumptions underlying our professional practice. Neither do we always consider possible long-term, as well as short-term, consequences of our actions. These consequences may be of a personal nature, for example, the effects of classroom events on a child's self-image. They may be of an academic nature, for example, a child's intellectual achievement. Finally, they may be of a social nature, for example, the cumulative effects of school experience on a child's life chances.

1 THE NEED FOR REFLECTIVE TEACHING

Every day teachers are faced with dilemmas which have to be resolved, sometimes at great speed. These have been analysed by Berlak and Berlak (1981) and the framework which they developed is a simple but very powerful one. The importance of their analysis derives from the fact that, although they studied only three schools in detail— one infant, one junior and one primary—they took great care to relate their analysis of the dilemmas which arose in the 'micro' world of the classroom to major factors, beliefs and influences in society as a whole. Such 'macro' factors, they argued, influence, structure and constrain the actions of teachers, children and parents. However, they do so in ways which are inconsistent, because of existing complexities and contradictions, hence the dilemmas which have to be faced. Their resolution calls for teachers to use their professional judgement to assess the most appropriate course of action in any particular situation. But what are the major dilemmas which have to be faced? Table 1.1 presents our version of some of them.

The reader will immediately have realized that these dilemmas, rather than express-ing simple options, call for judgements, with purposes and aims being borne very much in mind. In fact, they call for a reflective approach to teaching.

2 THE MEANING OF REFLECTIVE TEACHING

The notion of reflective teaching, around which this book is based, stems from Dewey (1933), who contrasted 'routine action' with 'reflective action'. According to Dewey, routine action is guided by factors such as tradition, habit and authority and by institutional definitions and expectations. By implication, it is relatively static and is thus unresponsive to changing priorities and circumstances. Reflective action, on the other hand, involves a willingness to engage in constant self-appraisal and develop-ment. Among other things, it implies flexibility, rigorous analysis and social awareness.

Dewey's notion of reflective action, when developed and applied to teaching, is very challenging. In this section, we review its implications by identifying and discussing what we take to be four essential characteristics. These are:

1. Reflective teaching implies an active concern with aims and consequences, as well as with means and technical efficiency.

2. Reflective teaching combines enquiry and implementation skills with attitudes of openmindedness, responsibility and wholeheartedness.

Table 1.1 *Common dilemmas faced by teachers*

Treating each child as a 'whole person'	Treating each child primarily as a 'pupil'
Organizing the children on an individual basis	Organizing the children as a class
Giving children a degree of control over their use of time, their activities and their work standards	Tightening control over children's use of time, their activities and their work standards
Seeking to motivate the children through intrinsic involvement and enjoyment of activities	Offering reasons and rewards so that children are extrinsically motivated to tackle tasks
Developing and negotiating the curriculum from an appreciation of children's interests	Providing a curriculum which children are deemed to need and which 'society' expects them to receive
Attempting to integrate various elements of the curriculum	Dealing systematically with each discrete area of the curriculum
Aiming for quality in school-work	Aiming for quantity in school-work
Focusing on basic skills or on cognitive development	Focusing on expressive or creative areas of the curriculum
Trying to build up cooperative and social skills	Developing self-reliance and self-confidence in individuals
Inducting the children into a common culture	Accepting the variety of cultures in a multi-ethnic society
Allocating teacher time, attention and resources equally among all the children	Paying attention to the special needs of particular children
Maintaining consistent rules and understandings about behaviour and school-work	Being flexible and responsive to particular situations
Presenting oneself formally to the children	Relaxing with the children or having a laugh with them
Working with 'professional' application and care for the children	Working with consideration of one's personal needs

3. Reflective teaching is applied in a cyclical or spiralling process, in which teachers continually monitor, evaluate and revise their own practice.

4. Reflective teaching is based on teacher judgement, informed partly by self-reflection and partly by insights from educational disciplines.

A reflective teacher, therefore, is one who constantly questions his or her own aims and actions, monitors practice and outcomes, and considers the short-term and long-term effects upon each child.

Each of these four characteristics will now be considered more fully.

2.1 Reflective teaching implies an active concern with aims and consequences, as well as with means and technical efficiency.

During the 1960s and the early 1970s, classroom practice in primary schools was guided by a particular philosophy of 'child-centredness', which embraced a specific set of generalized aims and attitudes. This philosophy has a long history, but in the post-war years it drew particular support from the work of child psychologists, such as Piaget (1926, 1950) and received official legitimation in the Plowden Report (Central Advisory Council on Education 1967). There appeared to be a broad consensus about the nature of 'good practice' in primary schools. However, child-centredness has been the subject of much criticism in more recent years. For instance, it has been accused of preventing rigorous thinking about the curriculum and of providing a relatively closed system of professional beliefs—an 'ideology'.

Whatever view is taken on this last issue, the fact remains that the broad consensus on the characteristics of 'good practice', which appeared to exist briefly, has now been shattered. Where there once seemed to be 'answers', there are now 'issues to debate' and many competing opinions.

This raises the questions of aims and values, on which a philosopher, John White, has proposed some challenging views (White 1978). White starts from the seemingly uncontroversial argument that, in a democratic society, decisions about the aims of education should be 'democratically' determined. As a corollary, he suggests that teachers should see themselves as 'interpreters' of political policy. It is this corollary which has important and radical implications for teachers.

Such a stance is very different from the idea of the autonomous professional with which many teachers have traditionally identified. Yet it can be argued that the existence of such autonomy is reasonable and practical only if ends, aims and values are thought to be shared in some sort of social consensus. Obviously, in such circumstances, judgements about the technical effectiveness of various types of teaching would best be derived from the educator on the spot. However, as soon as questions about educational aims and social values are seriously raised, then the position changes. The debate, therefore, quickly, and appropriately, extends to the political domain.

This does not mean that teachers, even as interpreters of policy, should simply 'stand by' in the procedure, for there are two important roles which they can play. In the first case, an appropriate metaphor for the teacher's role is, as White suggested, that of 'activist'. This suggests that primary school teachers are individual members of society who, within normal political processes, have the right to pursue their values and beliefs as guided by their own individual moral and ethical concerns. They should thus be active in contributing to the formation of public policy. Second, in their role as professionals, teachers must accept a responsibility for translating politically determined aims into practice. Further, having a genuine sense of professional responsibility means that teachers should be far from passive in this process. They should speak out if they view particular aims and policies as being impracticable, educationally unsound or morally questionable. In such circumstances, the professional skills, knowledge and judgements of teachers should be brought to bear on policy-makers directly. Hence, the reflective teacher should acknowledge the political process and be willing to contribute to it both as a citizen and as a professional.

In all of this there is an implicit and positive assumption that teachers are willing and able to consider aims, values and social consequences and to contribute to the formation of policy, whether it be at the classroom, school, local or national level. This will only be possible if teachers are reflective about what education is all about and what is worthwhile. Thus reflective teaching implies very serious consideration of ends as well as means. This is an issue which we feel has been relatively neglected in some teacher–education courses.

2.2 Reflective teaching combines enquiry and implementation skills with attitudes of openmindedness, responsibility and wholeheartedness.

This element of reflective teaching brings the focus on to skills and attitudes rather than aims, but the issues are closely related. In the first place, we would emphasize that reflective teaching requires a wide range of skills. These are necessary for teachers to be effective and they can be applied at several levels of activity. We will identify six types of skill, each of which contributes to a cyclical process of reflection (see section 2.3). Although it would be possible to begin at any point in the cycle, for convenience, the cycle will begin with the preliminary collection of information, analysis and initial evaluation. These preliminaries must take place before the first stage of planning. This is followed by action and further evaluation and reflection, which is then communicated and shared, before the whole cycle begins again at a more refined level.

Empirical skills. These relate to the essential issue of knowing what is going on in a classroom or school. They are concerned with collecting data and with describing situations, processes, causes and effects with care and accuracy. Two sorts of data are particularly relevant. Objective data—such as what people actually do, their behaviour—are important; but so are subjective data, which describe how people feel and think—their perceptions. The collection of both types of data calls for considerable skill on the part of investigators, particularly when they may be enquiring into their own classroom practice.

Analytical skills. These skills are needed to interpret descriptive data. Such 'facts' are not meaningful until they are placed in a framework which enables a reflective teacher to relate them, one with the other, and to begin to theorize about them.

Evaluative skills. Evaluative skills are used to make judgements about the educational consequences of the results of the practical enquiry. Evaluation, in the light of aims and values, enables the results of an enquiry to be applied to future policy and practice.

Strategic skills. Strategic skills take us directly into the realm of planning for action and anticipating its implementation, following the analysis which a reflective teacher carries out. Whether action is at the level of the classroom, school or local authority, consideration of how it may best be carried forward is vital.

Practical skills. Here we are directly concerned with the skills which are involved in action itself. A reflective teacher is one who is able to link analysis and practice and ends and means to good effect. To be highly analytical but ineffectual in practical matters is not a satisfactory balance, any more than the reverse situation would be.

Communication skills. Communication skills are necessary because reflective teachers are concerned about aims and consequences as well as means. They are likely to need and to want to communicate and discuss their ideas extensively with others. They are likely to need to establish their legitimacy and to gain the support of others in the processes of development in which they engage. Thus, they should be effective communicators.

Such skills are not sufficient in themselves for a teacher who wishes to engage in reflective teaching. Certain attitudes are also necessary and must be integrated and applied with the skills indicated above. Three essential attitudes, which were identified by Dewey and have been discussed further by Zeichner (1981/2), are openmindedness, responsibility and wholeheartedness.

Openmindedness

As Dewey put it, openmindedness is an

> active desire to listen to more sides than one, to give heed to facts from whatever source they come, to give full attention to alternative possibilities, to recognise the possibility of error even in the beliefs which are dearest to us.
>
> (Dewey 1933, p. 29)

Openmindedness is an essential attribute for rigorous reflection because any sort of enquiry which is consciously based on partial evidence only weakens itself. Thus we use it in the sense of being willing to reflect upon ourselves and to challenge our assumptions, prejudices and ideologies, as well as those of others. However, to be openminded about evidence and its interpretation is not the same thing as declining to take up a value-position on important social and educational issues. This point brings us to the second attribute which Dewey saw as a prerequisite to reflective action, 'responsibility'.

Responsibility

Intellectual responsibility, according to Dewey, means

> to consider the consequences of a projected step; it means to be willing to adopt these consequences when they follow reasonably. . . . Intellectual responsibility secures integrity.
>
> (Dewey 1933, p. 30)

The position implied here is clearly related to the issue of aims which we discussed above. However, in Dewey's writing the issue is relatively clearly bounded and he seems to be referring to classroom teaching and to school practices only. Zeichner goes considerably further when, in considering teacher education, he points out that

> Because of the intimate relationships between the school and the social, political and economic contexts in which it exists, any consideration of the consequences to which classroom action leads must inevitably take one beyond the boundaries of the classroom and even of the school itself and beyond the consideration of educational principles alone. . . . An exclusive focus on the level of the classroom and on educational principles alone does not enable the student teacher to contemplate the kinds of basic structural changes that may be necessary for his or her responsibility to be fully exercised. The attention of student teachers remains focused on the amelioration of surface symptoms in individuals and not on an analysis of the social conditions that stand behind, and at least partially explain, the existence of those symptoms.
>
> (Zeichner 1981/2, pp. 6–7)

Here, Zeichner is asserting the inevitable consequence of relating means and ends in education with systematic openmindedness. Moral, ethical and political issues will be raised and must, he argues, be considered so that professional and personal judgements can be made about what is worth while. It clearly follows that an instrumental approach to teaching is not consistent with reflectiveness.

Wholeheartedness

'Wholeheartedness', the third of Dewey's necessary attitudes, refers essentially to the way in which such consideration takes place. Dewey's suggestion was that reflective teachers should be dedicated, single-minded, energetic and enthusiastic. As he put it,

> There is no greater enemy of effective thinking than divided interest. . . . A genuine enthusiasm is an attitude that operates as an intellectual force when a person is absorbed, . . . The subject carries him on.
>
> (Dewey 1933, p. 30)

Together, these three attitudes are vital ingredients of the 'professional' commitment which needs to be demonstrated by all those who aim to be reflective teachers.

2.3 Reflective teaching is applied in a cyclical or spiralling process in which teachers continually monitor, evaluate and revise their own practice.

This characteristic refers to the process of reflective teaching and provides the dynamic basis for teacher action. The conception of a classroom-based, reflexive process stems from the teacher-based, action–research movement of which Lawrence Stenhouse was a key figure. In 1975 he argued that teachers should act as 'researchers' of their own practice and should develop the curriculum through practical enquiry. Various alternative models have since become available (Kemmis and McTaggert 1981; Elliott 1981; Ebbutt 1983) and, although there are some significant differences between them, they all preserve a central concern with self-reflection.

Teachers are principally expected to plan, to make provision and to act. Reflective teachers also need to monitor, observe and collect data on their own and the children's intentions, actions and feelings. This evidence then needs to be critically analysed and evaluated so that it can be shared, judgements made and decisions taken. Finally, this may lead teachers to revise their classroom policies, plans and provision before beginning the process again. It is a dynamic process which is intended to lead through successive cycles, or through a spiralling process, towards higher-quality teaching. This model is simple, comprehensive and certainly could be an extremely powerful influence on practice. It is consistent with the notion of reflective teaching, as described by Dewey, and provides an essential clarification of the procedures for reflective teaching. Figure 1.1 represents the key stages of the reflective process.

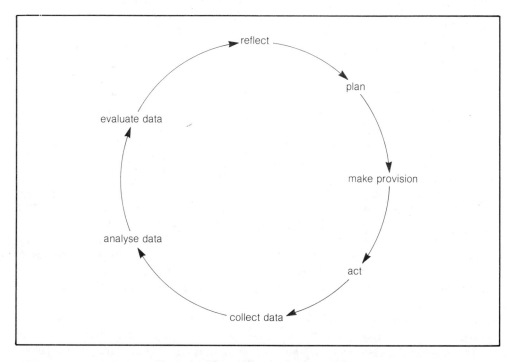

Figure 1.1 The process of reflective teaching

2.4 Reflective teaching is based on teacher judgement, informed partly by self-reflection and partly by insights from educational disciplines.

Bolster (1983) has provided an analysis of teachers as classroom decision-makers and concluded that teacher knowledge commonly has certain clearly defined negative characteristics. He suggests that it is particularistic in the sense that it is specific and pragmatic, and, as a corollary, it is resistant to change. Bolster argues that 'teacher knowledge' is based on individual experiences and is believed to be of value if it 'works' in practical situations. Therefore, since it 'works', there is little incentive to change, even in the light of evidence supporting alternative ideas or practices.

However, Bolster's position does not seem to recognize adequately the very real strengths of the knowledge which teachers can develop. For an alternative view it is possible to draw on Donald Schon's work (1983) on the characteristics of the 'reflective practitioner'.

Schon contrasts 'scientific' professional work, such as laboratory research, with 'caring' professional work, such as education. He calls the former 'high hard ground' and sees it as supported by quantitative and 'objective' evidence, whereas the 'swampy lowlands' of the caring professions involve more interpersonal areas and qualitative issues. These complex 'lowlands', according to Schon, tend to become 'confusing messes' of intuitive action. He suggests that, although these 'messes' tend to be highly relevant in practical terms, they are not easily amenable to rigorous analysis because they draw on a type of knowledge-in-action, that is, knowledge that is inherent in professional action. It is spontaneous, intuitive, tacit and intangible, but it 'works' in practice. Schon also argues that it is possible to recognize reflection-in-action, in which adjustments to action are made in the light of experience. As he puts it:

> When someone reflects-in-action, he becomes a researcher in the practice context. He is not dependent on the categories of established theory and technique, but constructs a new theory of the unique case. His enquiry is not limited to a deliberation about means which depends on a prior agreement about ends. He does not keep means and ends separate, but defines them interactively as he frames a problematic situation. He does not separate thinking from action. . . . His experimenting is a kind of action, implementation is built into his enquiry.
>
> (Schon 1983, p. 68)

While Schon's position has much to commend it, we would argue that it lacks balance. For instance, there is a great focus on 'unique cases', which can lead to isolationism. There is also much emphasis on constructing 'new theory', which can lead to failing to make use of existing research findings. It can also be argued that a consideration of wider social issues and of the need to generalize and form policies appears to be underplayed in Schon's work.

Rather than seeking to construct alternative modes of enquiry, we prefer to advocate attempts to maximize the potential for collaboration between teachers and researchers in relevant disciplines. For such collaboration to be successful, it must be based on a frank appreciation of each other's strengths and weaknesses. While recognizing the danger of unjustified generalization, we can identify these strengths and weaknesses (see Table 1.2).

We arrive, then, at a position which calls for attempts to draw on the strengths of teachers and researchers and by doing so to overcome the weaknesses which exist in both positions. This is what we mean by our statement of the fourth characteristic of reflective teaching: that it should be based on 'informed teacher judgement'. The collaborative endeavour which is implied here underpins the structure of each subsequent chapter of this book.

Table 1.2 *Comparison of researchers' and teachers' knowledge*

	Strengths	Weaknesses
Researchers' knowledge	Often based on careful research with large samples and reliable methods	Often uses jargon unnecessarily and communicates poorly
	Often provides a clear and incisive analysis when studied	Often seems obscure and difficult to relate to practical issues
	Often offers novel ways of looking at situations and issues	Often fragments educational processes and experiences
Teachers' knowledge	Often practically relevant and directly useful	Often impressionistic
	Often communicated effectively to practitioners	Often relies too much on situations which might be unique
	Often concerned with the wholeness of classroom processes and experiences	When analysing, is sometimes unduly influenced by existing assumptions

NOTES FOR FURTHER READING

The dilemmas in educational decision-making, which suggest that reflection is a continually necessary element of teaching, are analysed in:

Berlak, H. and Berlak, A. (1981) *Dilemmas of Schooling*. London: Methuen.

Two works by Dewey which have influenced our thinking are:

Dewey, J. (1916) *Democracy and Education*. New York: Free Press.
Dewey, J. (1933) *How We Think: A Restatement of the Relation of Reflective Thinking to the Educative Process*. Chicago: Henry Regnery.

The recent work of Zeichner on reflective teaching is also very stimulating. See, in particular:

Zeichner, K. (1981/2) Reflective teaching and field-based experience in pre-service teacher education, *Interchange*, **12**, 1–22.
Zeichner, K. (1986) Content and contexts: neglected elements in studies of student teaching as an occasion for learning to teach, *Journal of Education for Teaching*, **12** (1), 5–24.

On the potential gains which are claimed to derive from self-evaluation and classroom enquiry see:

Carr, W. and Kemmis, S. (1986) *Becoming Critical*. London: Falmer Press.
Elliott, J. (1980) The implications of classroom research for professional development, in Hoyle, E. and McGary, J. (eds.) *World Yearbook of Education*. London: Kogan Page.
Ruddock, J. and Hopkins, D. (1985) *Research as a Basis for Teaching*. London: Heinemann.
Stenhouse, L. (1983) *Authority, Education and Emancipation*. London: Heinemann.

For a range of views on the nature of professional knowledge and its relationship to more theoretical analyses see:

McNamara, D. and Desforges, C. (1978) The social sciences, teacher education and the objectification of craft knowledge, *British Journal of Teacher Education*, **4** (1), 17–36.
Schon, D. A. (1983) *The Reflective Practitioner*. London: Temple Smith.
Van Manen, M. (1977) Linking ways of knowing with ways of being practical, *Curriculum Inquiry*, **6**, 205–28.

For case studies of teachers' practical reasoning see:

Clandinin, D. J. (1986) *Classroom Practice: Teacher Images in Action*. London: Falmer Press.
Elbaz, F. (1983) *Teacher Thinking: A Study of Practical Knowledge*. London: Croom Helm.

Chapter 2

Social Contexts, Teachers and Children

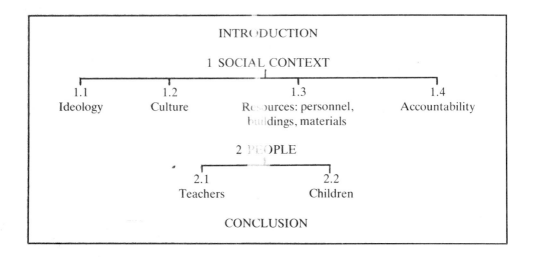

INTRODUCTION

1 SOCIAL CONTEXT

| 1.1 | 1.2 | 1.3 | 1.4 |
| Ideology | Culture | Resources: personnel, buildings, materials | Accountability |

2 PEOPLE

| 2.1 | 2.2 |
| Teachers | Children |

CONCLUSION

INTRODUCTION

This chapter is intended as an introduction and brief review of a wide-ranging set of social issues which are important for teachers in primary schools. It will provide a context and theoretical framework for the more specific factors regarding teaching and learning which will be considered in Part 2.

Figure 2.1 represents the way in which the relationships between these factors have been conceptualized in this book.

We would argue that social influences permeate everything that happens in schools and classrooms and, as we suggested in Chapter 1, awareness of such issues is an important contributing element of reflective teaching.

We begin this chapter by discussing the social context and by establishing a theoretical framework.

1 SOCIAL CONTEXT

A particular theoretical position underpins this chapter and, indeed, the book as a whole. At the core of this position is the concept of a dialectical relationship between society and individuals. This suggests the existence of a constant interplay of social forces and individual actions. On the one hand, the decisions and actions which people

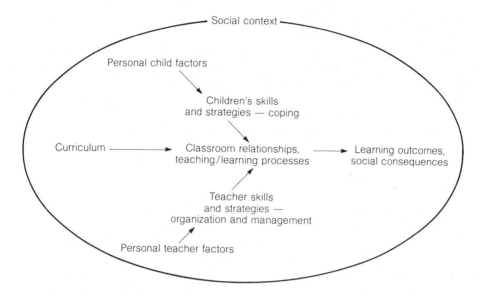

Figure 2.1 Factors in classroom teaching and learning

make and take in their lives are constrained by social structures and by the historical processes which brought about such structures. On the other hand, each individual has a unique sense of self, derived from his or her personal history or biography. Individuals have a degree of free will in acting and in developing understandings with others. Sets of these understandings, which endure over time, form the basis of cultures. Such understandings can also lead to challenges to established social structures and thus to future changes.

For example, there are differences between various social groups in terms of power, wealth, status and opportunities (Halsey 1986, Reid 1977). However, individuals, each with their own background and sense of self, will react to such factors in a variety of ways. Some in powerful positions might wish to close ranks and defend themselves by suggesting that their position is inherited by right or earned by merit. Some among those who are less fortunate may accept the social order or even aspire to success in its terms. Others may try to contest it, for, of course, to be able to question existing social arrangements is a fundamental right in our democratic societies.

There is, thus, an ebb and flow in social change, a process of tension and struggle. At opposite poles are action and constraint, voluntarism and determinism, biography and history.

We believe that a reflective teacher has responsibilities within this process which should not be avoided. With this in mind, we will now discuss four aspects of the social context which we feel are particularly significant for practice in primary schools: ideology, culture, resources and accountability. The influence of each can be traced at national, regional, local and school levels so that, although such issues sometimes seem distant, they affect children and teachers in classrooms in very real ways.

1.1 Ideology
A dictionary definition of ideology states that it means a 'way of thinking'. However, particular sets of ideas are often used, consciously or unconsciously, to promote and legitimize the interests of specific groups of people. Indeed, if a particular way of thinking about education is dominant at any point in time, it is likely to be an important

influence on teachers' actions. It would emphasize particular issues and frame the ways in which teachers might respond.

For instance, in the post-war years, and up to the early 1970s, there was a significant degree of consensus about the aims of State education—a prevailing ideology. In an era of economic expansion, prominent goals included striving towards equality of opportunity and making the best use of the nation's resource of young people. In primary education, the Plowden Report (Central Advisory Council on Education 1967) provided official support for child-centred teaching methods and thus legitimated the particular way of teaching which became known as 'progressivism'. The focus was on the 'growth' of individual children, on their all-round development and on the quality of classroom relationships.

However, in the early to mid-1970s, with economic recession gradually deepening and confidence decreasing, the progressive ideology was challenged. Indeed it was seen by some to represent an ideology of 'trendy teachers and educationalists'. Documents, such as the 'Black Papers' (e.g., Cox and Dyson 1969), suggested that many attempts to implement Plowden lacked 'rigour', particularly in terms of curriculum design and organization, and that standards had fallen. A 'Great Debate' was initiated by James Callaghan, the Labour Prime Minister (Callaghan 1976), and a 'core curriculum' was proposed to ensure that education kept 'in touch with the fundamental need for Britain to survive economically' (DES 1977).

Since then, ideological debates have been sharpened enormously by the publication of unprecedented numbers of reports and prescriptive documents by the DES and HMI. Initiatives from successive Conservative administrations have centred on increasing the number of subject-specialist teachers who could act as 'consultants' in primary schools; proposals for a core curriculum and for testing children's achievement at certain ages; developing systems of teacher appraisal; and providing particular types of inservice opportunities to support such changes.

Each of these proposals has been initiated in the belief that it will help to raise academic standards. However, a reflective teacher needs to examine each proposal in terms of its intended effects and its likely consequences and in terms of any existing research evidence. For example, a recent study of PGCE students showed that, when talking about lesson planning, few of them referred to their own knowledge or to ideas that might have originated from their specialist degree (Calderhead and Miller 1986). Their practical experience and related discussions seemed to be more powerful influences on their professional development than their subject studies.

In terms of examining the intended effects and likely consequences of recent proposals, some historians have argued (for example, Simon 1985) that, by such means, attempts are being made to make the education system more effective as a means of 'social control'. In other words, existing inequalities are to be accepted and reproduced. Indeed, authors such as Althusser (1971) have seen education systems within capitalist societies as forms of 'ideological state apparatus' which are designed for precisely this purpose. On the other hand, sociologists such as Collins (1977) argue that educational policies and provision are the product of competing interest groups and that control and power is more diffuse.

In any event, the recent degree of 'advice' and legislation from central government has radically challenged what previously had been a very decentralized system, so that the priorities, structures, centres of control and accountability are all being re-appraised.

Thus, the dominant patterns of thinking about primary-school practice have changed considerably in recent years. Teachers are often required to respond to such development as new priorities supplant old ones. Awareness of the concept of ideology makes it more likely that the values or interests that may lie behind new proposals will be considered by reflective teachers.

1.2 Culture

Cultures can be seen as sets of shared perspectives and as the products of people acting together. Cultures can develop from collective activity and from the creative responses of groups to situations. Furthermore, it must also be recognized that cultures endure over time and can thus represent sets of ideas, perspectives, values and practices into which individuals are likely to be socialized. The playground cultures of children provide an example here. In one sense, children in friendship groups develop unique and particular ways of perceiving school life. Indeed, they use these as a means of understanding school and coping with it (Davies 1982). Yet, at the same time, continuities in children's culture, from generation to generation, seem to provide a context which young children absorb (Opie and Opie 1959; Sluckin 1981).

Several other kinds of culture are likely to affect teachers. For instance, the catchment area and the community which the school serves provide another cultural context. This is bound to influence and be influenced by the perspectives of parents, children and teachers. Few communities, however, can be characterized as single, united entities. Among the many divisions which may exist are those relating to race, language, religion, social class and to political or personal values. The existence of such cultural diversity is particularly important in many inner-city schools and reflective teachers are likely to wish to explore the relationship between cultures in the home and school very carefully indeed. A great deal of research has shown problems arising when working-class cultures are regarded as being deficient by those in schools (for example, King 1978; Sharp and Green 1975) and institutionalized forms of racism are likely to result if teachers fail to take appropriate account of the perspectives of minority ethnic groups (Willey 1984).

There are also likely to be cultures among the adults within each school. Those which are particularly important for teachers are the professional ones which develop out of the staffroom—that backstage area where tensions are released, feelings are shared and understandings about school life are developed. This is the territory of the classroom teacher, and the resulting teacher cultures usually provide a source of solidarity and sympathy when facing the daily pressures of classrooms. While colleagues may be stimulating and supportive of experimentation, they can also become protective of existing practices and inhibit innovation. Furthermore, there is sometimes a tendency for staffroom talk to avoid important educational issues which might be contentious and might thus begin to break down the sense of solidarity which teacher cultures are, in a sense, collaboratively created to provide.

Despite this element of constraint and limitation in some aspects of teacher cultures, it should be remembered that they develop in response to particular conditions and work experiences in a school (Denscombe 1980). One crucial factor here is the availability and nature of resources, and it is to this issue that we now turn.

1.3 Resources: personnel, buildings, materials

Adequate resources are essential in education and we will distinguish three types here: people, buildings and materials. In both quality and quantity, these resources have an impact on what it is possible to do in schools and classrooms (Stewart 1986).

Many people are involved in the life of a successful primary school and, for this reason, collaboration and team-work are needed, irrespective of status. Apart from the head and the teaching staff, there are many others, such as cleaners, dinner supervisors, cooks, secretaries, classroom ancillaries, and caretakers, who all have very important supportive parts to play. However, it is arguably the case that, from the educational point of view, the number and quality of classroom teachers is the major factor in determining what is done and what it is possible to do in school. Teachers themselves are the most important resource.

Buildings are also an important influence on what goes on in schools. The interior design of schools and classrooms is an important factor to consider in planning activities, routines and timetables. The quality of the school environment will also be influenced by aesthetic considerations, and schools vary considerably in terms of the degree of consideration which is given to this issue. Many schools still date from the last century, particularly in rural and inner-city areas. These are often built on a 'central' model, with classes leading from a large hall, or on a 'linear' model, with classes strung out along a corridor. Buildings from the early 1970s are particularly notable for 'open-plan' designs. Reflective teachers are likely to be concerned about the quality of the learning environment and will aim to maximize the learning potential of the buildings and space which they have available. In one sense, buildings have an obvious fixed quality and are a source of constraint; on the other hand, it is surprising what uses and activities creative imaginations can produce.

Materials are the bread-and-butter consumables of a school and are largely funded out of the capitation allowances—a small sum per pupil which each school receives from the local education authority. Most of the items of expenditure are likely to be of direct educational relevance, such as paper, pencils, games, books, equipment, creative and artistic materials. However, many schools also have to pay for things like cleaning materials and their telephone bill out of capitation. These can form a considerable proportion of the total. The net result is that the mere cost of some activities can be a constraint on engaging in them, whatever educational value they might be thought to have.

All these resources have to be paid for and, on a national basis, education can appear to be expensive. For instance, the projected cost of the maintained school sector in 1986/7 was £14.7 billion. Nevertheless, education still costs less than defence, the social services and the health service and forms only about 10 per cent of total government expenditure. At the local level, though, education is by far the largest item in council budgets: about 70 per cent in some cases, of which the most significant item is teachers' salaries. Despite the large total cost, one should not forget that, at the primary-school level, capitation in 1985/6 was both relatively low and very variable between local education authorities. In 1984, it ranged between £12.80 and £22.13 (DES 1985b).

Further resource differences emerge due to the fact that a considerable contribution to total school incomes can be made by parental fundraising. For instance, HMI (DES 1985b) reported a variation for single schools between £70 and £9000. It seems likely that social divisiveness will be increased by such parental funding because of the wide differences in the distribution of parental wealth and incomes in different local areas and regions of the country.

Thus, the level of resourcing in particular classrooms is dependent on a combination of school-based decisions and fundraising, on the deliberations of local councils and on the policies of national governments. A good deal of political, as well as professional, judgement is involved at all points (Hewton 1986).

While resources structure the material conditions in which teachers work, the actions which they might take are also likely to be influenced by the degree of autonomy which they feel they have. For this reason, we now focus on the issue of accountability.

1.4 Accountability

Teachers in the public education system are paid, through the taxation and rating systems, to provide a professional service. However, the degree of accountability and external control to which they have been subject has varied historically and is a subject of considerable debate at present.

In the first part of this century, the 'payment by results' system of the late 1800s, although superseded, still left a legacy in the form of imposed performance requirements in reading, writing and arithmetic. Handbooks of 'suggestions' for good practice were published regularly, as guidelines, but were not enforceable. However, from the 1920s teachers began to develop greater professional autonomy and in this they benefited from the acquiescence of successive governments (Lawn and Ozga 1986). In particular, the independence of head teachers within their schools, and of class teachers within their classrooms, emerged to become established principles. After the Second World War, as professional confidence grew, this independence extended into the curriculum: so much so that, in 1960, it was described by Lord Eccles, Minister for Education, as a 'secret garden' into which central government was not expected to intrude. Such confidence was probably at a high point in the early 1970s.

Since then, the change in the ideological, economic and political climate has resulted in teachers coming under increasing pressure: first, to increase their 'accountability'; and second, to demonstrate their 'effectiveness'. Some of the products of this concern can now, in the late 1980s, be seen. For instance, regarding accountability, local education authorities have been required to report to the DES on the curriculum in their schools; while at a local level, both the rights and the numbers of governors drawn from parents, industry and the community are being increased and governors must present an annual report to parents.

Thus, there are two levels of development. The first is towards the production of initiatives from central government. The second is the strengthening of parental participation in school governing bodies. These developments have been presented as a necessary reduction in the influence of the 'producers' (seen as teacher unions, administrators and theorists) and as enabling educational provision to be 'shaped by the users'.

On the issue of teacher assessment, there have been signs of the profession responding through the negotiation of procedures with local authority employers. There has also been a significant increase in school-based, self-evaluation schemes (McMahon *et al.* 1984; Rodger and Richardson 1985) and in classroom-based research (Rowland 1984; Hustler, Cassidy and Cuff 1986). On the other hand, the pressure for forms of external appraisal is also growing. Reports from HMI inspections of schools are now published and standards of attainment for children as young as 7 years old have been proposed so that the 'effectiveness' of schools and teachers can be judged. In an historical review of such developments, Grace has suggested:

> We are now in a period where the social and political context of state-provided schooling in Britain is reminiscent in a number of ways of the climate of reaction in the 1860s. There is a growing emphasis upon tighter accountability; a required core curriculum and a concentration upon basics. The role and strength of the inspectorate is being reappraised and changes can be expected in the ideology and practice of inspection at all levels. Both teacher training and the work of teachers in schools are to be subject to more surveillance and to the application of more specific criteria for the assessment and evaluation of competence.
>
> (1985, p. 13)

Accountability is thus an important aspect of social context because it highlights both legal requirements and areas of independent and consultative decision-making. Further, it has considerable implications for each teacher's work-experience itself, depending on the influence of governors and parents and the nature of teacher-assessment schemes (Sallis 1987). It is likely to remain an area of much flux and considerable contest, particularly between the government and teacher unions. For all these reasons, accountability is a very important issue for a reflective teacher.

In a sense, too, it is an issue which crystallizes many of the considerations which are raised more generally by a focus on the social context of schooling. What relationship does education have to society? Should it be a relatively autonomous system or should it be under tighter forms of control? The history of our education system provides many fascinating instances of attempts to resolve such questions (Silver 1980) and there are plenty of related current issues on which a reflective teacher might reflect. In particular, though, and following the dialectical model of social change which we discussed above, the issues of accountability, autonomy and control pose questions of a personal nature for teachers. How should each individual act?

2 PEOPLE

Within the dialectical model, which conceptualizes the constant interaction of social structures and individuals, personal factors are the counterpart of social context. For instance, classroom life can be seen as being created by teachers and children as they respond to the situations in which they find themselves. Thus, as well as understanding something of the factors affecting the social context of schooling, we also need to consider how teachers and children respond. We begin by focusing on teachers.

2.1 Teachers
Teachers are people who happen to hold a particular position in schools. We make no apologies for wishing to begin by asserting this simple fact, for it has enormous implications. Each person is unique, with particular cultural and material experiences making up his or her 'biography' (Sikes, Measor and Woods 1985). This provides the seed-bed for their sense of 'self' and influences their personality and perspectives (Mead 1934). The development of each person continues throughout life, but early formative experiences remain important. Indeed, because personal qualities, such as having the capacity to empathize and having the confidence to project and assert oneself, are so important in teaching, much of what particular teachers will be able to achieve in their classrooms will be influenced by them. Of even greater importance is the capacity to know oneself. We all have strengths and weaknesses and most teachers would agree that classroom life tends to reveal these fairly quickly (Nias, forthcoming). Reflective teaching is, therefore, a great deal to do with facing such features of ourselves in a constructive and objective manner and in a way which incorporates a continuous capacity to change and develop.

Teachers, as people, have opinions, perspectives, attitudes, values and beliefs. Thus, the particularly human attribute of being able to review the relationship of 'what is' and 'what ought to be' is one which teachers often manifest when considering their aims and examining their educational values and philosophies. While there has always been a good deal of idealism in the thinking of teachers of young children, there has also always been a concern with practical realism. Indeed, a very important factor which influences teachers' perceptions in the classroom is that the teacher has to 'cope', personally as well as professionally, with the classroom situation. For this reason, we would suggest that a fundamental element of classroom coping, or survival, is very deeply personal, for it involves teachers, with a particular image of their self, acting in the very challenging situation which classrooms represent. In this, it is important to remember that what it is possible to do in classrooms is constrained by the basic facts of large numbers of children, limited resources, compulsory attendance and the external expectations which exist about what should and should not take place (Hargreaves 1978; Pollard 1982).

In such circumstances, teachers face acute dilemmas between their personal and professional concerns and the practical possibilities (Berlak and Berlak 1981). They are forced to 'juggle' with their priorities as they come to terms with classroom situations.

The final set of personal factors about teachers to which attention will be drawn, relates to their position as employees. The first aspect of this is that teachers are workers and have legitimate legal, contractual and economic interests to maintain, protect and develop (Ozga and Lawn 1981). Some balance has to be struck between educational expectations and what it is reasonable to ask of people who happen to earn their living from teaching. In addition, it should never be forgotten that teachers also have their own personal lives outside the classroom. Both male and female teachers have family responsibilities, as well as other interests which may be important to their own personal development. In a very real sense then, teachers, especially the females who make up the vast majority of primary teachers, experience the pressure of having two 'jobs'.

2.2 Children

As with the personal factors associated with teachers, the most important point to make about children is that they are thinking, rational individuals. Each child has a unique 'biography'. The way in which they feel about themselves, and present themselves in school, will be influenced by their understandings of previous cultural, social and material experience (Richards and Light 1986). Their sense of 'self' and their emerging personality will be at relatively early stages of their development—a fact which may well leave each child rather vulnerable when confronted with the challenges of school life.

Perhaps the most important fact for teachers to consider is the huge range of attributes and experiences which children may bring to school. Factors, such as sex, social class, race, language development, learning styles, health and types of parental support, are so numerous and so complex in their effects that, although broad but important generalizations about patterns of advantage and disadvantage can be made (Osborn, Butler and Morris 1984), it is foolish to generalize in specific terms about their ultimate consequences. This caution is made even more necessary if it is acknowledged that factors in children's backgrounds can influence, but not determine, consequences.

Coming between the children's backgrounds and their educational development is the whole issue of how children actually respond to their circumstances and, indeed, of how teachers provide for them. Like teachers, children have to learn to cope and survive in classroom situations in which they may well feel insecure. We would argue that children's culture and the support of a peer group are considerable resources in this. However, such cultural responses by children can also pose dilemmas in class when children try to satisfy personal interests by attempting to please both their peers and their teacher. Creative strategies are called for and these may cover a range from conformity through negotiation to rejection. Once again then, we wish to highlight the importance of the subjectivity of the perspectives which teachers and children develop as they interact. Such perspectives are likely to be a great influence on the motivation which children feel and on the ways in which learning is approached.

Above all, though, we must never forget that children are placed in the role of 'pupils' for only part of each day (Calvert 1975). It is no wonder that families and peer groups are important to them. A reflective teacher, therefore, must aim to work with parents and with an understanding of child culture for the benefit of each child.

CONCLUSION

It has often been suggested that schools make little difference to educational outcomes. In this respect it is interesting to see the results of extensive recent research in inner London (Mortimore *et al.* 1986) which shows very clearly that the quality of junior schools makes a considerable difference to children's social and intellectual progress. If we can extrapolate the finding to primary schools more generally, we can dispense with the argument that schools and teachers can have little effect on children in the face of their socio-economic circumstances or backgrounds. Indeed, we can replace it with the assertion that the quality of schools and teachers matters a great deal.

Our intention in this chapter has been to discuss the relationship between society as a whole and the people who are involved in primary education. This is because we believe that school practices and classroom actions are influenced by the social circumstances within which they occur. We have also argued that individuals can have effects on future social changes. A theoretical framework of this sort is important for reflective teachers. Such change can only be fully effective when social awareness is developed and when individual responsibilities for professional actions are taken seriously.

NOTES FOR FURTHER READING

On the theoretical framework which has been introduced, two classic books may be helpful:

Berger, P. L. (1963) *Invitation to Sociology: a Humanistic Perspective*. New York: Doubleday.
Mills, C. W. (1959) *The Sociological Imagination*. Oxford: Oxford University Press.
(Chapter 1 of Mills and Chapters 4 and 5 of Berger are particularly relevant.)

For a readable analysis of modern British society, which illustrates aspects of this framework, see:

Halsey, A. H. (1986) *Change in British Society*. Oxford: Oxford University Press.

For a more difficult but very worthwhile analysis of education, individual action and society, see:

Apple, M. W. (1982) *Education and Power*. London: Routledge & Kegan Paul.

Three very different illustrations of the uses of the basic framework are provided by:

Connell, R. W., Ashden, D. J., Kessler, S. & Dowsett, G. W. (1982) *Making the Difference: Schools, Families and Social Divisions*. Sydney: Allen & Unwin.
Hammersley, M. (ed.) (1986) *Controversies in Classroom Research*. Milton Keynes: Open University Press.
Humphries, S. (1981) *Hooligans or Rebels?* Oxford: Blackwell.
(Humphries is based on oral histories and analyses the education of working-class children. Connell *et al.* is an analysis of school processes and Australian society. Hammersley contains a section which illustrates debates about the relationship of classroom resource to 'macro' social issues.)

Regarding primary education more specifically, there are a number of useful sources available. Two general reviews which locate primary school practices within a social and historical context are:

Marriott, S. (1985) *Primary Education and Society*. London: Falmer Press.
Stewart, J. (1986) *The Making of the Primary School*. Milton Keynes: Open University Press.

Two case studies which specifically attempt to trace links between individual actions and the wider social context are:

Pollard, A. (1985) *The Social World of the Primary School*. London: Holt, Rinehart & Winston.
Sharp, R. and Green, A. (1975) *Education and Social Control*. London: Routledge & Kegan Paul.

A recent report from a House of Commons Committee also provides fascinating information and documentation of the effects on primary education of public debates and Government policies over the past ten years:

House of Commons (1986) *Achievement in Primary Schools*, Third Report of the Education, Science and Arts Committee. London: HMSO.

For keeping abreast of new developments and policies, there are a number of useful newspapers and magazines:

Times Educational Supplement (weekly)
Child Education (monthly)
Junior Education (monthly)

Chapter 3

Investigating Classrooms

INTRODUCTION

1 APPROACHES TO RESEARCH

2 ISSUES TO BE CONSIDERED WHEN PLANNING CLASSROOM ENQUIRY

3 TECHNIQUES FOR COLLECTING DATA

CONCLUSION

INTRODUCTION

The relationship between 'researchers' and teachers has often been an uneasy one. Teachers have frequently identified a number of particular reasons for this state of affairs. First, teachers claim that researchers do not seem to focus on the kinds of concerns which teachers have. Second, researchers appear to be rather distant: they come to do research about teachers and their classrooms, but without clearly explaining the purpose or the methods. Hence the whole operation appears shrouded in mystery. Third, the results are often presented through complicated statistical procedures or are heavily embedded in obscure language. Consequently, many teachers have disclaimed research as 'less than useful' (Cane and Schroeder 1970; Freeman 1986).

Alternatives to this situation include researchers working alongside teachers in a collaborative way, or teachers becoming their own researchers. In the latter case, this would mean that teachers would need to develop the necessary techniques to research their own classrooms.

Such developments raise important issues, the first of which relates to the nature of research itself. Research is traditionally characterized as being 'objective'—reliable, valid, generalizable and credible (Shipman 1981). If the research were done by an involved insider, such as teachers in their own classrooms, would the research still be able to meet these criteria? If not, would this matter? In particular, would such research, which would be likely to be small-scale, provide a basis for theoretical explanations and generalizations? Again, if not, would it matter?

Such doubts have been raised about the feasibility of teachers becoming 'teachers-as-researchers'. Indeed, teachers are frequently aware of the discrepancies between their 'espoused theory' and their actual practice, and between their own descriptions of the practice and the descriptions made by others of the same practice (Elbaz 1983). Most of us realize how difficult it can be to 'see' what we are doing while we are in the middle of doing it. However, because it is difficult, it does not mean that it is not possible or that it is not worthwhile to try!

The model of a reflective teacher, as outlined in Chapter 1, suggests that critical reflection and systematic investigation of our own practice should become an integral part of our daily classroom lives. Such self-examination should lead to an improvement in our teaching judgements and help us to have a more professional control over our own development and that of others. Self-appraisal and professional awareness should provide the basis for a professional autonomy and reduce the perceived threat from 'outside' accountability.

If this is to happen, then an appreciation of the major issues involved in research and some knowledge of the main enquiry techniques available are essential. This chapter has been written as an introduction to such matters. Readers are strongly advised to follow up issues and techniques in which they may be particularly interested via the Notes for Further Reading section.

The chapter begins by examining two issues: the nature of traditional forms of research and the status of the main alternative forms. It will then consider a range of possible research techniques which teachers could use in their own classrooms.

1 APPROACHES TO RESEARCH

Four main research approaches can be identified. The first is the 'classical' scientific model which has traditionally laid great emphasis on quantitative data—for instance, by classifying and measuring behaviour. This approach is sometimes called 'positivistic'. A second approach is offered by some sociologists and focuses on structural features of society—for example, social inequalities, which are frequently measured and quantified. Such features are also examined in relationship to their historical, economic, cultural and political contexts. This may be referred to as the 'macro-sociological' approach. The third approach is 'interpretive' research, which emphasizes qualitative aspects of the situation being researched—for instance, by analysing people's perceptions. It is sometimes referred to as being 'phenomenological'. The final approach is one which has been developed in recent years by curriculum specialists working alongside teachers. This 'action research' is concerned with self-evaluation and the direct improvement of classroom practice.

The classical model is based on the research style which has served the physical sciences for many years. Its characteristic stages are:

- to recognize and define a problem;
- to accumulate observations;
- to classify the data;
- to develop an hypothesis;
- to design a controlled experiment to test the hypothesis;
- to analyse and interpret new data;
- to form generalizable explanations.

The hallmarks of this classical model are, therefore, that the investigation has an hypothesis, which is testable and replicable, which provides an explanation and is generalizable. When such research is referred to as 'scientific', it is usually to highlight two features which are believed by some to be crucial: that it is 'systematic' in the way the research is carried out and that it is 'objective' in the interpretation of the data collected and in the conclusions drawn. How far such research is 'scientific' in practice and whether this is still a suitable model for some areas of the physical sciences (for example, astrophysics or microbiology as just two examples) is in dispute in the scientific community itself (Capra 1982).

When this model is transferred to the social sciences, certain inadequacies are evident. For instance, it is very much more difficult to test an hypothesis in a classroom situation with the same rigour as one might expect in a laboratory experiment. It is more difficult because we cannot isolate the variables being examined and we cannot control all the myriad factors which might influence the test. In addition, we are dealing with human beings for whom we must have proper ethical concern about the way in which they, as with all living things, are treated. Further, because of the complexity of the classroom and because of the ethics of any such research, any 'experiment' can never be replicated exactly. Researchers have had to rely on sophisticated statistical methods to try to measure the impact of variables. Notwithstanding this, these difficulties weaken the claim that such research can provide generalizable explanations. For all these reasons, the argument runs, such study cannot properly be called scientific research.

There has been a long tradition in education research of following the classical model as exactly as is humanely possible. For example, much of the laboratory-based psychological testing and measurement research has been of this nature (for example, Cattell and Kline 1977). Similarly, the extensive work on teacher effectiveness in classrooms in the USA during the 1960s and 1970s (for example, Flanders 1970) used systematic observation techniques. These are still positively regarded for some purposes (for example, Galton, Simon, and Croll 1980).

The second, 'macro-sociological', approach has many features which distinguish it from the 'classical' model. In the first place, it is far more wide-ranging, for it is based on the assumption that specific situations, practices and perspectives can only be understood in relationship to their historical, economic and cultural contexts. Also, it rejects narrow forms of positivistic empiricism, which tend to prevent such wide-ranging factors being considered. In addition, it uses various forms of theorizing to try to make sense of such social structures, their processes and developments. Among a number of forms of theorizing, the most important influences on educational analysis have been structural functionalism (for example, Parsons 1951, 1959), structural Marxism (for example, Bowles and Gintis 1976) and cultural Marxism (for example, Apple 1982a). The latter two offer ways of examining the tensions and dialectical forces of change or development within education and society.

One major criticism that has often been made of this style of research is that it fails to address the subjective perceptions of the people who are the subjects of a study. This concern has led to the development of an alternative 'interpretive' form of sociological research.

The origins of this 'interpretive' approach can be traced to anthropology and the concern to understand, describe and analyse the cultures of particular societies and groups. Among the 'ethnographic' methods which were developed are participant observation and interviewing. These techniques (which we will discuss in more detail later) are explicitly 'qualitative', rather than 'quantitative', and are concerned with opinions and perceptions rather than only observable facts or behaviour. Interpretive researchers tend to aim, in the first place, simply to describe the perspectives, actions and relationships of the people whom they are studying. Typically, they study a limited number of cases in depth and try to achieve a view of the whole situation in a way which is seen to be valid by the participants. This process requires the personal involvement of the researcher and is rarely a neat, linear progression of research stages. The approach is pragmatic and flexible, as the researcher seeks data and understanding (Burgess 1984; Hammersley and Atkinson 1983). The outcome of such research is usually a detailed case study within which concepts, relationships and issues are identified and analysed. Glaser and Strauss (1967) provided the classic statement of the challenge of such work when they argued that interpretive sociologists should start from the grounded base of people's perspectives and, through the simultaneous collection, classification and analysis of data, should develop systematic and theoretically refined perspectives of the social institutions and relationships which they study.

Interpretive research has strengths and weaknesses, as with the classical model. Indeed, in many respects, they can be seen as complementary. For instance, a phenomenological researcher's 'generation' of theory may be balanced by a positivistic researcher's 'testing' of theory; qualitative data on perspectives may be balanced by quantitative data on behaviour; and a focus on detailed whole cases may be balanced by generalizing from sampling across cases.

Whatever their differences and the degree of their complementarity, these alternative approaches to social science each share one important feature: they have all tended to distance themselves from actual practice. It is only very recently that a direct concern with practical action has emerged (Finch 1986; Shipman 1985; Woods and Pollard 1987). It has been argued that to understand thoroughly is a precondition of acting effectively, and there is clearly some merit in this point. However, a quite different approach has also been developed, which seeks to improve and understand practice through the direct action and involvement of practitioners.

This approach has been termed 'action–research' and was originated by Lewin (1946). His model for change was based on action *and* research. It involved researchers, with teachers or other practitioners, in a cyclical process of planning, action, observation and reflection before beginning the whole process all over again.

Further development of this model was instigated by Stenhouse (1975) and elaborated by Elliott and Adelman (1973) in their work with the Ford Teaching Project, based at the Centre for Applied Research in Education at the University of East Anglia. It was this generation of researchers who coined the term 'teacher-as-researcher' to refer to the participants in the movement they helped to create. This encouraged teachers to assume the role of researcher in their own classrooms as part of their professional, reflective stance.

The approach has been criticized for encouraging a focus on practical classroom ideas while wider, structural factors are accepted as unproblematic (Barton and Lawn 1980/81; Whitty 1985). However, Carr and Kemmis (1986) argue that such work provides a means of 'becoming critical'. They suggest that action–research involves

- the improvement of practice
- the improvement of the understanding of the practice by the practitioners
- the improvement of the situation in which practice takes place

(1986, p. 165)

Overall, they, like Stenhouse (1983), see the potential of action–research as being 'emancipatory': releasing practitioners from 'the often unseen constraints of assumptions, habits, precedents, coercion and ideology' (Carr and Kemmis 1986: 192).

Thus, we have identified four major forms of research in this section: the classical or positivistic, the macro-sociological, the interpretive or qualitative and, lastly, action–research. The position which we have adopted in this book borrows a great deal from action–research in terms of the processes of enquiry which we suggest. In addition, its sense of purpose draws on macro-sociological issues. With regard to specific substantive topics, we aim to utilize the findings and methods of both positivistic and interpretive approaches to research as well. However, regardless of whichever approaches to research or enquiry are adopted, there are certain basic questions which have to be addressed and these form the subject of the next section.

2 ISSUES TO BE CONSIDERED WHEN PLANNING CLASSROOM ENQUIRY

Before any research can begin there are general decisions to be taken, concerning the overall design of the study. The most significant of these design issues will be discussed below.

1. *Which facet of classroom life should be investigated and why?* Identifying the 'problem' for investigation is sometimes a problem in itself. We do not always have a particular problem in mind, but merely want to explore first and see what emerges. Dillon (1983) offers a threefold categorization of the kinds of problems that might be explored: existing problems which we can already recognize; emergent problems which we discover in our initial investigations; and potential problems which we anticipate might develop if we took a particular course of action. The issue chosen for investigation may emerge from any of these three types of problem.

2. *What data to collect and how?* This decision is very important, for it must be remembered that no data can ever wholly represent the events or phenomena which are studied. Therefore, data should be selected which are valid indicators of what it is we want to study. Judgements about which data to collect are thus crucial, so that we do not distort the 'picture'. It is important to remember that what we choose to collect and how we will collect it affect what we find and, therefore, our understanding of the situation. Thus, however objectively we try to collect data, the choice of methods inevitably results in some distortion. One way of limiting this problem is to use several methods so that data on a single issue is collected in several ways. This is known as 'methodological triangulation'. However, our choice must, to a certain extent, be determined by what is feasible, given the time we can set aside to collect data and the time we can spend analysing it.

3. *How can we analyse, interpret and apply the findings?* The basic strategy is to look for patterns, for places where regularities and irregularities occur. In order to do this, the data have to be sorted using various sets of criteria. All patterns of frequencies, sequences and distributions of activity are likely to be of interest. In addition, it is also important to look for spaces and omissions—where something does not occur which might have been expected to. Where examples of co-occurrence exist, they can be misinterpreted as implying a cause–effect relationship. Such judgements should be viewed with caution until further data reinforce the pattern.

The important question of interpreting findings leads us into the issue of the relationships between research and the theoretical explanations to which it can lead.

We would argue that theorizing is an important and integral part of reflective teaching. This is because it represents an attempt to make sense of data and experience. It is also an opportunity to develop creative insights and an occasion to consider any discrepancies between 'what is' and 'what ought to be'. In a sense, we are all theorists in our everyday lives in the ways in which we develop hunches and use our intuition. This might be a starting-point, but, as reflective teachers, we would need to go further. In particular, we would want to generate theory relatively systematically and consciously. One way of doing this is to engage in a continuous process of data collection, classification and analysis of our own practice. The 'theory' which emerges is likely to be professionally relevant and may also offer insights with regard to other cases. This kind of theory resembles what Glaser and Strauss (1967) refer to as 'grounded theory'; in this sense, that which is developed from and grounded in our own experiences.

Such theorizing is particularly important for conceptualizing teaching and learning processes and for developing a language with which they can be discussed and refined (Hargreaves 1978). Grounded theory, developed from the study of individual cases, is valuable. However, such particular 'micro' studies can only offer a partial analysis of social and educational structures, processes and practices. This is where macro-sociological models can help (Mills 1959) by offering explanations which may challenge 'common-sense' assumptions and place particular events in a wider context (for example, Apple 1982a; Archer 1979; Bourdieu and Passeron 1977; Carnoy and Levin 1985; Halsey 1986; Whitty 1985). Such studies may well raise more issues than they resolve, but they are likely to make an important contribution to the sense of commitment and social responsibility which we have identified as being characteristic of reflective teaching. Furthermore, there is nothing to prevent reflective teachers from developing their own theories and conceptualizations of the relationships between education, the individual and society.

For the most part though, reflective teachers are likely to be concerned more directly with specific aspects of their practice. This calls for the use of a range of techniques for gathering data, which we will now review.

3 TECHNIQUES FOR COLLECTING DATA

For many teachers, busy teaching, it is difficult to collect the information we need to make the necessary day-to-day decisions and judgements, much less the information needed for anything more systematic and research-like. Our usual impressionistic data are collected sporadically and are often incomplete. They are selective and are probably based on what we have found in the past to be useful (one of the reasons it is so difficult to break out of old habits). They are also subjective, because we have so few chances of discussion to help us to see things from any other viewpoints. More helpful forms of data might be:

- descriptive (rather than judgemental)
- dispassionate (and not based on suspicions and prejudice)
- discerning (so that they are forward-looking)
- diagnostic (so that they lead us into better action)

Some of the main forms of alternative techniques are outlined below and references for their future consideration are also provided in the Notes for Further Reading section at the end of this chapter.

Document analysis
It can be revealing to examine official school documents. This might include the brochure for parents containing basic information about a school. Similarly, curriculum policy documents for staff (for example, maths policy or language policy) should provide some guidelines to their thinking—their aims, values and commitments. The contents of such documents are likely to indicate the assumptions held by their author(s) about how children learn, what they should learn, why, and how it should be taught. Indeed, attempting to devise such policies is an excellent way to clarify assumptions, either individually or collectively as a group.

Working papers, which might have been produced for staff development meetings, may also throw light on the issues discussed during the formation of school policies. Similarly, minutes of governors' meetings, documents from community organizations, communications from the school to the community (for example, notice-boards/letters/bulletins) can also be of value to the reflective teacher.

However, all such documents tend to be general statements of areas of agreement and hence gloss over the internal debates. It is important, therefore, to read 'between the lines' and to be aware of what is not included as well as the issues that are included. Any written planning devices, such as school policy documents, attempt to describe what is expected in terms of the intended curriculum. They do not, of course, include what is actually conveyed through the 'hidden' curriculum. Distinguishing between these two aspects is a very important task for a reflective teacher (see Chapters 5 and 11).

Curriculum matrices and checklists
Chapter 6 outlines a number of different forms of matrix which could be used to analyse the balance between the components of the curriculum—for example, in terms of concepts, knowledge, skills and attitudes. These can be used for planning purposes as well as for monitoring the children's progress.

Checklists can be formed by listing any items on which a teacher/researcher wishes to focus—for example, specific social behaviours, particular concepts, knowledge, skills and attitudes. The process of devising a checklist can be very helpful in assisting us to articulate our aims, so that they can be itemized and shared with others. Checklists can be used to monitor progress in greater detail than that which can be easily fitted into a matrix form.

Using personal constructs and socio-metric techniques
These are structured methods of indirectly finding out about the way people think and feel about each other.

Personal constructs are evident in our thinking when, for example, we appraise or comment on children. They can be identified by asking teachers to comment 'off the top of their heads' about the children in their class. The usual procedure is to ask each teacher to identify similarities and differences between pairs of children, often by using the class register as a 'neutral' list. In this way it is possible to elicit relatively instinctive reactions and the actual 'constructs', or criteria, which are used by the teacher. Such a procedure is usually more effective than asking teachers to consider, in abstract, what constructs they think they might use to distinguish children. Having obtained such a list, it is then possible to classify the constructs—for example, those which are academic, physical and social; or in terms of the children's behaviour towards the teacher or towards other children. The patterns which may emerge could highlight underlying assumptions that teachers have about what school is for and how they perceive the children.

Socio-metric techniques have been developed to help children and teachers gain insights into friendship patterns (Evans 1962). The basic procedure is to ask children, in confidence, to name three children with whom they would like to work or play. This can also, with care, be extended to ask children to identify anyone with whom they would not like to work or play. The friendship groupings which emerge from an analysis of these choices can then be represented in diagrammatic form, known as a socio-gram. Such representations provide a visual display of social relationships: mutual pairs and groups (where choices are reciprocated); clusters of friends (though not all with recipro-cated choices); isolates and even rejectees. However, neither of these techniques tells the whole story. They only provide information which the respondents choose to give. They provide information about what respondents say they feel, but they do not say why. Nevertheless, the data are structured and descriptive and can provide a starting-point for analysing further aspects of the attitudes and relationships between teacher and child, and between children.

Audio-recording, video-recording, photography

Recording what happens inside a classroom, by any of these techniques, provides a very valuable source of information, for they 'fix' events which are so fleeting. This is valuable for no one can have ears and eyes everywhere—even the most alert of teachers misses a great deal of what goes on.

Audio-recording of a class discussion is a common and simple procedure. However, tape recorders often only pick up a few of the children, or perhaps only the teacher's voice. Nevertheless, the procedure can provide information about how many children participate, which ones, how, and with what effect. It can also show the amount, type and distribution of teacher talk—a very worthwhile, though often saluatory experience.

Recording small groups or pairs is technically easier and can similarly provide valuable insights into the language strategies used and into social dynamics. Children usually forget about the recorder, though its presence may affect some—either to put on a performance or to clam up. Therefore, time should be allowed for familiarization. An alternative is to attach a radio microphone to an individual child for a period of time. The main advantage of this is that the quality of the recording is frequently excellent. Finally, it must be remembered that it takes time to play back the tapes: at least three times the length of the recording is often needed to listen to it and to distinguish who said what. Still more time will be needed for transcription.

However, audio-recording inevitably cannot record non-verbal aspects of any discussion. Because looks and silences can speak volumes, this is where video-recording can provide valuable information. Again, the presence of cameras is likely to affect some children and may distort the normality of the classroom, but, if done periodically, the novelty usually soon wears off. New models of video-cameras, with automatic focusing and low-light adjustment facilities make videoing a relatively easy task.

Photography is a much less obtrusive form of visual recording, especially if 'fast' (with a high ASA/ISO rating) film is used so that flash is not needed. Photography, of course, only captures 'frames' of action rather than the sequence of action itself, though stop-frame techniques can overcome this to some extent (Adelman and Walker 1975). Nevertheless, it is a cheaper and easier medium in which to work than video.

Each of these forms captures and records what is said or done. They can, therefore, be used as descriptive data, leaving us to analyse and infer our own explanations. Alternatively, we can discuss them with the participants and use them to gain insights into their interpretations of the same events.

Systematic observation

This is a way of observing behaviour in classrooms by using a schedule, or list of categories, of probable behaviour. The categories are chosen by the observer or reflective teacher who has decided which ones are important to the issue in hand. Each category is then 'checked off' as the behaviour is observed. The technique assumes that the teacher has already carried out sufficient preliminary, exploratory investigations to be able to decide which behaviours are relevant. Nevertheless, having devised the schedule, it can be a very quick and easy-to-administer technique for collecting information. The method can be adjusted to any situation and can be made practical for a teacher to operate during a teaching session.

There are two main differences in the use of such schedules. First, there are those which are 'checked off' each time there is any sign of the listed behaviours. This is called a 'sign' system. The other type of schedule is 'checked off' at predetermined time intervals and can be referred to as a 'timed' system.

Information collected in this way can easily be quantified, and the frequencies and distribution patterns of the listed behaviours can be calculated. It might be useful, for example, in finding out how much use is made of the book corner and who seems to use it most. It can be used to find out how individual children, perhaps with special educational needs, seem to spend their day. It could be used to note how teachers distribute their time among different children; which children seek attention; which ones avoid it; or which ones get 'forgotten'. Another common use is to measure the possible differences in the ways teachers interact with boys and with girls.

To reduce the possibility of misrepresenting the behaviour which is seen, it is often considered advisable to use categories which can be clearly identified and involve little interpretation by the teacher (that is, low-inference categories rather than those which involve high levels of inference). An example of a low-inference category would be 'child talks to neighbour' rather than 'child helps neighbour'. Further, to make it easier to code quickly in a busy classroom situation, it is advisable to use categories which do not overlap—exclusive rather than inclusive categories. Exclusive categories would be 'teacher asks open question', 'teacher expands child's response', rather than 'teacher discusses'.

Such information can only indicate what happens and not why. The technique is designed to be selective, but might distort the picture. For instance, it focuses on frequencies and not on sequences of behaviour and it relies on the appropriateness of the predetermined categories on the schedule.

Questionnaires, inventories

Both these forms of data collection use questions and statements to stimulate responses to set items. Questionnaires are usually given to the respondents to fill in (which, therefore, demands a certain level of writing skill). Inventories are usually used to structure a discussion (for example, between teacher and child so that the teacher can collect data about the children in a standardized and systematic fashion). Both techniques can be used for collecting factual information as well as opinions. Hence, they may provide data about what people do or think, and also why.

The format of each of these techniques can be closed (e.g. asking for specific data or yes/no responses) or open (e.g. asking for general and discursive responses). Responses can also be open or closed (e.g. closed items might be set in terms of ranking a given number of items or rating alternatives). Both the closed techniques are problematic in that they assume equal 'distances' between the orderings, and that respondents start from the same 'base-line'. Further, the wording of the format is important, so that the respondents do not misunderstand, nor should they be led to respond in a particular way. For example, some words are highly emotive and can exaggerate responses. Sometimes people react differently to a positive statement compared to a negative statement. The alternative, open form of response encourages a 'free' answer. This, of course, makes greater demands on the respondents' writing abilities. It also poses the problem of how to categorize a wide range of replies which such an item may well evoke.

Despite these problems in the presentational format of these techniques, they can be useful ways of collecting certain kinds of data. Questionnaires can be used to provide information to include on school records. They can be used to try to discover how respondents feel about aspects of classroom life: for example, they can be used as feedback on a particular lesson or topic of work. Questionnaires are also useful in that they can be filled in independently of the teacher and thus not interrupt the flow of teaching time. On the other hand, inventories can be useful precisely because they encourage the teacher to set aside time to talk individually to children and to go beyond the setting and marking of classroom activities. For example, inventories can be useful to record children's general interests in and out of school; their reading habits (Strang 1972); or general concerns which can help the teacher and child to understand each other better.

Children's logs, diaries and writings

These forms of written data are more informal. Logs and diaries, for instance, can be kept by children, or teachers, to record work in process and also their response to it. For example, children may note what they like/don't like; what they find hard/easy; what they would like/not like to do next. They can also be used by parents and thus serve as a regular part of the home–school communication system (Burgess and Adams 1980).

In addition, children's writing can contribute to generating greater understandings between teacher, child, and also parents. By providing a free context in which children can explore and imagine, it can give them the opportunity to examine what is as well as what might be. All such information could be useful to the teacher by providing evidence from others' viewpoints about situations, both within and beyond the classroom. However, in the written form, the full meaning of such evidence may remain unclear. It can, of course, form the basis for discussion, so that meanings can be explored. The understandings thus gained can be used to negotiate subsequent classroom activities, and to support the children in the situations they face.

Interviews and discussions

Both these techniques are oral, and both are interactive. They can be used to find out what the participants think or do, and why. They can also be used to explore and negotiate understandings because of the possibility of immediate feedback and follow-up. However, because of the person-to-person situation, some people may feel threatened—by the 'interviewer' or the other participants. The success of these techniques of data collection rest heavily on the relationships established and the way in which they are conducted. Both forms can be used with varying degrees of formality and structure. The term 'interview' is usually reserved for the more formal, more structured one-to-one situations.

Participant observation

In contrast to systematic observation, participant observation does not aim to observe pre-selected behaviours and record them on structured schedules. It is more exploratory in intention and, therefore, adopts a more open-ended method of recording. This is usually done in the form of field-notes which contain detailed memos of incidents, impressions or issues that, at the time, appeared to be significant. Such field-notes may record individual or group activity. They may include observed conversations or periods of silence, together with features of the situations in which conversations or events took place. The participant observer will also often try to discuss the situation observed to elicit the participants' interpretations of events. Thus the observer's, teacher's and the children's views will be sought, and a process of triangulation may be employed.

Although this may be a time-consuming procedure, such records can contain a wealth of information. Over a period of recording, it is normally possible to discern recurring themes which may lead to a greater understanding of the complex whole of a classroom environment. This technique, because it is relatively 'free-wheeling', can be particularly comprehensive and responsive to the unique features of the situation.

However, field-notes can also generate an enormous quantity of wide-ranging data from which it may be difficult to draw conclusions. On studying such notes, the teacher may identify specific insights which it might prove fruitful to follow up in greater detail. The follow-up could then be in terms of a further set of more focused observations, designed to test out an emerging idea. Alternatively, the teacher may decide to use another technique to provide a further source of insights. Follow-up analysis may then be of a more structured nature and lead to firmer conclusions.

CONCLUSION

This chapter has provided a brief introduction to some of the theoretical issues and practical techniques of undertaking classroom research as reflective teachers. We would advise readers to follow up other more detailed references, such as those given below. However, 'doing research' is not just about collecting data. The next stage is to be able to identify the issues which the data reveal. It is also important to be able to interpret the data and to design further investigations to refine our understandings. We need to be able to relate our findings to those of others and to consider our results in the context of the current debates about educational issues. Finally, as reflective teachers and collaborating professionals, we need to be able to turn our data into action and articulate what we are doing and why to others.

Part 2 is designed to help to put this reflection into practice.

NOTES FOR FURTHER READING

These notes are more extensive than those provided for other chapters. It is important that suggestions on methodology are followed up to provide detailed information on techniques prior to their use.

Gathering information about the existing state of knowledge on educational issues is obviously important. Abstracts, journals and research indices are available in good libraries. Two useful reviews of recent work are:

Cohen, L., Thomas, J. and Manion, L. (1982) *Educational Research and Development in Britain, 1970–1980*. Slough: NFER.
Hartnett, A. (ed.) (1982) *The Social Sciences in Educational Studies: A Selective Guide to the Literature*. London: Heinemann.

For general overviews and discussion of the most common research methods used in the study of education, see:

Cohen, L. and Manion, L. (1980) *Research Methods in Education*. London: Croom Helm.
Open University (1979) *Research Methods in Education and the Social Sciences*, Course DE304. Milton Keynes: Open University Press.

Useful books to focus our thinking on important research issues are:

Hammersley, M. (1986) *Controversies in Classroom Research*. Milton Keynes: Open University Press.
Shipman, M. (1981) *The Limitations of Social Research*. London: Longman.
Shipman, M. (ed.) (1985) *Educational Research: Principles, Policies and Practice*. London: Falmer Press.

Approaches to Research
The classical 'scientific' research tradition is discussed in:

Popper, K. R. (1968) *The Logic of Scientific Discovery*. London: Hutchinson.

For useful guides to the application of this approach in education see:

Borg, W. R (1981) *Applying Educational Research: A Practical Guide for Teachers*. New York: Longman.
Cohen, L. (1976) *Educational Research in Classrooms and Schools: A Manual of Materials and Methods*. London: Harper & Row.

An excellent and extensive series of pamphlets on particular methods is provided by:

Rediguides, Nottingham University School of Education.

Statistical analysis would be helped by books such as:

Cohen, L. and Holliday, M. (1979) *Statistics for Education*. London: Harper & Row.

For a quite different, critical perspective see:

Radical Statistics Education Group (1982) *Reading Between the Numbers: a Critical Guide to Educational Research*. London: BSSRS publications.

The methods which are appropriate to macro-sociological approaches are, in one way, properly seen as being those involved in conceptualizing the links between individuals, classroom practices and wider social structures. The classic book is:

Mills, C. W. (1959) *The Sociological Imagination*. New York: Oxford University Press.

For a more recent example, see:

Whitty, G. (1985) *Sociology and School Knowledge*. London: Methuen.

A rather different approach to macro-sociology issues is through the collection of survey data. A book for guidance in this method is:

Fink, A. and Kosecoff, J. (1986) *How to Conduct Surveys: A Step by Step Guide*. London: Sage.

Excellent examples of work using a survey approach are:

Halsey, A. H., Heath, A. F. and Ridge, J. M. (1980) *Origins and Destinations*. Oxford: Oxford University Press.
Osborne, A. H., Butler, N. R. and Morris, A. C (1984) *The Social Life of Britain's Five-Year-Olds*. London: Routledge & Kegan Paul.

Interpretive research has a long history. A general collection of papers, in which the major methodological issues are discussed, is:

Burgess, R. G. (ed.) (1982) *Field Research: A Sourcebook and Field Manual*. London: Allen & Unwin.

Further discussions of these issues can be found in:

Burgess, R. G. (1984) *In the Field: An Introduction to Field Research*. London: Allen & Unwin.
Hammersley, M. and Atkinson, P. (1984) *Ethnography: Principles in Practice*. London: Tavistock.

There is one book on qualitative methods which has specially been written for teachers who want to engage in their own studies:

Woods, P. (1986) *Inside Schools*. London: Routledge & Kegan Paul.

Books which provide advice on the use of a variety of methods within an action–research approach are:

Hook, C. (1981) *Studying Classrooms*. Victoria: Deakin University Press.
Hopkins, D. (1986) *A Teacher's Guide to Classroom Research*. Milton Keynes: Open University Press.
Walker, R. (1986) *Doing Research: A Handbook for Teachers*. London: Methuen.

For guidance on designing an action–research study for classroom or school use:

Elliott, J. (1981) 'Action Research: A framework for Self-Evaluation in Schools'. Teacher–pupil Interaction and the Quality of Learning Project, Working Paper No. 1. Cambridge: Cambridge Institute of Education.

Kemmis, S. and McTaggert, R. (1981) *The Action Research Planner*. Victoria: Deakin University.

Open University (1980) *Curriculum in Action: Practical Classroom Evaluation*. Milton Keynes: Open University Press.

Illustrations of action–research studies are becoming more easily available. See for instance:

Barr, M., D'Arcy, P. and Healy, M. K. (eds.) (1982) *What's Going On? Language/Learning Episodes in British and American Classrooms, Grades 4–13*. Montclair: Boynton/Cook.

Hustler, D., Cassidy, T. and Cuff, T. (eds.) (1986) *Action Research in Schools and Classrooms*. London: Allen & Unwin.

Nixon, J. (ed.) (1981) *A Teachers' Guide to Action Research*. London: Grant McIntyre.

Being a Reflective Teacher

Chapter 4

Who Are We? Considering Ourselves as Teachers and the Children as Pupils

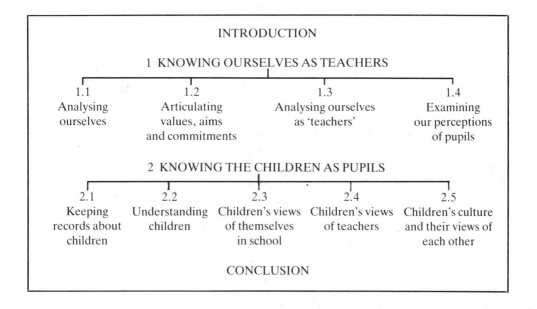

INTRODUCTION

1 KNOWING OURSELVES AS TEACHERS

1.1	1.2	1.3	1.4
Analysing ourselves	Articulating values, aims and commitments	Analysing ourselves as 'teachers'	Examining our perceptions of pupils

2 KNOWING THE CHILDREN AS PUPILS

2.1	2.2	2.3	2.4	2.5
Keeping records about children	Understanding children	Children's views of themselves in school	Children's views of teachers	Children's culture and their views of each other

CONCLUSION

INTRODUCTION

In the first section of this chapter we focus on ourselves as teachers and pay particular attention to three central issues: the qualities of ourselves as unique individuals; our strengths and weaknesses in taking on the role of teacher; and the values and commitments which we hold. The second section focuses on understanding children as pupils.

1 KNOWING OURSELVES AS TEACHERS

In considering ourselves as teachers, the first step is to examine the person we are. We could do this in terms of social, cultural and educational background, experience and qualifications, position, interests and personality. These factors make up our 'personal biography' and together they can be seen as contributing to the development, within each of us, of a unique sense of 'self': a conception of the person we are.

It is argued by some social-psychologists that this sense of self is particularly important because of the way in which it influences our perspectives, strategies and actions (Secord and Backman 1964). This is as true for teachers and children in classrooms as it is for anyone else (Hargreaves 1972). Each individual is thus seen as having a 'self-image' which is based on a personal awareness of the characteristics which he or she possesses and an awareness of how others see 'self'. Individuals may also have a sense of an 'ideal-self', that is, of the characteristics which they may wish to develop and of the type of person which they might want to become. An individual's self-esteem is, essentially, an indicator of the difference between the self-image and the ideal-self.

The concept of ideal-self introduces the question of values, aims and commitments which individuals hold and to which they aspire. This is important because individuals in society, whether teacher or child, actively interpret their situation in terms of their values, aims and commitments. Furthermore, teachers' values have considerable social significance because of the responsibilities of their professional position. Thus, reflective teachers need to consider their own values carefully and be aware of their implications.

This brings us to a second set of factors connected with the 'roles' which are occupied by a teacher, or by a pupil too. While teachers and pupils do not simply act out particular roles, it is certainly the case that expectations have developed about the sort of things that each should do. These expectations come from many sources: for example, head teachers, parents, governors, advisers, the Government and the media. Furthermore, they are frequently inconsistent. Teachers and pupils, thus, have to interpret these pressures and make their own judgements.

Few teachers, however committed, can hope to fulfil all their aims if the context in which they work is not supportive. For instance, some parents may have a different set of educational priorities from our own; staff may take up another value position; the established practices of the school may not support the particular styles of teaching which we would wish to adopt; or the resources which we need may not be available. For reasons such as these, teachers must continually adapt; they must both know themselves and the situations in which they work, and they must be able to make astute strategic judgements as they seek to achieve personal and professional fulfilment and to resolve the dilemmas posed by idealism and pragmatism.

Thus, knowing oneself as a person, establishing a clear set of values, aims and commitments, and understanding the situation one is in are three essential elements in any reflective consideration of teaching. These issues are examined in more detail below.

1.1 Analysing ourselves

Recent studies of primary-school teachers by Nias (1984a, 1984b) have shown that most people enter the profession with a strong sense of personal identity and of personal values. Nias reported that this sense of self was so strong that many teachers saw themselves as 'persons-in-teaching' rather than 'teachers' as such. Clearly, if this is so, then the openness and willingness to change and develop, which is implied by the notion of reflective teaching, is dependent on the qualities and degree of confidence of each teacher's sense of self and on the relationship of 'self' to 'role'. One issue of particular interest is Nias's argument about achieving personal fulfilment from teaching. She suggests that this is most likely when there is a congruence between each teacher's personal sense of self and the ways in which they are expected to present their self in school—their public display.

This raises a number of important points, particularly the need to develop self-knowledge. Easen (1985) has provided a useful framework for developing such understanding. He suggests that we can distinguish between a set of characteristics which we see as being part of ourselves (as representing our self-image) in contrast to a set of attributes which other people attach to us on the basis of observation and interaction with us. There is also an unknown area of potential for self-development.

Using a model of this sort one can distinguish between the following:

- our public display: aspects of ourselves which we recognize and others also see.
- our blind spots: aspects of ourselves which others see but we do not recognize.
- our dreamer spots: aspects of ourselves which we know are there, or would like to be there, but of which others are unaware.
- our untapped reservoir: our unknown potential, of which we are also unaware.

These aspects are indicated in Figure 4.1.

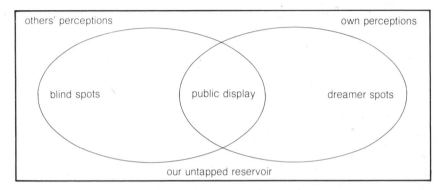

Figure 4.1 Diagram to show seen and unseen aspects of 'self'

Understanding oneself is not something which one can simply 'do' and complete in a single activity. It is something which develops over time. In Practical Activity 4.1 (see over), our main purpose is simply to draw attention to the centrality of such self-awareness for the reflective teacher.

However, it is necessary to consider the fact that developing such self-awareness can involve a process of self-discovery which may, at times, be threatening and painful. The work of Carl Rogers (1961, 1969, 1980) is useful here. Rogers writes as a psychotherapist who has developed what he calls a 'person-centred' approach to his work. His central argument is

> that individuals have within themselves vast resources for self-understanding and for altering their self-concepts, basic attitudes and self-directed behaviour.
>
> (1980, p. 115)

In addition to the focus on inner self-development, Rogers also suggests that personal development is facilitated by genuine acceptance by others. This has great relevance for professional and personal development in teaching. In particular, it points to the importance of working collaboratively with colleagues and developing open, trusting relationships. Such relationships should not only provide an alternative source of insights into our own practice, but should also provide the support to face and deal with whatever issues may be raised.

1.2 Articulating values, aims and commitments

In beginning to consider personal values, it is important to establish a basic point: that our perspectives and viewpoints influence what we do both inside and outside the classroom. The values we hold are frequently evident in our behaviour and, thus, in our teaching.

PRACTICAL ACTIVITY 4.1

Aim: To analyse dimensions of our 'selves'.

Method: Think of specific and memorable incidents in which you were centrally involved. Try to identify the most prominent characteristics of yourself which they reveal.

Try to identify:
1. Dreamer spots . . .   1.
   (parts you would like to develop)   2.
                                                      3.

2. Blind spots . . .   1.
   (parts you do not often face up   2.
   to)   3.

3. Public display . . .   1.
   (how you try to present yourself)   2.
                                                      3.

4. Untapped reservoir . . .   1.
   (parts you think might be there)   2.
                                                      3.

It would probably be beneficial to do this exercise with a friend. It could help you to deepen your understandings, share and explain your perceptions, while providing mutual support.

Follow-up: Clearly, the challenge of being a reflective teacher is intimately bound up with reflection on such personal issues. It is about replacing blind spots with insights, about developing dreams and ideals into realities, about tapping potential and facilitating learning.

Identifying values and aims is difficult, and so, too, is trying to identify what to look for in the classroom that would tell us whether we were putting our aims into practice. Reflective teachers need both to identify values, aims and commitments and to consider indicators of their actual implementation. Only then will they be able to judge whether what they do really matches what they say they believe.

Many attempts have been made to group such beliefs and link them to educational ideologies. These value positions and ideological perspectives can be labelled in many different ways—itself a challenging activity for a reflective teacher. We have identified five positions below which we feel are, or have been, particularly important.

Liberal romanticism. An example of this is the highly individualistic, 'child-centred' view of education focusing on the unique development of each child, a view which values diversity and individual difference. This is the ideology which was celebrated by the Plowden Report (Central Advisory Council on Education 1967).

Educational conservatism. A perspective that emphasizes the transmission of established social values, knowledge and culture through a subject-orientated approach which also has a particular emphasis on upholding 'standards'. This was the explicit ideology of the 'Black Papers' (for example, Cox and Dyson 1969) and is evident in the manifesto of the Hillgate Group (1987).

Economic pragmatism. An instrumental approach focusing on the individual's acquisition of useful skills. Where the emphasis shifts to directing individuals to acquire skills economically useful to society, the term 'economic revisionism' is sometimes used. This approach is evident in many of the current changes in post-16 education and in the vocational training sponsored by the Manpower Services Commission.

Social democracy. This is characterized by an egalitarian value-position and a focus on the relationship between education as an instrument of social change. This was a prevalent ideology in the post-war years and, for a period, seemed to have a degree of all-party support.

Social reconstructionism. An approach which is based on a commitment to develop education as a means of combating inequalities in society. It also supports positive action on such issues as sexism, racism, social class, disability, rights and the distribution of power and wealth. Many recent policies of the Inner London Education Authority reflect this approach.

Such value-positions deserve serious consideration. A clearly defined perspective is necessary so that practical policy can be initiated. The lack of explicitly stated values and aims often results in an inconsistent commitment to implement any relevant policy. Approaching this in another way, Eisner and Vallance (1974) distinguish three main aspects upon which varied value-positions are held. They suggest these are best represented as continua:

individual ⟷ society
(i.e. whether education should meet the individual's need, compared with the education system being geared to produce individuals to meet the needs of society)

values ⟷ skills
(i.e. whether education should focus on developing children's sense of values or on developing their skills without reference to a moral and ethical context)

adaptive ⟷ reconstructive
(i.e. whether education should prepare individuals to fit into the present society or should equip them to change it)

By separating these three elements, it may be possible to clarify where each of us stands, regarding our value-positions. For example, a person may place herself at the 'individual' extreme of the first dimension, the 'skills' extreme of the second dimension and the 'adaptive' extreme of the third dimension. Therefore, such a person would be committed to an educational system which aimed at developing individuals with instrumental skills able to fit into the given present society, without ethical concerns for the needs of society as a whole or any desire to consider the possibilities and processes of change.

The importance of identifying our value-positions is twofold. Firstly, it can help us to assess whether we are consistent in what we, as individuals, believe and how to reconcile differences which exist between colleagues working together. Secondly, it can help us to assess whether what we believe is consistent with how we behave: that is, if our 'philosophy', or values, is compatible with our 'pedagogy', or aims and action.

PRACTICAL ACTIVITY 4.2

Aim: To consider available policy statements from local education authorities, school brochures or Government guidelines on gender, race or children with special needs.

Method: We suggest that a variety of policy statements are discussed with colleagues with a view to identifying both underlying value-positions and practical implications.

We provide an example from parts of a report on *Girls and Mathematics* produced by the Royal Society and the Institute of Mathematics and Its Applications (1986). The document states:

Mathematics plays an important part in many aspects of our daily lives, and a thorough grounding in mathematics is thus essential for all girls and boys during their education and training. . . . There is disturbing statistical and anecdotal evidence that girls, as a group, are seriously underparticipating and underachieving in mathematics in comparison with their male counterparts, and increasingly so after age 11; many individuals, however, are successful. There is no convincing or conclusive evidence that the discrepancy can be adequately accounted for by innate or genetic disability at mathematics in girls. Urgent and coordinated action by all those concerned with the mathematical education of girls is needed, if girls are to fulfil their abilities.

At primary level girls and boys achieve the same overall performance in mathematics, although differences occur in relation to specific topics. Despite this, both teachers and pupils regard maths as a subject at which boys are likely to achieve a higher overall performance than girls, and teaching styles and expectations are modified often unconsciously. By the end of primary school boys have developed more confidence than girls in the fields of mathematics that are the most important at secondary school.

Recommendations

(i)   Positive expectations of girls in their mathematics by teachers will foster positive attitudes to the subject from girls.
(ii)   Expect boys as well as girls to complete a mathematical problem that involves applied as well as arithmetical aspects . . .
(iii)   Encourage girls to use constructional toys, apparatus and equipment (e.g. Technical Lego and wheeled vehicles) that develop visuo-spatial skills.
(iv)   Use mathematics textbooks in which girls as well as boys are shown actively using mathematics in pleasure and enjoyment. Write to publishers when books show bad practice.
(v)   Introduce problem-solving skills and an experimental approach to mathematics early through group-work and cooperative teaching styles, and avoid a right versus wrong approach. Encourage all pupils to talk about mathematics and attempt to listen to each other so as to bring a 'social' (perceived as 'female') element to teaching.
(vi)   Avoid praising neatness and tidiness in girls' work for its own sake; do not confuse neatness with clarity of thought.
(vii)   Provide girls and boys with genuinely equal opportunities to be familiar with the use of microcomputers in their learning of mathematics.

(viii) Promote the use of mathematics for girls in many activities outside school.

(ix) Encourage women teachers to participate fully in in-service training programmes and to take more responsibility for portraying themselves as confident and happy with mathematics.

(x) Draw attention to women who use and enjoy mathematics.

Conclusions

If all the recommendations outlined above were implemented there would undoubtedly be an improvement in the way in which girls view mathematics. Nevertheless, in the world outside school there are strong pressures in many aspects of life to confirm sexual stereotypes, and these are likely to change only slowly in response to equal opportunities legislation. Traditional perceptions of mathematics as a 'male' subject persist and it is vital that they change. Improvements in girls' participation and achievements in mathematics will only occur when everyone perceives the problem and works towards the same objectives.

Follow-up: Discussion of such documents should bring questions about educational aims and commitments into the open, and thus expose them to debate.

For instance, although official support has, for some time, been given to a child-centred (liberal romantic), so-called 'progressive' ideology, there is considerable evidence that, in practice, it is not nearly so widespread as it was once thought. Both HMI (DES 1978a) and the ORACLE survey (Galton, Simon and Croll 1980) found only limited evidence for 'progressive practices'. In order to try to identify our own 'pedagogy', we need to specify particular behaviours which can act as 'indices' of our value-positions.

In a sense, the whole of this book is dedicated to helping us to identify additional indices, such as those listed in Table 4.1, whereby we can more precisely analyse our own behaviour and its consequences in the light of our own beliefs.

PRACTICAL ACTIVITY 4.3

Aim: To identify individual value-positions.

Method: Try to place yourself along each of the three continua discussed above and clarify where your 'position' is.

Follow-up: Having tried to do this, you may find other dimensions need to be added as well—or taken away. This exercise can be extended so that a whole group could identify their 'positions'. Then it is possible to clarify areas of conflict and reassess policy issues in the light of such discussions. Consider the implications each 'position' may have for teaching styles. A reflective teacher will also need to consider to what extent classroom behaviour is consistent with expressed beliefs.

Table 4.1 *Characteristics of pedagogy*

Progressive	Traditional
1. Teacher as guide to educational experiences (e.g. pupils participate in curriculum planning)	1. Teacher as distributor of knowledge (e.g. pupils have no say in curriculum planning)
2. Active pupil role (e.g. learning predominantly by discovery techniques)	2. Passive pupil role (e.g. accent on memory, practice and rote)
3. Intrinsic motivation (e.g. enjoyment and fulfilment emphasized, interests followed)	3. Extrinsic motivation (e.g. rewards and punishments used: points and penalties)
4. Integrated subject matter and flexible timetable	4. Separate subject matter and rigid timetable
5. Concerned with personal/social/academic potential: accent on cooperative groupwork, and creative expression	5. Concerned with academic standards: accent on competition and correct expression
6. Continuous informal forms of monitoring	6. Periodic formal testing and assessments
7. Teaching not confined to classroom base	7. Teaching confined to classroom base

---

PRACTICAL ACTIVITY 4.4

Aim: To identify general aims which you hold for the children's learning.

Method: List your 'top ten' aims, and number them in order of importance.

Follow-up: How do your aims relate to your 'value-position'? How do your aims compare with those of your colleagues? What are the implications of any similarity or difference?

1.3 Analysing ourselves as 'teachers'

Any set of aims makes certain demands of a teacher. In this section, we will consider the personal demands of the relationships between a teacher and the other adults with whom they work. This theme will be further developed in Part 3 of this book. Relationships between teachers and children will also be discussed briefly here, but are the main focus of Chapter 5.

We suggested earlier, following Nias (1984a, 1984b), that being a teacher involves accepting particular responsibilities and establishing particular kinds of relationships with the people with whom we work. These have to be achieved within the context of other people's expectations of a 'teacher'.

The first set of relationships with other adults to be considered here are those with parents. It is increasingly being argued that the educational experiences which are provided by parents and teachers should not be separated by conventional boundaries of 'home' and 'school' (Cullingford 1985). For this reason, parents may want to participate more fully in their child's education than in the past. Teachers are now being encouraged to regard parents as 'partners' in the educational process. For some, this is seen as a threat and as a move towards de-professionalizing teachers. For others, it is seen as a welcome and positive change where home and school work together for the greater benefit of the child.

Other professionals are also involved in the educational process. In particular, with moves towards the integration of pupils with special educational needs—in part, resulting from the Warnock Report (DES 1978b) and the 1981 Education Act—we can expect other specialist staff to be working in the classroom, alongside the teacher. This may be in addition to peripatetic and ancillary staff. Hence, teachers have to be able to manage not only themselves and their children, but also a team of other adults as well.

A final set of relationships that we have to be able to develop is with other teaching colleagues on the school staff. With pressures to produce school policies in all curricular areas and to strive for progression and continuity, we can expect to operate more closely with colleagues than perhaps was common in the past (Campbell 1985). This may call for new levels of openness and for frank exchange, professional trust and cooperation.

PRACTICAL ACTIVITY 4.5

Aim: To consider the advantages and disadvantages of other adults working in the classroom.

Method:

1. List the different adults who might work in a primary classroom, their status (e.g. parent, ancillary, etc.), and the possible kinds of tasks they might do. Try to identify advantages/disadvantages, possibilities/limitations of their involvement.

2. List the qualities that you would look for in the different adults whom you would like to take up particular roles in your classroom.

This may best be done if you have had experience of these kinds of situations, or with colleagues who can perhaps share their experiences with you.

Follow-up: From such an exercise, it may be possible to draw up proposals for maximizing the potential of such classroom support and for minimizing possible problems.

Changes in the professional role of teachers may make considerable demands on our personal and social attributes, as well as on our pedagogic skills. They also make demands on our willingness and capacity for change. We need, therefore, to consider our aims in the light of the many demands which are made upon us.

PRACTICAL ACTIVITY 4.6

Aim: To identify the demands that teaching makes of us as individuals.

Method: Divide the page into two vertical columns. In the left-hand column, make a list of the aims you have for yourself as a teacher, as you did in Practical Activity 4.4. In the right-hand column, make a list of the personal qualities, skills or knowledge which are needed to implement each aim.

Follow-up: Review the qualities, skills and knowledge which are required. Consider which ones, personally, would be easy to exercise and which ones might be more difficult. Try to identify steps that could be taken to help to meet any discrepancies.

Perhaps the most important aspect of analysing self involves considering whether what it is 'to be a teacher' is compatible with how we see ourselves 'as a person'. For some, there may be a conflict between these two images, particularly for student teachers who may be more used to thinking of themselves as 'learners'. For example, certain aspects of 'being a teacher' have been described as being willing to take a leadership role, to be 'in authority'. This may result in a conflict between personal values and aims and other people's expectations of a teacher's role.

A final aspect, which at many different times in our teaching lives we need to consider, is the question of career. We have to make decisions concerning what part 'being a teacher' is going to play in our lives. We have to decide how we are going to balance the demands of the job with our own personal 'self' needs: for example, our own family or social life.

1.4 Examining our perceptions of 'pupils'

Just as it was important to understand what we expect of ourselves as 'teachers', so, too, it is important to understand what we expect of 'pupils'.

All of us are likely to have preconceptions and prejudices about what children should be like as pupils. For instance, it has been found that teachers are affected by the sex, race or social class of the children and even by their names (Meighan 1981). If, as teachers, we hold such preconceptions, it can result in treating children in different ways, according to these preconceptions. The children then respond differently, which reinforces our original preconceptions. Such labelling, or stereotyping, can lead to a phenomenon known as a 'self-fulfilling' prophecy and can result in considerable social injustices (Brophy and Good 1974; Nash 1976). The reflective teacher, therefore, needs to question the bases for any differential treatment of the children in the class. This means examining the evidence upon which we base our conceptions of individual children. We need to try and ensure that opinions are based on impartial appraisal, systematic and full observations and discussions, rather than prejudiced, haphazard and instant assessments.

Teachers do, of course, have to develop ways of understanding, interpreting and grouping children in order to respond effectively in the immediate classroom environment. However, this should be done with regard for the demands of a particular situation or activity and not become a form of permanent categorization for all classroom situations.

PRACTICAL ACTIVITY 4.7

Aim: To find out our responses to members of our class.

Method: Write down the names of the children in your class (without referring to the register or any lists). Note which order you have listed them in and which names you found hard to remember.

Follow-up: What does the order tell you about which children are more memorable than others, and for what reasons? How does this reflect those you get on with best, those with problems, children who are withdrawn, those you would like to forget . . .? Are there any differences between the sexes, races, abilities?

PRACTICAL ACTIVITY 4.8

Aim: To understand our perceptions of 'pupils'.

Method: Use the list from Practical Activity 4.7 of the children in your classroom to generate the 'personal constructs' which you employ. To do this, look at each adjacent pair of names and write down the word that shows how those two pupils are most alike. Then write down the word which shows how they are most different.

Follow-up: When you have done this with each pair, review the characteristics that you have identified.

1. What does this tell you about the characteristics by which you distinguish children? What additional qualities do the children have which these constructs do not seem to reflect and which perhaps you do not use?

2. Consider the constructs and note any patterns which might exist: for example, whether some constructs are used more with boys than girls, children from different class/race/religious backgrounds. There may also be a variety of constructs which relate to such things as academic ability, behaviour towards teachers or to other children or physical attributes.

3. Having reviewed the constructs you use, to what extent do they reflect differences which are relevant to appraising the children's educational needs? What implications are there for classroom policies and practice? What changes might you wish to make in the constructs you use?

---

2 KNOWING THE CHILDREN AS PUPILS

Developing an understanding of children as pupils requires that a reflective teacher should accumulate basic information about each child, as well as develop personal knowledge and rapport. However, this raises some important issues of a practical, ethical and educational nature which are associated with record-keeping. We discuss these issues first before moving on to consider the sorts of knowledge and understanding of children which might be developed.

2.1 Keeping records about children

As teachers, we need information about children on which we can base our policy decisions and classroom judgements. We need to be able to collect information, organize it, analyse it and use it effectively. One of the main educational reasons for keeping records is so that a better match can be made between children and tasks. Another, of a more general sort, is to provide information about the breadth and balance of the curriculum in which a child is engaged. A third reason arises because, as responsible and committed professionals, teachers need a means of judging their own effectiveness in the classroom—one criterion of which is the children's progress. Nor should it be forgotten that teachers are providing a public service and are accountable to their head teacher, to school governors, to parents and to the children. Records may be needed so that they can account for themselves. More immediately though, record keeping is a necessary part of everyday monitoring of teaching. Records should help in future planning, provision and action—hence, forming a vital link in the reflective spiral.

At the same time, though, any record-keeping system must be practical to operate. Inappropriately elaborate and time-consuming systems are likely to be discarded. There may be elements of record systems—perhaps to do with curriculum activities— that children could maintain for themselves.

While good reasons for keeping records exist, the whole question of records and of 'files' is an explosive one. The issue reflects more general concerns about the central accumulation and recording of information about individuals, whether it is medical information, financial, criminal or anything else. Indeed, most of us would probably want to know what was being kept on us and many people take the view that this should be a right.

When working with young children, it is normally accepted that parents should assume such rights. In fact, though, the present legal position gives such rights, formally, only to the parents of children who have been 'referred' for the assessment of special educational needs. However, there are signs that open record systems are spreading. Indeed, there may be gains, not only ethically, but from the quality of the records which are likely to be kept and from the deeper partnership with parents which could result.

It is useful to think of the range of alternative forms in which information could be kept. For example, teachers often note observations and jot down comments in an exercise book. Some schools use a standardized pro forma employed by all staff. Certain local education authorities have devised sheets or profiles, with a given set of criteria, for all schools to use. A more elaborate method is to put pupil information on to a computer data base, where it can be easily updated and quickly accessible. This, of course, needs to be used with careful regard to the Data Protection Act 1985.

PRACTICAL ACTIVITY 4.9

Aim: To identify information about the children which it is important for you, as their teacher, to know and record.

Method: Make notes, under the following headings, of:

1. What information do you think is important for you as a teacher to know about children in your class?

2. Why is it important?

3. How would you use it?

4. How would you record it?

5. How would you check on the objectivity and fairness of the record?

6. To whom would you make it available?

Follow-up: Asking such basic questions could provide a check on the keeping of records. Any information which is not demonstrably useful to teaching, recordable and ethically sound should be reviewed.

2.2 Understanding children

Just as we looked at personal and personality factors in the teacher, so a similar kind of 'biographical' knowledge about each child is valuable in understanding them as individual people and as learners. Many schools already collect information about each child's medical history, family history and educational history, but such records, although sometimes helpful, rarely convey an impression of the 'whole child'. For this reason, profiles are kept in some schools about each child's progress, together with examples of their work at different ages. Information about hobbies and interests, abilities and tastes in reading, progress and interest in mathematics and so on might be kept alongside records about each child's social attitudes and behaviour.

Such records may provide a starting-point for understanding each child, in terms of the material and social circumstances as well as their development in school. It, thus, provides a context for understanding children. However, such records cannot replace the awareness which will come from personal contacts with children and their parents.

PRACTICAL ACTIVITY 4.10

Aim: To construct a biographical perspective of a child.

Method:
1. Present open-ended opportunities where a child can write, draw, talk or otherwise communicate about herself or himself. Discussions about favourite books or TV characters can be revealing.

2. Observe and take notes on the child's general behaviour in the playground and in the classroom.

3. If possible, discuss the child with parents and other teachers.

4. Summarize key points.

Follow-up: Accumulating such information can take time and will only develop gradually. Nevertheless, it could provide a valuable profile of the specific and unique characteristics of an individual. Then it is necessary to consider what implications it has for shaping the learning experiences that are appropriate for each child.

It is often argued that the 'needs' of the learner should be seen as the starting-point for teaching and learning policies. However, the notion of appropriate needs is a very problematic one, since it begs questions about prior aims, and judgements about what is worthwhile (Dearden 1968; Barrow 1984). Nevertheless, it may be valuable for us as reflective teachers to articulate what we see as the basic 'needs' of every child which we commit ourselves to trying to meet.

Maslow (1954) identified three classes of needs:

- primary needs . . . for food, sleep and shelter
- emotional needs . . . for love and security
- social needs . . . for acceptance by peers

This is not dissimilar from those suggested by Kellmer-Pringle (1974), who identified four basic types of needs for young children:

- the need for love and security
- the need for new experiences
- the need for praise and recognition
- the need for responsibility

Within each of these areas, it might be possible to identify many further needs. This could be attempted in the specific context of one's class, though one would have to be careful to guard against adversely labelling the children in the process.

PRACTICAL ACTIVITY 4.11

Aim: To identify some needs of a selected number of children in one's class and to establish an order of priority.

Method: List the children's names and beside each name record your judgement of that child's key needs.

Follow-up:
1. Consider which criteria you used in deciding 'key' needs. Was your choice based on the fact that you value certain needs more than others and believe them to be of greater importance in themselves?

2. Examine the needs that you have listed and see if any pattern exists across the class which could form a common basis for planning activities.

3. Identify needs which are specific to individual children and consider how you could make provision for them.

A final set of issues in understanding children involves psychology, for studies of the development of children's thinking have had an enormous impact on teaching in schools, particularly through the work of Piaget (1926, 1950) and Bruner (1964, 1968). A key concept in Piaget's theory is that of 'equilibriation': a process through which children reorganize their 'cognitive structures' following a new experience which may have appeared to conflict with their previous understandings. It is argued that children's apparently spontaneous interests reflect their motivation to restructure existing understandings, that is, to move beyond states of 'disequilibriation' (Wadsworth 1978).

Piaget proposed the existence of cognitive schema of increasing complexity, each being dependent on those preceding it. These schema are commonly known as 'stages':

- sensori-motor stage (approx. birth–2 years)
- pre-operational stage (approx. 2–7 years)
- concrete operational stage (approx. 7–12 years)
- formal operational stage (approx. 12 years onwards)

Alternatively, Bruner suggested the existence of three modes of representing our understandings which are used *throughout* a person's development:

- enactive (physical–motor, conveying meaning through action)
- iconic (conveying meaning visually–pictorially)
- symbolic (using words as symbols for meanings they stand for)

A reflective teacher might wish to consider the characteristics of the thinking of each child in their class. Is there evidence of children at particular 'stages'? Are children being given a range of opportunities for developing new understandings? Are children encouraged to convey their understandings in a variety of ways?

There have been a number of criticisms of Piaget's work. Other psychologists, such as Donaldson (1978), have demonstrated that children's cognitive abilities are greater than those reported by Piaget. Such findings emerge when children are observed in situations which are meaningful to them, and in which they have shown considerable social competence (Richards and Light 1986). From a different perspective, sociologists, such as Walkerdine (1983), have argued that Piaget's stages and his developmental psychology have become part of child-centred primary school ideology. By this means, they have become established criteria and concepts through which teachers classify, compare and, thus, control children.

One simple conclusion which might be drawn from these criticisms is that children should never be underestimated. They may have limited experience and knowledge, but they have the capacity to engage in logical processes of 'intellectual search' (Tizard and Hughes 1984) at a very young age.

2.3 Children's views of themselves in school
The members of the class, both teachers and children, will have opinions of each other, and these opinions may well affect individual children. However, what children think of themselves is also important. Children may be highly anxious and continually under-value themselves. Conversely, others may seem over-confident. Some may be very well aware of their own strengths and weaknesses, while others may seem to have relatively naïve views of themselves. Children may be gregarious, or loners, or they may be lonely. Whatever the image of themselves and feelings about school, it is likely to help a teacher to know what they are (see Practical Activity 4.12). It may also be helpful for some children to reflect upon them.

PRACTICAL ACTIVITY 4.12

Aim: To identify how children feel about themselves in a school context.

Method: Children can be asked to complete 'Me at School' sheets (Mortimore *et al.* 1986). They should be completed by each child individually and can be administered to a whole class simultaneously. Each item can be read out by the teacher. Children should put a cross in the box which is 'most true for me'.

The children's responses will give an indication of their overall feelings about themselves at school and the items can be scored and aggregated. Scoring is from 1 to 5 left to right for items 1, 3, 5, 6, 7 and 9. It is reversed for items 2, 4, 8, 10 and 11. If an item is missed, code 0. If two or more marks for the same item are made, then score 9.

If a more specific analysis is required, then the following groups of items can be identified:
- 3, 7 and 10 relate to relationships with other children
- 1, 2 and 8 relate to anxiety
- 4, 5 and 9 relate to learning
- 6 and 11 relate to behaviour

ME AT SCHOOL

MY NAME _____

TODAY'S DATE _____

	Always	Usually	Sometimes	Usually	Always	
A	A	A	A and sometimes B	B	B	B

1.
I am happy and contented ☐ ☐ ☐ ☐ ☐ I am unhappy, nervous or worried

2.
I find it difficult when I am put in new situations or meet new people ☐ ☐ ☐ ☐ ☐ I find it easy when I am put in new situations or meet new people

3.
I am easygoing and it takes a lot to make me lose my temper ☐ ☐ ☐ ☐ ☐ I am irritable and quarrelsome

4.
I find it hard to concentrate on work and I am easily distracted ☐ ☐ ☐ ☐ ☐ I can concentrate on my work and I am not easily distracted

5.
I am keen to learn and I am interested in finding out about things ☐ ☐ ☐ ☐ ☐ I am not very interested in learning or finding out about things

6.
I am well behaved and I do what my teacher tells me to do ☐ ☐ ☐ ☐ ☐ I am naughty and I don't do what my teacher tells me to do

	Always A	Usually A	Sometimes A and sometimes B	Usually B	Always B	
A						B

7.

I am helpful and kind to other children ☐ ☐ ☐ ☐ ☐ I bully or am spiteful towards other children

8.

I'd rather be on my own than be with other children ☐ ☐ ☐ ☐ ☐ I'd rather be with other children than be on my own

9.

I keep going if work is hard and I like to try and find the answer to difficult problems ☐ ☐ ☐ ☐ ☐ I give up easily if work is hard and I don't like trying to find the answer to difficult problems

10.

Other children think I am unkind and spiteful ☐ ☐ ☐ ☐ ☐ Other children think I am kind and helpful

11.

My teacher thinks I am naughty and don't do as I'm told ☐ ☐ ☐ ☐ ☐ My teacher thinks I am well behaved and I do as I am told

Follow-up: The results of such an exercise would be to give scores which should indicate those children with positive as well as negative perceptions of themselves at school. However, a questionnaire is only one way of tapping such feelings. Results have to be interpreted cautiously and followed up by further observations and discussions. Such an analysis could provide a basis for reviewing issues, such as ways of creating opportunities for individuals to feel successful in class or for looking at ways in which the children relate to each other.

A central strategy in the development of positive self-concepts among children in school lies in encouraging individuals to identify qualities within themselves which they can value. It is important to provide opportunities where a wide range of qualities can be appreciated. In classrooms where competitive achievement is greatly emphasized, some children may quickly come to regard themselves unfavourably, or else learn to resent and oppose the values and the teacher. It is, however, possible to create a climate where many different qualities are valued and where children are encouraged to challenge themselves to improve their own individual performance. In this way, the dignity of the individual child can be protected and individual effort and engagement rewarded. (These ideas are extended in Chapter 5, section 3 and Chapter 10, section 3.)

One of the ways of establishing such a climate is to encourage children to evaluate their own work and to set their own personal goals.

PRACTICAL ACTIVITY 4.13

Aim: To encourage children to evaluate themselves and to review their work.

Method: This can be done informally, for example, when a story is brought for marking, the child can be asked for his or her opinion on it. More formally, perhaps at the completion of a project, children could fill in a comment form to indicate what they had liked best/least about it; what they had found easy/difficult about it; what they had learnt from it (content and skills); what they think they need to practise more or try harder at, etc. Another excellent strategy, if the children can write freely, is to ask them to keep a journal in which they can review their achievements on a regular basis.

Follow-up: Such procedures will reveal specific difficulties which children experience and help the teacher to match future tasks appropriately. However, it is necessary to consider what difficulties some children might experience. How could the teacher help them to articulate their own needs?

2.4 Children's views of teachers

If we are trying to negotiate a positive working relationship with children, it is important to know how each of the individuals involved in the relationship view each other. Hence, it is important to know how children perceive their teachers.

A considerable amount of evidence has been collected in this area (Blishen 1969; Makins 1969; Meighan 1978). Much of the evidence suggests that children like teachers who 'make them learn'. They expect teachers to teach, by which they seem to mean to take initiatives and to be in control. On the other hand, they also like teachers who are prepared to be flexible and to respond to the different interests of the individuals in the class. Children dislike teachers who have favourites or who are unpredictable in their moods. Most children like a teacher who can sometimes 'have a laugh'. Hence, it seems that children like teachers who are firm, flexible, fair and fun.

PRACTICAL ACTIVITY 4.14

Aim: To find out children's criteria for a 'good teacher'.

Method: Hold a discussion (with the whole class, or in small groups which can then report back to the whole class) on what makes a good teacher. Perhaps the discussion could be couched in terms of suggestions for a student on how to become a good teacher. Discussions with children on such a topic must obviously be handled very carefully and only with the agreement of any teachers who are involved.

Follow-up: Such information can be interesting in two ways:
1. It reveals something of the children's expectations of what it is to be a 'teacher'.
2. It can serve as a useful form of feedback on a teacher's effectiveness in communicating his or her conception of 'being a teacher' and in implementing his or her values, aims and commitments. It could also lead to a reconsideration of those values, aims and commitments.

PRACTICAL ACTIVITY 4.15

Aim: To provide an opportunity for children to analyse the teaching they experience.

Method: At the end of a term, when children in some schools receive reports from teachers, it would be possible for children, also, to write 'reports' on their teacher, or, on the work they have done that term. They could comment on what they have enjoyed and why, and what they have not enjoyed and why.

Follow-up: Such reports could be of particular interest to student teachers at the end of their period of teaching in a school.

PRACTICAL ACTIVITY 4.16

Aim: To find out children's views on school.

Method: Children could be asked to write a story of their ideal school, or their policies if they were the head teacher.

Follow-up: Consider the pattern of ideas which emerges. Is there any consensus? What practical suggestions emerge? What implications do the children's views have for us? How should we respond?

2.5 Children's culture and their views of each other

So far, the focus has been on the teacher, the child and their mutual perceptions. However, it is most important to remember that, although the teacher is a central figure, classrooms are a meeting-place for many children; indeed, Jackson (1968) referred to 'the crowd' as being a salient feature. How children learn to cope with being one of a crowd and how they relate to each other is of consequence. This can affect how well the children settle in the class socially, and, in turn, may affect their learning. There is, thus, a social dimension to classroom life.

Children's culture has been described by Davies (1982, p. 33) as the result of children 'constructing their own reality with each other' and 'making sense of and developing strategies to cope with the adult world'. Thus, it reflects the children's collective perspectives and actions, many of which can be interpreted as defensive responses to children's relative dependence on adults.

Children's play is, therefore, an important means by which they can identify with each other, establish themselves as members of a group, try out different roles and begin to develop independence and responsibility. Young children often make friends with those who are immediately accessible and with whom they share common experiences (Rubin 1980). Typically, their friends are children who live close by, who are in their class or who are the children of their parents' friends. When peer groups begin to form, each individual is likely to have to establish their membership of the group in a number of ways. For example, each member may be expected to contribute and conform to the norms which are shared by the group: for example, liking similar games, toys and TV programmes; supporting the same football team or pop group; liking the same fashions. Group members will also be expected to be loyal to each other, 'stand up for their mates', play together and share things.

A further feature of children's culture is status. As children try to establish their individual identities among their peers, each will be valued in particular ways. Sometimes this value will be based on prowess in the playground: for example, in skipping, football, fighting. In addition, the identity which children develop through their school-work and their relationship with teachers may influence the way children are perceived by their peers. Where this is the case, there are clear implications for us as teachers. This process of differentiation of children, in terms of their status with both teachers and with other children, affects their own self-image. The process starts during the early years at school and has been found to increase during children's school lives. It may lead to a polarization of pro-school and anti-school cultures (Lacey 1970). Hence, the status and self-image of the children have significant consequences for the children's development during their school years—and these can last into their adult lives.

Teachers may wish to know something of the patterns of children's friendships to use this information to sustain a positive learning atmosphere and so that friendships might be used as the basis of grouping arrangements in classrooms.

For reasons of this sort, trying to establish the friendship patterns within the classroom may be of particular interest. Many teachers feel that they 'know' their class well and several friendship groupings may be clearly identifiable. Nevertheless, friendship is very complex, and with younger children may be highly fluid. Constructing a sociogram can begin to capture some of this complexity.

Friendships can be a source of much pain and distress. It is also easy to fail to notice things, such as that an outgoing child may actually lack a particular friend of his or her own. Socio-metric analysis can help in developing this sort of awareness and sensitivity, but there are other ways. For instance, Sluckin (1981) spent many hours watching children in their playgrounds. He observed their 'playground code', which encompas-

PRACTICAL ACTIVITY 4.17

Aim: To try to identify the class friendship patterns.

Method:

It is possible to construct a socio-gram to indicate friendships.

1. Each child can be asked, confidentially, to write down the names of the three people with whom he/she would most like to play, or with whom he/she would most like to do a particular classroom activity.

2. If desired, children could also be asked for the names of those with whom they would least like to play or work.

3. Having collected the data, friendship groupings can then be picked out and plotted. It is often easier to start with the reciprocal choices, where these are also positive (i.e. two or more children name each other as children with whom they would like to play, or work).

4. Where the choices are positively reciprocated, write down the names, linked with a double-headed arrow (i.e. $\longleftrightarrow$).

5. Where the choice is not reciprocated, link the names with a single-headed arrow (i.e. $\rightarrow$).

6. Where a negative choice is reciprocated (that is, there is mutual dislike), link the names with a dotted, double-headed arrow (i.e. $\longleftarrow\cdots\cdots\longrightarrow$).

7. Where a negative choice is one-way, link the names with a dotted single-headed arrow (i.e. $\cdots\cdots\longrightarrow$).

From the diagram thus created (which will probably take more than one attempt), it should now be possible to isolate various features, such as:

- Clusters (i.e. three or more pupils who show mutual, positive relationships—a clique).
- Pairs (i.e. two pupils who show mutual choices).
- Isolates (i.e. those whom no one positively chooses but towards whom no one displays negative feelings).
- Rejectees (i.e. those who are negatively identified and actively disliked).

Follow-up: A number of questions need to be considered:

1. Are there any isolates or rejectees? If this results in any negative behaviour on the part of any children, what can a teacher do to help all the children in their social development, so that they learn to handle differences in positive ways and try to find ways by which they can accept each other? At the same time, it is important to remember that some children may choose to be outsiders for a time: they may be very cautious in establishing relationships and may, at first, prefer to be loners.

2. Have groups emerged which are based on race, social class, ability or sex? To what extent are these reflections of criteria used in the school?

3. Have the friendship patterns discovered got any implications for classroom management policies (e.g. seating and collaborative groupwork activities)? Is understanding a particular individual, or group, enhanced by greater knowledge of their place in the children's social structure?

sed things such as ways of behaving, establishing status and resolving disputes. Observing, in a consciously focused way on such issues, could be valuable.

CONCLUSION

The process of engaging in activities such as those suggested in this chapter should help us as teachers to place our aims in a realistic personal perspective. If the many unconscious influences on our teaching can be made explicit, it is easier to identify where we are being most successful and where perhaps our aims and our practice do not match as well as they might. It is also possible, by trying to make the implicit explicit, to be more aware of how we get to know children and of the evidence upon which we base our understanding. Furthermore, by becoming more aware of the children's perceptions of us as teachers, of their culture and their perspectives on each other, we are more likely to be able to take account of their needs when planning and making provision for classroom activities.

NOTES FOR FURTHER READING

A very accessible and insightful introduction to the importance of considering the 'self' of teachers and children remains:

Hargreaves, D. H. (1972) *Interpersonal Relationships and Education*. London: Routledge & Kegan Paul.

A classic sociological analysis of these matters is:

Goffman, E. (1959) *The Presentation of Self in Everyday Life*. New York: Doubleday.

Easen provides many suggestions for coming to understand our 'selves' more clearly:

Easen, P. (1985) *Making School-Centred INSET Work*. London: Croom Helm.

The following paper is a particularly sensitive account of the challenges which are posed for primary-school teachers:

Nias, J. (1984a) The definition and maintenance of self in primary teaching, *British Journal of Sociology of Education* **5,** (3).

See also:

Nias, J. (forthcoming) *Becoming and Being a Primary School Teacher*. London: Methuen.

A considerable amount of work on teacher-biography has been conducted in recent years. This illustrates links between the personal and professional spheres of activity and demonstrates effects on careers. Among the best are:

Ball, S. J. and Goodson, I. F. (1985) *Teachers' Lives and Careers*. London: Falmer Press.
Connell, R. W. (1985) *Teachers' Work*. London: Allen & Unwin.
Sikes, P. J., Measor, L. and Woods, P. (1985) *Teacher Careers*. London: Falmer Press.

On questions of aims, values and commitments, there are a number of useful philosophical analyses. See for example:

Bantock, G. H. (1980) *Dilemmas of the Curriculum*. Oxford: Martin Robinson.
Barrow, R. (1975) *Moral Philosophy for Education*. London: Allen & Unwin.
Peters, R. S. (1966) *Ethics and Education*. London: Allen & Unwin.
Straughan, R. and Wilson, J. (1983) *Philosophising about Education*. London: Holt, Rinehart & Winston.

The largest empirical study of primary teachers' aims is reported in:

Ashton, P M. *et al.* (1975) *The Aims of Primary Education: A study of Teachers' Opinions.* London: Macmillan.

Ashton, P. M. (1981) Primary teachers' aims 1969–77, in Simon, B. and Willcocks, J. (eds.) *Research and Practice in the Primary Classroom.* London: Routledge & Kegan Paul.

For an analysis of commitments at a more immediate and personal level, see:

Nias, J. (1981) Commitment and motivation in primary school teachers, *Educational Review* (33), 181–190.

For an excellent historical analysis which demonstrates the importance of considering aims and value-positions within their social context, see:

Grace, G. (1978) *Teachers, Ideology and Control.* London: Routledge & Kegan Paul.

Materials designed to provoke thinking about these issues are available in:

Grant, K. A. (ed.) (1984) *Preparing for Reflective Thinking.* Boston: Allyn & Bacon.

A comprehensive account of research on the effects of teachers' expectations on pupils is provided in:

Meighan, R. (1981) *A Sociology of Educating.* London: Holt, Rinehart & Winston.

See also:

Part 3 of Hammersley, M. (ed) (1986) *Case Studies in Educational Research.* Milton Keynes: Open University Press.

The most comprehensive collections of advice and ideas on keeping records about children are:

Clift, P., Weiner, G. and Wilson, E. (1981) *Record Keeping in the Primary School.* London: Longman.

Shipman, M. (1983) *Assessment in Primary and Middle Schools.* London: Croom Helm.

On children's 'needs', see:

Kelmer-Pringle, M. (1974) *The Needs of Children.* London: Hutchinson.

For philosophical discussions of the difficulties in identifying needs, in particular of the values which must be inherent in any such attempt, see:

Barrow, R. (1984) *Giving Teaching back to Teachers.* Brighton: Wheatsheaf.

Dearden, R. F. (1968) *The Philosophy of Primary Education.* London: Routledge & Kegan Paul.

Two useful books which introduce and apply psychological findings to the school context are:

Child, D. (1981) *Psychology and the Teacher.* London: Holt, Rinehart & Winston.

Fontana, D. (1981) *Psychology for Teachers.* London: Macmillan.

Other excellent books on children's cognitive development, which also provide clear critiques of Piagetian theory, are:

Donaldson, M. (1978) *Children's Minds.* London: Fontana.

Donaldson, M., Grieve, R. and Pratt, C. (eds.) (1983) *Early Childhood Development and Education.* Oxford: Blackwell.

A comprehensive book on the importance of children's sense of self in education is:

Burns, R. B. (1982) *Self-concept Development and Education.* London: Holt, Rinehart & Winston.

There are a number of interesting books on children's culture, friendships and perspectives. A collection which illustrates such work is:

Pollard, A. (ed.) (1987) *Children and Their Primary Schools: A New Perspective.* London: Falmer Press.

Other useful books which focus on specific issues are:

Calvert, B. (1975) *The Role of the Pupil.* London: Routledge & Kegan Paul.

Davey, A. (1983) *Learning to be Prejudiced.* London: Edward Arnold.

Rubin, Z. (1980) *Children's Friendships*. London: Fontana.
Sluckin, A. (1981) *Growing up in the Playground*. London: Routledge & Kegan Paul.
Willes, M. (1983) *Children into Pupils*. London: Routledge & Kegan Paul.

The three books below are more wide-ranging in their coverage:

Davies, B. (1982) *Life in the Classroom and Playground*. London: Routledge & Kegan Paul.
Goodnow, J. and Burns, A. (1985) *Home and School: a Child's Eye View*. Sydney: Allen & Unwin.
Pollard, A. (1985) *The Social World of the Primary School*. London: Holt, Rinehart & Winston.

Chapter 5

How Are We Getting on Together? Considering Classroom Relationships and Discipline

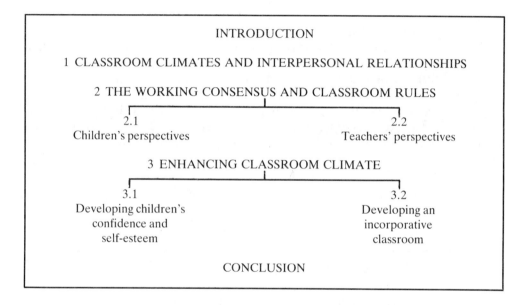

INTRODUCTION

1 CLASSROOM CLIMATES AND INTERPERSONAL RELATIONSHIPS

2 THE WORKING CONSENSUS AND CLASSROOM RULES

2.1	2.2
Children's perspectives	Teachers' perspectives

3 ENHANCING CLASSROOM CLIMATE

3.1	3.2
Developing children's confidence and self-esteem	Developing an incorporative classroom

CONCLUSION

INTRODUCTION

The quality of classroom relationships is commonly regarded as being very important, but it is also extremely intangible. As we suggested in Chapter 2, it has played a prominent part in the child-centred ideology which has influenced primary practice for many years. It is also considered to be important in facilitating learning, in providing both teacher and children with a sense of self-fulfilment and, in addition, it is often seen as the basis for a positive, purposefully disciplined working atmosphere. Yet, classroom relationships is a subject which often seems to defy analysis. Perhaps this is because relationships are the product of such very particular, complex, and subtle personal interactions between teachers and children.

Despite such inherent difficulties, the issue is of such importance that reflective teachers are likely to have it almost constantly in mind. This chapter sets out a framework for consideration of the issue. The framework is based on various analytic models of classroom relationships and is largely derived from interpretive studies.

This chapter is in three main parts. It is particularly concerned with the importance of the mutual awareness of classroom rules, with the monitoring of children's perspectives and with developing positive and incorporative classroom strategies. It also addresses the issue of our own feelings towards children.

The chapter begins, in a more general way, by considering some of the insights on classroom climates and interpersonal relationships which have been developed by social-psychologists.

1 CLASSROOM CLIMATES AND INTERPERSONAL RELATIONSHIPS

The influence of classroom environments on teachers and children has been a research topic for many years. One obvious question which emerged was how to define the 'environment'. Withall (1949) answered this by highlighting the 'socio-emotional climate' as being particularly significant. Indeed, he attempted to measure it by classifying various types of teacher statement: learner supportive, problem structuring, neutral, directive, reproving and teacher self-supportive. Understanding of the topic moved on when researchers began to define classroom environment in terms of the perception of teachers and children, rather than relying on outside observers (see Moos 1979; Walberg 1979). Further developments in this field have been comprehensively reviewed by Fraser (1986). He also provides a way for teachers to investigate the climate in their own classrooms—the 'My Classroom Inventory' (Fraser and Fisher 1984). This can give direct and structured feedback on children's feelings about classroom life and could be used, for example, at the beginning and end of a school year (see Practical Activity 5.1).

PRACTICAL ACTIVITY 5.1

Aim: To 'measure' overall classroom climate at a particular point in time.

Method: Each child will need a copy of the inventory opposite. As a class (or in a group) the children should be asked to circle the answer which 'best describes what their classroom is like'. The items could be read out in turn for children to give a simultaneous, but individual, response.

Scoring of answers can be done using the 'teachers' column. 'Yes' scores 3 and 'No' scores 1, except where reversed scoring is indicated (R). Omitted or undecipherable answers are scored 2.

There are five scales, made up by adding scores on the various items indicated, i.e.

Satisfaction (S)	Items 1, 6, 11, 16, 21
Friction (F)	Items 2, 7, 12, 17, 22
Competitiveness (Cm)	Items 3, 8, 13, 18, 23
Difficulty (D)	Items 4, 9, 14, 19, 24
Cohesiveness (Ch)	Items 5, 10, 15, 20, 25

Follow-up: Mean scores for each scale will provide some indication of the quality of the overall classroom climate and may raise issues for further consideration. (It should be noted that the inventory reproduced here is a short form of a longer inventory and is not a statistically reliable measure of the feelings of individuals.)

NAME _____

SCHOOL _____

CLASS _____

Remember you are describing your *actual* classroom	Circle your answer	For teacher's use
1. The pupils enjoy their schoolwork in my class.	Yes No	
2. Children are always fighting with each other.	Yes No	
3. Children often race to see who can finish first.	Yes No	
4. In our class the work is hard to do.	Yes No	
5. In my class everybody is my friend.	Yes No	
6. Some pupils are not happy in class.	Yes No	R
7. Some of the children in our class are mean.	Yes No	
8. Most children want their work to be better than their friend's work.	Yes No	
9. Most children can do their schoolwork without help.	Yes No	R
10. Some people in my class are not my friends.	Yes No	R
11. Children seem to like the class.	Yes No	
12. Many children in our class like to fight.	Yes No	
13. Some pupils feel bad when they don't do as well as the others.	Yes No	
14. Only the smart pupils can do their work.	Yes No	
15. All pupils in my class are close friends.	Yes No	
16. Some of the pupils don't like the class.	Yes No	R
17. Certain pupils always want to have their own way.	Yes No	
18. Some pupils always try to do their work better than the others	Yes No	
19. Schoolwork is hard to do.	Yes No	
20. All of the pupils in my class like one another.	Yes No	
21. The class is fun.	Yes No	
22. Children in our class fight a lot.	Yes No	
23. A few children in my class want to be first all of the time.	Yes No	
24. Most of the pupils in my class know how to do their work.	Yes No	R
25. Children in our class like each other as friends.	Yes No	

For teacher's use only

S___   F___   Cm___   D___   Ch___

The use of instruments, such as the 'My Class Inventory', can provide a helpful description of children's collective feelings and thus go some way towards representing the classroom climate. However, such techniques arguably fail to grasp either the subtleties of the interpersonal relationships to which many primary school teachers aspire, or the dynamic complexity of teacher–pupil interaction.

One excellent source of insights on relationships is the work of Rogers (1961, 1969) on counselling. He suggests that three basic qualities are required if a warm, 'person-centred' relationship is to be established: acceptance, genuineness and empathy. If we apply these to teaching, it might suggest that acceptance involves acknowledging and receiving children 'as they are'; genuineness implies that such acceptance is real and heartfelt; while empathy suggests that a teacher is able to appreciate what classroom events feel like to children. Rogers introduced the challenging idea of providing 'unconditional positive regard' for his clients and perhaps this can also provide an ideal for what teachers should offer children. Good relationships are, according to Rogers, founded on understanding and on 'giving'. Rogers's three qualities have much in common with the three key attitudes of the reflective teacher, discussed in Chapter 1. Being able to demonstrate acceptance and genuinely empathize requires 'openminded-ness' and a 'wholehearted' commitment to the children. It also necessitates 'responsibil-ity' when considering the long-term consequences of our feelings and actions.

However, this analysis is not fully adequate as a guide to classroom relationships, because additional factors are involved. For a number of reasons, the warmth and positive regard which teachers may wish to offer their class can rarely be 'unconditional'. In the first place, they are constrained by their responsibility for ensuring that the children learn adequately and appropriately. Secondly, the fact that they are likely to be responsible for relatively large numbers of children means that issues of class management and discipline must always condition their actions. Thirdly, the fact that teachers, themselves, will have feelings, concerns and interests in the classroom means that they, too, need to feel the benefit of a degree of acceptance, genuineness and empathy if they are to give of their best. Good relationships in classrooms must, then, be based on teachers having earned their respect, their authority and their personal security. Without this, a mutual positive regard between teachers and their classes cannot be developed. Instead, the children are likely to regard the teacher as 'soft' or as 'muddled'.

If, as reflective teachers, we are to take full account of the interpersonal climate in our classrooms, we need a form of analysis which goes beyond description and measurement. It needs to recognize both the rate at which things can happen in classrooms and the inevitable power relationships between teachers and children. One such form of analysis, we suggest, is offered by adopting an interpretive approach and, in particular, by using the concept of a 'working consensus'.

2 THE WORKING CONSENSUS AND CLASSROOM RULES

The concept of 'working consensus' (Hargreaves 1972) helps us to identify the factors involved in the dynamics of relationships between teacher and children. A working consensus is based on a recognition of the legitimate interests of other people and on a mutual exchange of dignity between the teacher and the children in a class. Embedded in this is a tacit recognition of the coping needs of the other and a shared understanding that the 'self' of the other will not be unduly threatened in the classroom (Pollard 1985).

In a classroom, both teachers and children have the capacity to make life very difficult for each other and a pragmatic basis for negotiation thus exists. However, a positive relationship, or working consensus, will not just appear. To a very great extent, the development and nature of this relationship will depend on initiatives made by teachers, as they try to establish rules and understandings of the way they would like things to be in their classrooms.

Children expect such initiatives from teachers and they are unlikely to challenge their teacher's authority to take them, so long as the teacher acts competently and in ways which children regard as 'fair'. However, it is also the case that, through negotiating the working consensus, the children recognize the greater power of the teacher. As they do so they also expect that the teacher's power will be partially circumscribed by the understandings which they jointly create within the classroom.

Understandings and 'rules' develop in classrooms about a great many things. These might include, for example, rules about noise levels, standards of work, movement and interpersonal relationships. The first few weeks of contact with a class—the period of 'initial encounters' (Ball 1981)—is a particularly important opportunity during which a teacher can take initiatives and introduce routines and expectations (Hamilton 1977). This is often a 'honeymoon period' when teachers attempt to establish their requirements and the children opt to play a waiting game. However, both the 'rules' and the teacher's capacity to enforce them are normally tested by the children before long, for children usually want to find out 'how far they can go' and 'what the teacher is like' when pressed.

As a working consensus is negotiated, both overt and tacit rules are produced. These are normally accepted by the majority of the class and become taken for granted.

While some classroom rules are overt, there are many more which are tacit. Awareness of this is very important for all teachers, but it is especially necessary for a student teacher who is likely to be working with children who have already established a set of understandings with their class teacher. Two things have to be done: the first is to find out what the rules are; the second is to check that when attempting to enforce and act within them, student teachers are doing so in ways which will be regarded as 'fair'. This is essential if teachers are to establish the legitimacy of their actions in the eyes of the children.

The concept of 'fairness' is vitally important in establishing a working consensus. Because of this, reflective teachers need to develop a variety of ways of monitoring children's perspectives and the criteria by which they make judgements about teachers. For this reason, a number of possible techniques are suggested below.

PRACTICAL ACTIVITY 5.2

Aim: To identify the overt and tacit content of classroom rules.

Method:
1. Asking the children is the obvious first step. With care, this can be done either in discussion or might be introduced as a written activity. Children usually enjoy such activities, but they will obviously tend to produce more information on the overt rules than on the tacit ones.

2. The best way to gather information on tacit rules is to study the patterns which exist in what people do. Observation, using a notebook to record such patterns, is one possibility. Another way is to record the events which lead to children being reminded of 'the way we do things here' or to being 'told off'. These could be noted during observation, or a video-cassette recording could be made of a session for later analysis.

Follow-up: Knowing the overt and tacit content of rules in a classroom makes it easier to evaluate social situations accurately, to act with the competence of a 'member' and to use such rules in achieving goals.

To be unaware of classroom rules and understandings is likely to produce a negative response from the children, because actions which they regard as incompetent or unfair will inevitably be made.

PRACTICAL ACTIVITY 5.3

Aim: To check that we are acting in ways which are regarded as being 'fair'.

Method: Again, the only really valid source of information on this is the children. While it is possible to discuss the issue openly with them, it is probably less contentious and just as satisfactory to watch and note their responses to teacher actions. This should be a continuous process for teachers who are sensitive to the way their children feel about school, but it is worth while to focus on the issue from time to time. Both verbal and non-verbal behaviour could be noted and interpreted—the groans and the expressions of pleasure, the grimaces and the smiles. From such information, and from the awareness to be gained from such an activity, it should be possible to analyse classroom actions in terms of the classification which is discussed below.

One obvious but important point to note here is that not all the children will feel the same about teacher actions. This requires careful consideration (see Chapter 10).

Follow-up: The feedback, which this activity should produce, could contribute to the smooth running of the classroom and to the maintenance of the working consensus. If rules, which were previously established, are being broken by a new teacher, then the children are likely to become resentful. If classroom rules are not being maintained and enforced by the teacher, then the children may well consider the teacher to be 'soft' and may try to 'play him or her up' for a 'laugh' at their expense.

In addition to the content and legitimacy of classroom rules, on which practical activities have been suggested, there are several other aspects of rules which can also be productively considered. In particular, the 'strength' and the 'consistency' of rules can be identified.

The strength of rules indicates the extent to which situations or events are 'framed' by expectations. This concept is referred to as 'rule-frame' (Pollard 1980). It relates to the way in which action is constrained by understandings of appropriate behaviour which are developed for particular situations. For instance, one might compare the strong rule-frame which often exists in a hushed library, with the weak rule-frame which often exists in classrooms during wet dinner-breaks. For some purposes, such as a transition between phases of a session, one might want the rule-frame to be strong, thus ensuring very tight control. On other occasions, such as during an indoor play-time, a weak rule-frame may be perfectly acceptable and allows children much more choice. Situations of difficulty often arise where a strong rule-frame is expected by a teacher, but children act as if the rule-frame were weak. If this happens, a teacher has to act quickly to clarify and define the situation and to re-establish the rules in play.

Teachers can influence the degree of rule-frame by their actions, statements and movements. For example, an active, purposeful entry into a classroom is a clear signal that a teacher wants to get attention and one which will normally tighten the frame immediately. Conversely, acting rather casually, or withdrawing into conversation with a visiting adult, will usually cause the rule-frame to weaken and may result in children relaxing in their approach to activities.

The ability of a teacher to manage the strength of rule-frame has a great deal to do with classroom discipline. In particular, skilful management provides a means of pre-empting serious difficulties by giving clear expectations about acceptable be-haviour. By its very nature, though, the development of such understandings cannot be rushed and frequently needs to be reviewed explicitly by teachers and children.

The degree of consistency with which rules are maintained provides an underlying structure for learning sessions. Conversely, teacher inconsistency tends to reduce the integrity of the working consensus and the sense of fairness on which it is based. This, in turn, can lead to a variety of subsequent control difficulties.

Therefore, relationships between teacher and children, which derive from a working consensus, have important implications for discipline and control. Figure 5.1 provides a simple model which may help us to reflect on the types of action which teachers and children may make in classrooms when a working consensus exists. The most important distinction is between actions which are bounded by the understandings of the working consensus and those which are not. Five basic 'types of action' can be identified.

Teacher acts				Child acts
Unilateral	Within working consensus			Unilateral
Non-legitimate censure	Legitimate routine censure	Conformity	Legitimate routine deviance	Non-legitimate rule-framed disorder

Figure 5.1 A classification of types of teacher and child classroom action

Non-legitimate censure. This is the type of teacher action which children dislike and cannot understand. It often occurs when a teacher loses his or her temper or feels under great pressure. The effect of this action is that the children feel attacked and unable to cope. They perceive teacher power being used without justification. This action lies outside the bounds of the working consensus and is likely to lead to a breakdown in relationships.

Routine censure. This is the typical teacher response to children's routine deviance: a mild reprimand. It will be regarded by the children as legitimate in so far as such a reprimand will not threaten the dignity of a child nor be employed inappropriately. Censures of this type are within the bounds of the working consensus.

Conformity. These actions, by teachers or children, are 'as expected'. They are accord-ing to the tacit conventions and agreements of the working consensus.

Routine deviance. This is that type of mischief or petty misdemeanour which is accepted as being part of the normal behaviour of children. Talking too loudly, 'having a laugh' and working slowly are examples. Such activities are partly expected by teachers and are not normally intended by children as a threat. They are thus within the bounds of the working consensus.

Non-legitimate rule-framed disorder. This is a type of child action which teachers dislike and find hard to understand. It often occurs when a child or a group of children feels unable to cope with a classroom situation and thus seek to disrupt it. They are particularly prone to do this if they perceive themselves to have been treated 'unfairly' or feel that their dignity has been attacked. Action of this type usually reflects the cultural rules of peer groups and can be used to build up a type of 'solidarity' or an alternative source of positive self-esteem.

Many of the suggested practical activities below are designed to assist in the analysis of classroom relationships, using this basic classification. The central argument in what follows is that 'good relationships' are based on the existence of a negotiated sense of acceptability and fairness which teachers and children share. Therefore, it is important to begin by considering various ways of understanding children's perspectives.

2.1 Children's perspectives

Teaching can only be regarded as successful if the learners are learning. Generally speaking, for this to be achieved, the learners have to be motivated and achieve a sense

---

PRACTICAL ACTIVITY 5.4

Aim: To gather information on how children feel about curricular activities which they undertake in school.

Method:

1. One method, suitable for children for whom writing is not difficult, is simply to ask them to write a comparison of two activities which you choose. It may be worth structuring this at the beginning by getting the children to make notes under headings such as the ones below:

	Good things	Bad things
Activity 1		
Activity 2		

2. An alternative would be to carry out a similar exercise verbally. There is no reason why even very young children cannot participate in discussions about the activities which they like and dislike. Fairly open questions might be used, such as, 'Can you tell me about the things that you like doing best at school?' and 'Can you tell me about the things which you don't like doing?' These, if followed up sensitively by further enquiries to obtain reasons (and the results recorded), should soon show up the children's criteria and patterns in their opinions about your provision. The recording is important: when there is no record to analyse, it remains easy to collect such information informally and intuitively, but one is much more likely to fail to notice its message.

Follow-up: This activity should yield data of considerable importance for future planning and provision, and should be analysed to identify any patterns in the children's perspectives. If some children seem to be poorly motivated, to lack interest or to dispute the value of an activity, then the situation must be reconsidered and remedial measures taken.

of self-fulfilment through their classroom activities. They have to be involved in the process of learning and they have to appreciate that the effort which is required of them is worthwhile. It is thus very valuable to collect data from children on the subject of how they feel about the classroom activities in which they are required to engage. This information supplies a basic type of feedback on children's motivation and can be set alongside other diagnostic information about their learning achievements and difficulties.

The method suggested above involves direct comparison between classroom activities in different areas of the curriculum. Such comparisons are useful because they often highlight hidden issues.

Another important aspect of children's perspectives are their views on their own teacher—already introduced, in a general way, in Chapter 4.

This is a fairly well-researched issue and enquiry into it can yield good summary data on the way children feel about the quality of relationships and education in their classroom. Obviously, for professional reasons, teachers should only collect such information in their own classroom, or with the permission of other people who may be concerned. Research has invariably shown that children like teachers who are kind, consistent, efficient at organizing and teaching, patient, fair and who have a sense of humour. They dislike teachers who are domineering, boring, unkind, unpredictable and unfair.

Strict/soft are two common constructs which children use, with 'strict but fair' often being positively valued. 'Softness' is usually regarded as a sign of weakness.

Predictability is also usually important and children are often expert interpreters of the 'moods' of their teachers. Indeed, more generally, children's feedback to their teachers has been found to be both relatively accurate and reliable.

PRACTICAL ACTIVITY 5.5

Aim: To gather feedback from children about how they feel about their teacher.

Method: A direct method may be best for this activity, but it should be timed carefully to come at the end of a session or series of activities, perhaps at half-term or at the end of a topic. We suggest that the children are simply asked to rate their teacher on a scale such as the one below:

'Most of the time my teacher is . . . . . .'

Soft	1 2 3 4 5	Strict
Unfair	1 2 3 4 5	Fair
Boring	1 2 3 4 5	Interesting
Serious	1 2 3 4 5	Fun
Moody	1 2 3 4 5	Not moody

Follow-up: The results of any activities designed to elicit children's points of view should provide considerable food for thought for a reflective teacher.

2.2 Teachers' perspectives

So far, a number of suggestions have been made about how a teacher can take account of the perspectives, feelings and position of children. Now it is time to change the focus on to ourselves as teachers, for, as was discussed in Chapter 4, the self-image of a teacher is just as important to maintain as the self-image of the child. Good teaching has never been easy, because, to some extent, it has always meant placing the learner's needs before the teacher's. However, classroom relationships are a very special and subtle phenomenon. On the one hand, the nature of the working consensus is related to disciplinary issues and problems which are likely to confront the teacher. On the other, the quality of the relationships can, potentially, provide a continuous source of personal pleasure and self-fulfilment for a teacher.

If our own feelings as teachers are also an important factor in maintaining a positive working consensus, then ways of monitoring our feelings may be useful.

PRACTICAL ACTIVITY 5.6

Aim: To monitor and place in perspective our own feelings on classroom relationships.

Method: Probably the best way to do this is by keeping a diary. This does not have to be an elaborate, time-consuming one, but simply a personal statement of how things have gone and of how we felt.

The major focus of the diary will obviously be on relationships. It is very common for such reflections to concentrate in more detail on particular disciplinary issues or on relationships with specific individuals.

Diary-keeping tends to heighten awareness and, at the same time, it supplies a document which can be of great value in reviewing events.

We would suggest that, once a diary has been kept for a fortnight or so, some time is set aside to read it carefully and to reflect upon it with a view to drawing reasonably balanced conclusions about ourselves and our planning of future policies in the classroom. It would be better still to discuss the issues which are raised with a colleague or friend.

---

3 ENHANCING CLASSROOM CLIMATE

So far in this chapter we have argued that the nature of classroom climates and the quality of interpersonal relationships are fundamental to establishing a positive learning environment. Having identified ways of improving our understanding of both teachers' and children's perspectives of these issues, it is now time to consider ways of enhancing other aspects of the learning environment.

3.1 Developing children's confidence and self-esteem

Children often feel vulnerable in classrooms, particularly because of their teacher's power to control and evaluate. This affects how children experience school and their openness to new learning. A considerable responsibility is thus placed on teachers to reflect on how they use their power and on how it affects children.

PRACTICAL ACTIVITY 5.7

Aim: To assess the degree and type of positive reinforcement given to children.
Method: There are many possibilities here.

1. Self-monitoring, that is trying to remain conscious of the need to praise efforts and achievements which children make. This involves actively looking for possibilities, but they must be genuine. The essence of this activity is expressed in the phrase 'Catch them being good'. Awareness is also likely to be heightened if the learning stages of each child and the tasks in which they are engaged are thoroughly appreciated and matched (see p. 92). With regard to our own tendencies to 'be positive' or otherwise, a diary-type record is well worth keeping for a period.
2. Observing by colleagues. A colleague who is able to sit in on a session to observe will be able to provide invaluable feedback. A suggested observational schedule is:

Child's initial action	Teacher's reinforcing action	Child's response

A discussion would be very helpful after the session, particularly to identify any patterns in children's responses and to consider whether other appropriate opportunities for reinforcement are being missed.

3. Analysis of displays of children's work. Questions which might be asked include: Are the genuine efforts of all children represented? Does the quality of the display indicate that the work is valued?

4. Analysis of written feedback to children. Children's workbooks provide a permanent record of teacher responses to their efforts. A tally of 'types of comment' is an easy exercise. Some headings might be:

	Child A	Child B	Child C
Encouragement given: a phrase a sentence			
Diagnostic advice given			
Extension proposed			
No comment given			
Discouragement given			

Follow-up: There is a simple point to be made in considering attempts to be positive as a whole. If, as an outcome of this monitoring, it is found that some children do not receive adequate reinforcement, bearing in mind their apparent needs, then the teacher should both check that opportunities for praise are not missed and make provision so that genuine opportunities occur. These can then be monitored. This is another, motivational, aspect of the 'match' (see Chapter 6) which is very important for the personal development of any child.

There are two basic aspects of this. First, there is the positive aspect of how teachers use their power constructively to encourage, to reinforce appropriate child action and to enhance self-esteem. Secondly, however, there is the potential for the destructive use of such power. The second issue thus concerns the manner in which teachers act when 'rules' are broken. This can be negative and damaging, but skilful and aware teachers will aim to make any necessary disciplinary points yet still preserve the dignity of each child. Activities are suggested below to monitor each of these aspects, starting with 'being positive'.

'Being positive' involves constant attempts to build on success. The point is to generate suitable challenges and then to make maximum use of the children's achievements to breed still more. This policy assumes that each child will have some successes. Sometimes a child's successes may be difficult to identify. Such difficulties often reveal more about the inability of an adult to understand and diagnose what a child is experiencing. As the psychologist Adler argued many years ago (Adler 1927), irrespective of the baseline position, there is always an associated level of challenge—a target for learning achievement—which is appropriate and which can be the subject of genuine praise. It may range from producing a vivid story to forming a letter of the alphabet correctly, or from helping another child to sustaining a period of attention and concentration in story-time. The appropriateness of the achievement is a matter for a teacher to judge, but the aim should be to encourage all children to accept challenges and achieve successes.

This brings us to 'avoiding destructive action'. This is the second aspect of the teacher's use of power—the way in which control is used. On this issue, we want to focus on the dangers of 'flashpoints' in classrooms: the situations in which teachers 'lose their cool' and start to act unilaterally. All teachers would probably agree that a class of children has to be under control if purposeful and productive activities are to take place. However, a teacher's power can be exercised in many ways. In most situations, teachers try to be calm, firm and fair; they act within the bounds of the working consensus and use various types of legitimate 'routine censure' to maintain discipline.

However, there is a well-documented tendency for teachers to reprimand children over-personally when telling them off in the heat of the moment, rather than focusing positively on the activity in which they should have engaged. The effect of this can be that the children may feel attacked and humiliated, so that, rather than conforming more, the children 'want to get back at' the teacher who has 'picked on' them 'unfairly'. Here, the problem is that the teacher's action is 'unilateral' and lies outside the understandings of the working consensus. The normally recommended way of enforcing authority, while at the same time protecting the self-esteem of the child, is to focus on the action of the children for condemnation, rather than on the children themselves (Hargreaves, Hestor and Mellor 1975). A reprimand can then be firmly given, but the self-image of each child is left relatively intact. Each child can then conform with dignity if he or she so wishes, and the incident is contained within the bounds of the working consensus. This will be discussed further in Chapter 8, where we focus on classroom management and on further aspects of discipline.

Thus, reflective teachers are likely to attempt to use their power positively and constructively, and they will be particularly aware of the potential damage to relationships which can be produced by over-hasty reactions to some classroom crises.

A further type of reflection on relationships concerns the degree of involvement by children, which brings us to the notion of what we have called the 'incorporative classroom'.

3.2 Developing an incorporative classroom

An 'incorporative classroom' is one which is consciously designed to enable each child to act as a full participant in class activities and also to feel him- or herself to be a valued member of the class. This is what most teachers would wish, but there is plenty of evidence that, in the context of curriculum pressures and large class-sizes, it is difficult to achieve. A particular feature which often causes problems is that there are variations in both the quantity and quality of teacher attention which is given to different categories of children.

PRACTICAL ACTIVITY 5.8

Aim: To identify if, when interacting with children, there are any patterns in the quantity, quality or purpose of teacher–child contacts.

Method:
1. To assess the quantity of interaction, it may be advisable to enlist the help of a colleague as an observer or to make a video-recording of a session for later analysis. A simple schedule will be required on which to record contacts. This could distinguish between contacts with girls/boys, racial groups, abilities or personalities, etc. It is then possible to make a tally of the different kinds of contacts. Decisions about whether to try to record all contacts or whether to adopt a time-sampling technique will have to be taken. If the latter is chosen, some practice is essential for the observer. It is also possible to focus on an individual child and to monitor the contacts with just that child.

2. To assess the quality of contacts requires a different approach. By quality, we have in mind, following Rogers (1980), the 'genuineness, acceptance and empathy' that is conveyed through the contact. Subjective interpretations are more likely to play a dominant part in this analysis, so it is probably helpful to use a video, or for an observer to make field-notes about the nature of contacts made. Sharing perceptions with others afterwards is a valuable way of trying to interpret this aspect of the contacts.

3. Regarding the purpose of contacts, a schedule can be devised which lists different kinds of contact. This should be in terms of descriptive and visible actions (low inference), which do not overlap (exclusive categories): for example, 'instructional', 'managerial', 'social' and 'other' contacts. Data might then be collected by time-sampling or a tally. The results could then be analysed to try to identify any different patterns of contact between girls/boys, different races, abilities or personalities.

Follow-up: If patterns in teacher–child contact are identified, they need to be evaluated against the specific aims which we have for the class as a whole and for that particular child or children. By monitoring such patterns, we become more aware of them and thus more able to change them if so desired.

There are four fairly obvious categories around which such variations have often been found: ability (Bossert 1979), gender (Clarricoates 1981), race (Giles 1977) and social class (Rist 1970). Age could also be an important factor in vertically grouped classes. In addition, it is necessary to analyse and to be aware of the responses to school life of individual children, for each responds in different ways. It is very understandable if teachers tend to deal first with children whose needs press most or whose actions necessitate an immediate response. The problem which then arises is that some other children may be consistently passed over. Arguably, the needs of all the children in a class cannot be satisfied simultaneously by any teacher.

Classes vary in the degree to which differences between children and their abilities are valued. Such differences between people must inevitably exist, but a contrast can be drawn between classes in which the strengths and weaknesses of each child are recognized and in which the particular level of achievement of each child is accepted as a starting-point, and classes in which specific qualities or abilities are regarded as being of more value than others in absolute terms. In the case of the latter, the stress is often on achievements rather than on the effort which children may have made; the ethos is often competitive rather than cooperative. The success of some children is made possible only at the cost of the relative failure of others. The overall effect is to marginalize some children, while the work of others is praised and regarded as setting a standard to which other children should aspire. The quality of work is a very important consideration, but there are also many other factors to bear in mind. For instance, we would suggest that an incorporative classroom will produce better classroom relationships and more understanding and respect for others than one which emphasizes the particular success of a few.

Thus, there are some central questions which should be answered by a reflective teacher. Among them are those which are suggested in Practical Activity 5.9. This time it takes the form of a checklist.

PRACTICAL ACTIVITY 5.9

Aim: To consider the degree to which the classroom is structured and run so that each of the children can fully identify with class activities.

Method: There are several indicators which might be considered:

1. Which is emphasized most: the absolute achievement of children or the efforts which are made?

2. In decisions about the curriculum, are the interests of each of the children recognized and given appropriate attention and is the previous experience of each of the children drawn on?

3. How is the work of the class represented—in classroom displays, in assemblies, in more public situations? Are there some children whose work features more often and others whose work is seen less often?

4. Are children helped to learn to respect each other?

5. Does any unnecessary and divisive competition take place?

Overall then, teachers wishing to sustain an incorporative classroom will set out to provide opportunities for children to feel valued and to 'join in'. At the same time, they will attempt to eliminate any routines or practices which would undercut such aims by accentuating the relative weaknesses of some children (Prutzman *et al.* 1978).

CONCLUSION

Apart from increasing the happiness and educational achievement of individual children, teachers who are attentive to the particular needs of individuals and develop good relationships with the class as a whole are likely to find that they encounter fewer disruptive incidents; perhaps too, an expectation of being caring towards each other may spread among the children and be of longer-term benefit.

Finally, there are often some children with whom more specific efforts to develop good relationships may need to be made. Such cases might include particularly able children who may become bored; children who find school-work difficult and may become frustrated; children who have special educational needs; children who are new to the class or school; and children who have been upset by events in their lives over which they have little control, such as a bereavement, a break-up of their parents' marriage or unemployment. Such children need sensitive and empathic attention and they may need special help to express their feelings, to put them in perspective, to realize that their teacher cares about them and to feel that they have tangible and appropriate targets to strive for. Above all, such care enables children to take control of their situation, with the support of their teacher, to the extent that this is possible. However, teachers should guard against being amateur therapists. Child psychologists are available and they can be invited to give advice if circumstances require their help.

NOTES FOR FURTHER READING

A comprehensive review and bibliography of recent social-psychological work on classroom climate is:

Fraser, B. J. (1986) *Classroom Environment*. London: Croom Helm.

One of a number of classic books by Carl Rogers on 'person-centred' theory is:

Rogers, C. (1969) *Freedom to Learn*. New York: Merrill.

A more general overview of classroom relationships is provided by:

Brophy, J. E. and Good, T. L. (1974) *Teacher–Student Relationships*. New York: Holt, Rinehart & Winston.

For social-psychological discussion on rules as guides to behaviour see:

Collett, P. (ed.) (1977) *Social Rules and Social Behaviour*. Oxford: Blackwell.
Harré, R. (1974) Rule as a scientific concept, in Mischel, T. (ed.) *Understanding Other Persons*. Oxford: Blackwell.

On rules in educational contexts see:

Hargreaves, D. H., Hestor, S. K. and Mellor, F. J. (1975) *Deviance in Classrooms*. London: Routledge & Kegan Paul.

The interpretive approach to classroom relationships, which has informed much of this chapter, is discussed in detail in:

Pollard, A. (1985) *The Social World of the Primary School*. London: Holt, Rinehart & Winston.

Other closely related accounts can be found in:

Delamont, S. (1983) *Interaction in the Classroom*. 2nd edn., London: Methuen.
Woods, P. (1983) *Sociology and the School: An Interactionist Viewpoint*. London: Routledge & Kegan Paul.

The original use of the concept of working consensus is well worth following up. It can be found in:

Hargreaves, D. H. (1972) *Interpersonal Relationships and Education*. London: Routledge & Kegan Paul.

The 'art' of maintaining relationships while teaching is described by:

Woods, P. (1987a) Managing the primary school teachers' role, in Delamont, S. (ed.), *The Primary School*. London: Falmer Press.

On children's confidence and self-esteem, the two books below provide a research review and practical ideas respectively:

Burns, R. B. (1982) *Self-concept Development and Education*. London: Routledge & Kegan Paul.

Cranfield, J. and Wells, H. (1976) *100 Ways to Enhance Self-concept in the Classroom*. Englewood Cliffs, NJ: Prentice-Hall.

For a fascinating study of secondary-school classrooms in which collaborative learning methods were developed so that relationships became 'the basis for learning itself', see:

Salmon, P. and Claire, H. (1984) *Classroom Collaboration*. London: Routledge & Kegan Paul.

Other constructive and stimulating books which will support the development of classroom relationships are:

Orlick, T. (1979) *Cooperative Sports and Games Book: Challenge without Competition*. London: Writers & Readers.

Prutzman, P., Burger, M. L., Bodenhamer, G. and Stern, L. (1978) *The Friendly Classroom for a Small Planet*. New Jersey: Avery Publishing.

The growing literature on personal and social education is also relevant here. For an excellent introduction, see:

Pring, R. (1984) *Personal and Social Education in the Curriculum*. London: Hodder & Stoughton.

Chapter 6

What Are We Teaching and Learning Through the Curriculum?

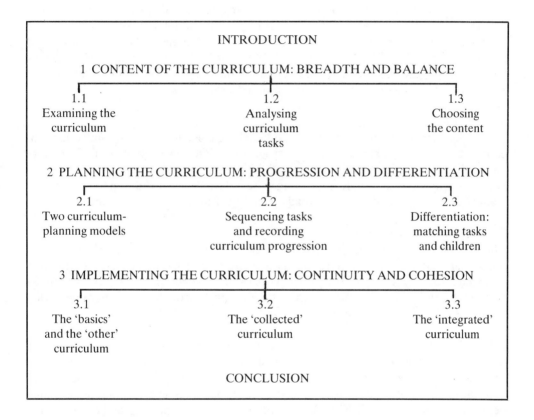

INTRODUCTION

1 CONTENT OF THE CURRICULUM: BREADTH AND BALANCE

1.1	1.2	1.3
Examining the curriculum	Analysing curriculum tasks	Choosing the content

2 PLANNING THE CURRICULUM: PROGRESSION AND DIFFERENTIATION

2.1	2.2	2.3
Two curriculum-planning models	Sequencing tasks and recording curriculum progression	Differentiation: matching tasks and children

3 IMPLEMENTING THE CURRICULUM: CONTINUITY AND COHESION

3.1	3.2	3.3
The 'basics' and the 'other' curriculum	The 'collected' curriculum	The 'integrated' curriculum

CONCLUSION

INTRODUCTION

The term 'curriculum' can be used in a number of different ways. It is important to distinguish between them because they mean different things to different people.

The official curriculum
This can be defined as 'a planned course of study' (i.e. an explicitly stated programme of learning intended for children). Such a course of study has three elements. First, there are intended activities, which are consciously planned, though they may not always actually take place. The planned activities focus on the learning which is intended to take place during school-time. It does not include learning which may additionally take place elsewhere, though it might include school-directed activities to be completed at home. Second, the official curriculum should include sequence and progression in the course of activities. Third, the planned course of activities should be designed so that it

challenges children appropriately and thus requires sustained application or study.

The hidden curriculum
The hidden curriculum is much less explicit. It refers to all that is learnt during school activities which is not a designated part of the official curriculum. It is what is 'picked up' about such things as the role of the teacher and the role of the learner; about the status and relationship of each; and about attitudes towards learning and to school. Children may also acquire ideas about the different ways boys and girls 'should' behave, or about differences 'because' of being black or white, middle class or working class.

Thus, the hidden curriculum is implicit within regular school procedures and curriculum materials. Much of what children learn from the hidden curriculum may not be intended. It may even go unrecognized and is often unexamined. It has been suggested by researchers in this field (Jackson 1968; Meighan 1981) that such implicit messages and mis-messages can have a profound effect on the self-image of children, upon their images of school and on their attitude to other social groups.

The observed curriculum
This is the curriculum that can be seen to be taking place in the classroom. It may, of course, be different from the intended official curriculum. If so, it may be useful to note and evaluate such differences. However, it must be remembered that what can be seen, in terms of activities, is not the same thing as how the teacher or children feel about it or what they learn through it, which leads to the next aspect of 'curriculum'.

The curriculum-as-experienced
This way of conceptualizing the curriculum identifies the parts of the curriculum, both official and hidden, which children actually experience from the observed curriculum and which they 'take away'. It is those parts of the curriculum which have an impact upon children. It could be argued that it is only the curriculum-as-experienced that 'educates'. The rest is forgotten.

In this chapter we focus on the official curriculum and examine three issues. In the first section we discuss the parameters and content of the curriculum and we focus on the issues of breadth and balance between different areas of learning. The second section addresses the question of analysing task demands and of planning a match between children and tasks. This includes finding ways of monitoring and recording the progression of tasks and the progress of each child. We also consider ways of differentiating between tasks and how to match them appropriately to children's needs. In the third section we discuss the issues of long-term continuity (so that consecutive learning is cumulative 'longitudinally') and cohesion (so that concurrent experiences interrelate and learning is linked 'laterally').

Practical activities here, as elsewhere in the book, provide opportunities for reflecting on the hidden and observed curriculum and on the curriculum-as-experienced.

1 CONTENT OF THE CURRICULUM: BREADTH AND BALANCE

1.1 Examining the curriculum
British primary schools have traditionally enjoyed considerable autonomy in choosing what is taught and how it is taught. Despite this, HMI's survey of 542 schools (DES 1978a) found there was a considerable overlap in the 'content' of the curriculum which

they observed. They listed 36 items which occurred in at least 80 per cent of classes. Of these items, 10 related to language skills and 12 to maths skills. Some more were concerned with social attitudes, such as reliability and consideration, while the remaining 7 were associated with aesthetic and physical education. What is noticeable is the continuing emphasis on the 'basics', despite considerable changes in the appearances and practices in primary schools, and despite wide-ranging aims and expectations which are continually emerging.

Currently, as we saw in Chapter 2, every school is required to set out its curriculum aims in publicly available brochures. Plans are being prepared to develop a framework for a 'core' curriculum within which individual schools would develop their overall curriculum. By such moves it seems likely that the curriculum will be subject to greater direction by central government. At the same time, plans are also being made to give parents a greater say in the curriculum of their children's school, thus affecting the professional educators' longstanding autonomy in this vital domain—which had at one time been regarded as a 'secret garden', into which the Secretary of State should not intrude.

However, the proposal for a curriculum framework raises major problems in terms of what should be in it, who should decide it and how often it should be reviewed. Such issues are highly contentious. Lawton has argued (1975, 1977, 1980) that the curriculum should be conceived as a selection from our 'common culture'. This, of course, begs a large number of questions about what is our 'common culture', particularly as part of that 'culture' is the respect for the diversity associated with different ethnic, gender, regional and social-class distinctions. Proposals for curricular decision-making, through discussion and cooperation at each level of the education system, may have an attractive appeal for some, but they may also obscure the very real problems which are likely to arise when different groups have contrasting perspectives and interests.

A reflective teacher, therefore, needs to consider the content of the curriculum very carefully, for, as teachers, we have a direct responsibility for what is taught. We need to examine the official content and the hidden messages of the activities which we select so that we can, more thoroughly, observe and monitor the curriculum as experienced by children.

The 1980s have witnessed a plethora of curriculum documents from a number of public bodies. These include 'The School Curriculum' (DES 1981), 'A View of the Curriculum' (DES 1980), 'The Curriculum from 5 to 16' (DES 1985a) and also 'Primary Practice' (Schools Council 1983). These documents represent different responses to a national, central concern about the curriculum.

The most comprehensive HMI document (DES 1985a) suggests that children should have access to a curriculum of similar breadth irrespective of their level of ability, the school they attend or their social circumstance, and that this can best be achieved within a framework that holds good for all students (DES 1985a, para. 3). HMI also believe that balance between curriculum components is important, though this balance need not be sought over each day, but rather over each term and year. Such a framework, it is argued, depends on unity of purpose, coherent action and debate, and on greater consistency in what is offered and expected of the learner (para. 7). The discussion document suggests that this requires careful selection and progression within the curriculum, as well as a thorough understanding of the educational needs of individual children so that tasks are appropriately differentiated (para. 5).

While many would agree with such proposals, they nevertheless raise some important questions. What exactly will the framework contain? How detailed will it be and what status will it have (i.e. advisory or compulsory)? What implications will this have for an increase in central control and the subsequent possible reduction of the much prized, professional autonomy of the individual classroom teacher? What will be the likely effects on the balance between individually and socially determined goals, between personal freedom and professional responsibility? Will such proposals affect the career structure of the profession and give greater opportunity to the 'subject specialist' or 'consultant' as opposed to the 'generalist' primary teacher?

A further issue concerns how the notion of a given framework relates to the notion of child-centred, self-motivated learning. For example, if teachers believe that the curriculum should be based on each individual child's interests and that children should be encouraged to initiate their own learning, does this conflict with the assumed advantages of every child having access to a similar curriculum? This issue revolves around our understanding of the term 'interests': whether we believe that the curriculum should be based on the self-expressed interests of children, or on areas of learning which are chosen as being in each child's interests and might therefore be centrally defined. The former might result in very varied and idiosyncratic learning experiences, while the latter would result in a common curriculum. We would have to decide whether we believe children are able to express their interests and whether we would accept all such interests as 'valid'. If not, what criteria would we use to decide which interests to 'allow'? If the curriculum is not to be based on the self-expressed interests of children, on whose interests will the curriculum be based? And, what thought will be given to what might 'interest' each child?

PRACTICAL ACTIVITY 6.1

Aim: To identify our value-position in relation to children's self-expressed interests.

Method: Ask the children what they are interested in and what they would like to do in school-time (or try to think what interests they have shown). Write down their ideas. Now consider this list and decide which ones would be acceptable and why, and which ones would not and why. What would you add and why?

Follow-up: Having reflected on the lists, preferably with a colleague, what conclusions can we each draw about how we value children's 'interests' and how we perceive the curriculum?

So far we have considered some aspects of the 'breadth' of the current primary curriculum and the implications of some of the suggestions to 'standardize' it. Now it is time to focus on the 'balance' of content which might be included within the curriculum. To begin this, we need to consider the range from which we may select and some of the possible ways of making this selection. As we have seen, there are many ways of conceptualizing the curriculum and there are also different ways of conceptualizing the contents. These differences rest partly on alternative views of 'knowledge'.

We would suggest that there are four main alternative positions regarding how knowledge is viewed. First, there are those who argue that different 'forms of knowledge' exist. These are thought to be distinguishable, philosophically, by the different ways of thinking and the different kinds of evidence which are employed in investigating them (Hirst 1965; Peters 1966). These different 'forms' are thought to be based on 'a priori' differences (i.e. logical and inherent differences). Such a view is referred to as 'rationalist' (Blenkin and Kelly 1981). Second, there are those who argue that knowledge is achieved through individuals interacting with the environment and restructuring their understanding through their experiences. Hence, knowledge is the application of intellect to experience. Proponents of this view can be termed 'empiricists' and it is evidenced in the writings of Dewey and Piaget. Third, a more sociological view suggests that knowledge can be constructed by groups of people, through their interactions with each other. Hence, they share their experiences and their perceptions of those experiences. In such an 'interactionist' approach, people are seen as developing a common sense of 'reality' (Berger and Luckman 1967). Finally, knowledge can be seen in the context of macro-social structures, and of historical forces, as being influenced by powerful social groups who define certain types of knowledge as being of high status. They may also attempt to control access to it (Young 1971).

It is the second, 'empiricist', view of knowledge which has been dominant in British primary-school rhetoric for some decades. The Hadow Report (Board of Education 1931), for example, urged that the curriculum should be 'thought of in terms of activity and experience rather than knowledge to be acquired and facts to be stored' (p. 93). Similarly, the Plowden Report (Central Advisory Council on Education 1967) argued that schools should lay stress on 'individual discovery, first-hand experience and on opportunities for creative work' (p. 187). It insisted that 'knowledge does not fall into separate compartments' (p. 187). Latterly, however, while recognizing this view, HMI have suggested (DES 1985a) that 'areas of learning and experience' can and should be identified and be used to form the basis of the curriculum.

Table 6.1 lists a version of the 'rationalists' forms of knowledge and the areas of learning and experience suggested by HMI.

Table 6.1 *Forms of knowledge and areas of learning and experience*

Forms of knowledge (Hirst 1965)	Areas of learning and experience (DES 1985a)
Empirical (physical and social sciences)	Scientific
	Technological
Mathematical	Mathematical
Aesthetic	Aesthetic and creative
Religious	Spiritual
Moral	Moral
Mental (values and intentions)	
Philosophical	
	Physical
	Linguistic and literary
	Human and social

Given the range of views about the nature of 'knowledge', it becomes clear that making a decision about breadth and balance within the curriculum is far from easy. A reflective teacher would have to question whether these distinctions were relevant to the framework of the curriculum, whether other aspects also needed to be considered, and what kind of balance was desirable (for example, equal proportions of time, or if not, in which proportions and why?).

PRACTICAL ACTIVITY 6.2

Aim: To consider the breadth and balance of official, intended curricular experiences during a day or week.

Method: Draw a matrix. List intended tasks at the left side and forms of knowledge/areas of experience along the top. Tick off the types of knowledge/areas of experience that the 'tasks' provided.

Follow-up: Review the 'breadth and balance'. What have you discovered about the curriculum? How useful and valid are distinctions between learning experiences? Compare this list with the lists of children's interests which were produced for Practical Activity 6.1. What kinds of differences emerge and what are the implications in terms of future curriculum planning?

PRACTICAL ACTIVITY 6.3

Aim: To evaluate an individual child's curricular experiences over one day or week.

Method: Note down each curriculum activity any one child actually does during this period.

Follow-up: What kind of breadth and balance exists in this observed curriculum? In classes where children can choose what they do or in which order, breadth and balance may be affected. When does this matter?

1.2 Analysing curriculum tasks

So far we have focused on the broad issues of breadth and balance in the curriculum. More detailed analysis is necessary to identify the various learning elements contained within the tasks set by teachers or initiated by children. This is a useful step for teachers to take, so that they can monitor, plan and provide a sequence of teaching–learning experiences.

In order to do this, it is necessary to decide how we wish to analyse learning experiences. Current practice (favoured by many Schools Council projects, as well as HMI) supports the division of the curriculum into knowledge, concepts, skills and attitudes—all of which may be considered as 'elements of learning' across the whole curriculum. We offer the following definitions:

Knowledge. The selection of that which is worth knowing and of interest. (See Practical Activity 6.1.)

Concepts. The generalizations and ideas which enable pupils to classify, organize and predict—to understand patterns, relationships and meanings, e.g. continuity/change, cause/consequence, interdependence/adaptation, sequence/duration, nature/purpose, authenticity, power, energy . . .

Skills. The capacity or competence to perform a task, e.g. personal/social (turn-taking, sharing), physical/practical (fine/gross motor skills), intellectual (observing, identifying, sorting/classifying, hypothesizing, reasoning, testing, imagining and evaluating), communication (oracy, literacy, numeracy, graphicacy), etc.

Attitudes. The overt expression of values and personal qualities, e.g. curiosity, perseverance, initiative, openmindedness, trust, honesty, responsibility, respect, confidence, etc.

The items listed above may provide a possible analytic framework, but they are not without problems. In particular, the concept of a 'skill' is fraught with ambiguity. Ryle (1967) introduced the distinction between 'knowledge that' and 'knowledge how' (i.e. knowing about something and knowing how to do something). The first came to be thought of as 'knowledge' and the second as a 'skill'. However, the distinction is not clear and an examination of current official curriculum documents will reveal (see, for example, DES 1980) that the term is used variously to mean a technique or a behaviour; to indicate the ability to execute a technique or behaviour; or even knowledge of a technique or behaviour.

Apart from attempting to define 'skill', it is important to identify the claims made for the usefulness of the term. Two particular claims can be distinguished. First, it is suggested that analysis of the component 'skills' of a task can provide a way of diagnosing difficulties and can thus assist in planning new learning provision. In many such instances, 'skill' has become associated with the mechanistic break-down of activities into components believed to contribute to the mastery of that activity. Second, and conversely, 'skills' are also heralded as being flexible and transferable. Therefore, it can be argued that skills are especially useful in a time of rapid change when particular knowledge may become rapidly obsolete. This sense of the term is used to encourage a consideration of what are thought of as key elements in learning to learn.

The commonly used term 'basic skills' also suffers from the ambiguities discussed above. On the one hand, 'basic skills' can be interpreted as 'initial prerequisites', as specifically instrumental to acquiring particular knowledge. This view assumes a linear, sequential mode of learning in order to achieve mastery. On the other hand, 'basic skills' can be interpreted as 'fundamental elements' underlying learning and basic to it in a range of contexts. In this view, learning is conceived more holistically and a commonality of learning strategies is assumed.

The attempt to define 'attitudes' and to distinguish them from 'skills' has raised further conceptual issues. This is particularly evident when considering social skills and attitudes. For example, what is the relationship between social behaviour and attitudes? Can they be contradictory? Does it require skill to be able to behave in a chosen way which may not be consistent with a particular attitude a learner holds?

Further, there is also a problematic relationship between attitudes and intellectual skills, for learners are likely to have 'feelings' about and attitudes towards what they are trying to learn. Hence, a reflective teacher may want to ask to what extent positive attitudes to learning foster intellectual development and to consider the role which motivation might play in learning.

Finally, it has been suggested that to master a skill it is necessary to understand the consequences of its use as well as its suitability (Elliott and Connolly 1974).

For all these reasons, it is important to understand links between skill categories and also to consider relationships between 'learning elements' (i.e. skills, attitudes, knowledge and concepts).

PRACTICAL ACTIVITY 6.4

Aim: To identify and select knowledge, concepts, skills and attitudes in a planned series of teaching–learning sessions, i.e. a 'curriculum forecast'.

Method:
1. Identify an intended age group and a time-span. Select a 'topic' (e.g. road safety) and list the knowledge, concepts, skills and attitudes which you expect to develop.

2. Using a grid similar to the one below, fill in the activities day by day, so that you can identify what opportunities for which elements of learning will occur.

	Knowledge	Concepts	Skills	Attitudes
Day/Week 1				
Day/Week 2 etc.				

Follow-up: How easy was it to identify and select elements in the four categories? Was it easier to think of an activity and then analyse it? How might this approach be refined to improve its usefulness as a tool of planning and analysis? What relationship between knowledge, concepts, skills and attitudes did you arrive at?

The purpose of analysing activities in this way is threefold. In the first place, it allows us to examine the breadth and balance of the provision we are planning, across the curriculum rather than only in terms of 'subjects'. Secondly, it encourages us to think more precisely about what we are trying to do. This should help to guide us in the questions we pose to support the children when they are engaged in activities. Thirdly, it provides a detailed framework which we can use to monitor the children's learning, which should help in identifying difficulties and then in planning future appropriate activities. The overall framework, from which we might select different items on different occasions, should provide a fine-grain analysis of tasks and assist us in the reflective cycle, as described in Chapter 1.

1.3 Choosing the content
It was suggested, in Chapter 1, that the hallmarks of the reflective teacher were openmindedness, wholeheartedness and responsibility. These three characteristics may be particularly useful in considering what the curriculum should contain and the criteria by which we should judge it.

The question of 'interests' has already been mentioned as one possible criterion, although an ambiguous one. Arguably, the reflective teacher should be openminded enough to be able to consider the 'interests' of all who are concerned with the process and results of the education system. However, teachers, as people who work directly with children, also have a particular social responsibility for the consequences of what is planned in the official curriculum, as well as for the hidden consequences of the curriculum-as-experienced. Questions of values and commitments and the use of judgement cannot be avoided.

Another possible criterion in the selection of content is 'relevance'. This, too, is almost as ambiguous as 'interests'. It can refer to that which is 'worthwhile' and intrinsically valuable or, alternatively, to that which is 'useful' and has an instrumental, practical function. As with the term 'interests', the term 'relevance' can be used in a short-term or a long-term context. It can also be used to refer to items which may have general application or to those with a specific use. Thus, the term is somewhat imprecise and, when used, calls for further discussion to clarify its intended meaning.

A third issue to consider, and one which may substantially affect the selection of content, is the question of 'resources' and, in particular, of 'first-hand experience'. The value of first-hand experience has been taken to lie in the opportunity it provides for children to interact directly with learning apparatus, real materials and events. For instance, in science, such learning experiences could encourage children to set up 'fair tests' and experiments to test their understanding. Hence, in the 'progressive ideology' of the primary school, considerable emphasis has been given to the importance of first-hand experience and to using resources from within the children's environment, which have, therefore, been said to be 'relevant'.

However, while the value of such interaction is usually accepted, the commitment to use resources within the children's environment and experience has received a mixed reaction from those involved with curriculum planning. It has been argued that too much reliance on children's immediate environment might result in limiting the children to that environment and thus in creating a rather parochial curriculum. Also, it has been suggested that children may feel bored if they only work on familiar territory. On the other hand, it can be argued that children may be able to relate meaningfully to an environment with which they can identify. They can be helped to examine it more closely, to value what they have around them and then be helped to move from the familiar to the unfamiliar.

Indeed, resources are available which can broaden the curriculum while still providing first-hand experience. For example, artefacts can be brought into the classroom or children can be taken out on visits. In addition, radio and television can play a role in providing vicarious first-hand experience. This, at least, allows each child to see and to experience other environments indirectly.

It is important to remember that no kind of resource is inherently better than any other. Each requires particular kinds of skills for a child to be able to learn from it successfully. For example, children need to learn how to listen actively to 'talks', to look carefully at objects on television, to read books and to set up experiments so that they can 'make knowledge their own' and develop 'ways of learning'.

Different resources have particular implications for the curriculum-as-experienced and for the skills, attitudes, knowledge and concepts which are likely to be developed through them. Resources should thus be seen to support a curriculum rather than as a means by which it is selected.

Finally, it is important to examine any selected curriculum content in terms of the values which it may convey, for this contributes to the hidden curriculum. Reflective teachers need to be alert to the fact that, by selecting particular areas of knowledge and particular activities, resources and experiences, they are also likely to be 'selecting' particular values and attitudes.

For instance, the very fact that the local environment is or is not used conveys certain attitudes that a teacher might have towards the 'value' of children's environment. Which artefacts, visits, programmes or books are chosen may also indicate to children that certain things are legitimate objects of learning, whereas others are not. Books used in school have been a particular focus of examination in terms of the hidden values that they contain. For example, analyses of the illustrations of children's reading schemes have shown considerable sex, class and race stereotyping: the girls help Mummy in the kitchen; the boys help Daddy wash the car; they mostly live in neat detached houses; and the characters are predominantly white. History books are often highly anglophile and geography books tend to show non-European countries as poor and the inhabitants as peasants. Few references are made to the sophistication of their cultures; to the impact of interaction between different civilizations; or, indeed, to the fact that European countries may also have economic problems. The difficulties in finding appropriate resources are diminishing, for publishers have now begun to address these problems.

PRACTICAL ACTIVITY 6.5

Aim: To identify the hidden curriculum in a selection of books for use in a primary school.

Method: Select a number of books which you might use to support a series of planned lessons (or a number of texts in your own specialist subject). Analyse the illustrations and then the text in terms of the values which are implicitly, and explicitly, conveyed. You might wish to identify values which relate to gender, class, race, religion or disability.

Follow-up: What conclusions can you draw about the hidden curriculum as evidenced in these books? How would you use such books? What could a reflective teacher do about any particular bias in books?

In summary then, one of the major difficulties in planning any course of studies is to identify, select and justify what we choose to provide and which classroom initiatives we will support. The basis of choice appears to be fourfold: value positions (which were discussed in Chapter 4); conceptions of the structure of knowledge (see section 1.1 above); assumptions about how children learn and how we teach (considered in Chapters 9 and 10); and, of course, the practicalities of the particular situation in which we work. In the next section, we will consider some ways of planning and recording curriculum tasks to help in monitoring, not only their breadth and balance, but also their progression and differentiation.

2 PLANNING THE CURRICULUM: PROGRESSION AND DIFFERENTIATION

So far, we have considered the issues of breadth and balance between the activities within the curriculum. The second set of issues we shall consider is that of progression and differentiation. The concept of 'progression' highlights the intended, cumulative outcomes in which a planned curriculum is expected to result: the expectation is that children should make progress in their learning, should build on and integrate their learning so that they deepen their understandings. The processes by which this can be achieved are, as we shall see, open to many interpretations, as are the natures of the final outcomes. 'Differentiation' highlights the importance of precisely distinguishing the nature of the demands which each activity makes. The purpose of this is to help teachers to match tasks and children as appropriately as possible, in the belief that greater progress will be achieved.

2.1 Two curriculum-planning models

One particular movement in curriculum planning, which became popular in America during the 1960s, has been called an 'objectives model'. Proponents of this approach aimed to provide ways of helping teachers to specify curriculum goals (Bloom *et al.* 1956; Tyler 1949). It was suggested that, having specified their objectives, the teachers would then be in a position to evaluate the curriculum and to monitor the children's progress more precisely. Teachers would thus have better evidence about their effectiveness.

Teachers were encouraged to list behavioural objectives (i.e. observable behaviour that could serve as evidence that the intended learning had taken place). For example, objectives might be 'that children learn to dress themselves'; 'that children will successfully use the four computation rules in number work'; or 'that children will design and perform tests to identify starch in foods'.

An extreme form of this kind of approach to learning can be seen in the materials produced for 'programmed learning'. However, severe criticisms were levelled at this model of curriculum planning. It was considered by some to trivialize learning and to ignore both qualitative aspects, such as aesthetic awareness and sensitivity, as well as attitudes and feelings that are less easily 'seen' in behaviour. In response to such criticisms, the notion of non-behavioural objectives was developed (e.g. 'that children will develop an appreciation of musical form'). Refinements were added so that distinctions between 'instructional' objectives and 'expressive' objectives could be noted (Eisner 1969).

Despite these modifications, two particular lines of objections were still raised. Although Tyler (1949) had suggested that objectives should specify the content to be learnt, as well as processes and skills to be engaged in, the objectives model was criticized for being more concerned with what was to be learnt as opposed to how it was learnt (i.e. more product orientated than concerned with the development of processes of learning). Furthermore, it was argued that precise specification of planned learning objectives might devalue the accidental or incidental learning which also often occurs during teaching–learning sessions. This would devalue the potential for spontaneity and for developing learning initiatives which derive from the children.

In contrast to the objectives model, a movement advocating a 'process model' emerged (e.g. Stenhouse 1975). This tried to shift concern from behavioural and non-behavioural goals and to focus on relating learning to 'principles of procedure' and to developmental processes of each child. In addition, the process model highlighted values and feelings associated with learning, together with on-going and open-ended aspects of learning. Thus, the suggested focus was on the total, developmental processes of learning, rather than on predetermined products or interim steps by which mastery of an identified product might be reached. In fact, the process model aimed to include both overall product and processes and to provide a more all-embracing framework. It was thought that this could permeate teacher–learner interaction; provide criteria for analysing that interaction; establish long-term guidelines; and help teachers decide priorities about which kinds of learning to reward.

The process model also made very different assumptions about learning. Advocates of the approach (e.g. Kelly 1982, 1986) support the notion of learning through the active engagement of learners in trying to resolve a conflict between their existing knowledge and the new situation being experienced. In particular, through active involvement and a degree of self-control over their own learning, it is believed that children can come to create their own understandings rather than just competently receive knowledge. It is also argued that, because each learner's knowledge and experiences are different, the situations from which each can successfully learn will be different. Individual patterns of learning, therefore, should be respected.

Given these alternative approaches to curriculum planning, we have to balance our views of the different ways in which particular children learn and their varied rates of learning, with our knowledge of the common patterns of development which children share. We also have to consider these approaches in the light of our own value-positions. The issues have again become especially important in the wake of HMI documents, such as 'The Curriculum from 5 to 16' (DES 1985a) and 'English 5–16' (DES 1984), where objectives figure prominently. We need to remember that clarity about what we do in the classroom, and our ability to identify and articulate our objectives and principles, does not have to result in mechanistic precision and uniformity, nor in restrictive pre-specification. For, as Hilda Taba argued:

> It is difficult to defend the 'frills' from current attacks because attainments, other than those in 'essentials', are not easily demonstrable . . . With a clear platform of objectives and more evaluation data, both the necessity and efficacy of many aspects of the school programme would be vastly more defensible . . .
>
> (Taba 1962, p. 199)

Over twenty years later, her words are still relevant, as is her suggestion that 'objectives are roads to travel along, not terminal points'.

PRACTICAL ACTIVITY 6.6

Aim: To identify learning objectives, as the basis for lesson plans.

Method: List the objectives which you hope will be achieved in activities for the next day/week.

Follow-up: Review the list you have made in terms of the balance between behavioural/non-behavioural objectives, and in terms of the balance between knowledge/concepts/skills/attitudes. Relate this to your value-position (see Practical Activities 4.3, 4.4). How useful do you think this exercise is in helping to analyse your curriculum plans?

Getting a suitable balance between these elements is a difficult task, as is getting a balance between flexibility and structure. Flexibility is recognized by many teachers as an important aid to learning, which can be achieved through differentiating tasks to meet individual needs. However, structure is also a key factor in planning to ensure progression. This can apply to the vertical continuity of tasks which develop over time (i.e. the extension of the task over consecutive days, weeks, terms and even years) and to horizontal cohesion between tasks (i.e. between concurrent daily tasks). Thus, while such continuity and cohesion are important, they must be balanced by the need for differentiated tasks to meet specific individual needs.

2.2 Sequencing tasks and recording curriculum progression

The sequencing of tasks within the curriculum raises two different sets of issues. First, a reflective teacher would need to consider whether tasks need to be sequenced in a particular order. If so, the second issue is to decide on criteria for sequencing the tasks. The choices depend on our view of knowledge and our view of how children learn. For example, if a curriculum is seen as a means of imparting specific knowledge selected because of its worth, interest, or relevance, then it is likely to be sequenced with reference to propositions about the logical structure of that knowledge and in terms of its conceptual basis. If, however, the curriculum is regarded as the accumulative experiences of the children interacting with their environment and with each other, then its sequence is less likely to be determined by the content *per se* than by the anticipated psychological patterns of children's learning. This may be less likely to fit a

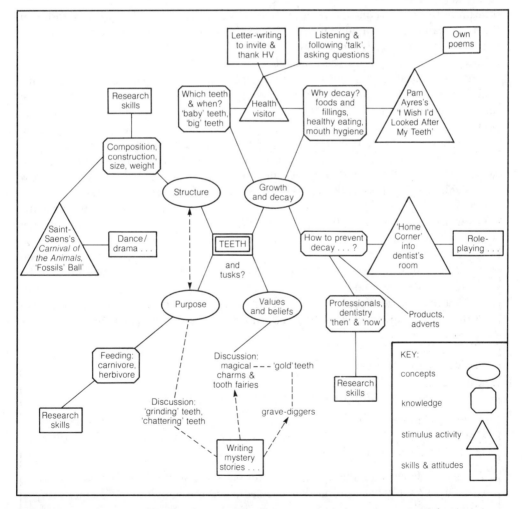

Figure 6.1 Planning the curriculum: 'topic web' recording opportunities for developing concepts, knowledge, skills, attitudes. Age: 7–8 years. Focus: Teeth.

neat linear model of learning, where certain forms of learning are seen as a step-by-step progression (Gagné 1975), but may be better represented by a spiral model, where children meet a concept or skill and then encounter it again later, when they may develop their understanding of it further (Bruner 1977). It may also be the case that children sometimes learn in leaps when something 'clicks' and they are able to consolidate or apply some new understanding (for an example, see Woods 1987b). A child may also 'miss out' certain steps/concepts which might seem to be logically related, but return to them at a later, psychologically relevant, point. Clearly differences in models of learning have serious implications when considering sequence within the curriculum.

Reflective teachers, having made decisions on how they believe children learn and, therefore, how the curriculum should be designed, then have to decide how they will record the observed curriculum as it is implemented in their classrooms.

One common practice in many primary schools is for teachers to spend part of their holiday planning next term's 'topic'. The plan is usually drawn out in a 'topic web' and illustrates the associated ideas and activities to be developed. It then serves as a blueprint to guide the progression of work during the coming weeks. This plan tends to result in pre-packaged learning experiences and is usually based on the teacher's interpretation of such concepts as 'interests', 'relevance' and 'worth'. An elaboration of this is to map out an extended web, which distinguishes between the concepts, knowledge, skills and attitudes that might develop (see Figure 6.1), or to represent these differences in matrix form (see Figure 6.2).

Alternative strategies are possible, which give wider options. The teacher may plan a preliminary short topic just to 'get things going' at the beginning of term. Then, if some interest emerges from the children's activities and discussions, it can become the focal point for an individual child, group or whole class. The teacher, building on what the children have shown interest in, might anticipate alternative lines of development and identify what knowledge or skills would be developed. Only some of these might be taken up by the children. Other aspects may be added. This can be recorded in a 'flow chart' which can be updated throughout the lifetime of the investigation. By this means, a record is provided which shows the activities anticipated by the teacher and the children's actual activities. Although the teacher need not pre-package the activities, it is important to anticipate possible avenues of investigation. This is necessary both to prepare resources and because some children are not always sure what they want to do next. Others always opt for the same kinds of activities and sometimes need to be guided into other areas so that their experiences are broadened. Figure 6.3 illustrates the way a teacher can keep a flow-chart type record of a topic as it develops its own pattern of skills, attitudes, concepts and knowledge across the curriculum.

PRACTICAL ACTIVITY 6.7

Aim: To make a record to show an intended sequence of tasks.

Method: Choose one of the approaches illustrated in Figures 6.1, 6.2 and 6.3. Continue to add possible tasks (activities) and plot the sequence of tasks indicating knowledge, concepts, skills, attitudes.

Follow-up: How might this approach be refined to improve its usefulness as a tool of analysis? On what criteria did you sequence the activities? Was there any progression?

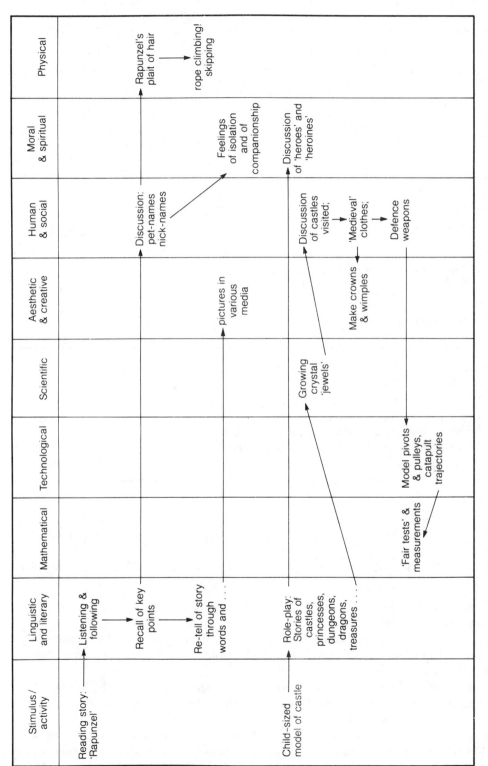

Figure 6.2 Planning a curriculum forecast: a student example of an on-going 'tabulated analysis' recording areas of learning and experience over a series of activities. Age 5–6 years. Focus: Fairy stories.

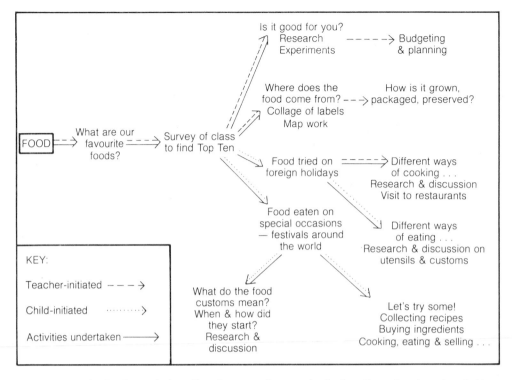

Figure 6.3 Monitoring the curriculum: flow chart recording growth of a class-directed project. Age: 9–10 years. Focus: Food.

2.3 Differentiation: matching tasks and children

Reflecting upon and analysing our curriculum, as suggested above, is an important prerequisite for differentiating tasks. This is necessary so that we can match tasks and children more appropriately, which in turn may help to promote learning progress. In trying to appraise this match, four stages are required:

- to discuss the perceptions and intentions of the teacher and the child
- to try to identify the child's existing knowledge, concepts, skills, and attitudes
- to observe the process by which the task is tackled
- to analyse and evaluate the product, or final outcome, of the task, so that future plans can be made

A mismatch could occur at any (or all) of the stages. To take an example at the first stage, a teacher could set a task for a particular purpose, but, if it were not explained adequately, then the child might misunderstand. Any task might be done 'wrongly', or it may be done 'blindly' (i.e. without seeing the point of it). Such a situation could have negative cognitive and affective outcomes.

There could also be a mismatch at the second stage. The task may be too hard for a child, because it requires certain knowledge which the child does not have.

A mismatch at the third stage can be illustrated by a task which may be set without an instruction to use certain apparatus, or to present the outcome in a certain way. However, the apparatus may not be necessary and may actually confuse the child, or the style of presentation may assume some skill which the child has not yet acquired. Any of these situations could result in negative cognitive and affective outcomes.

Additional problems could also arise from a mismatch at the fourth stage. For instance, teachers often 'mark' the end-product of children's learning. However, a high percentage of 'errors' cannot be assumed to relate to 'bad' work or 'poor' learning. The 'errors' can be very important clues as to the learning that has taken place. In this respect, they can be regarded as 'miscues' which indicate where misunderstandings may have occurred. Nevertheless, miscues can themselves be misinterpreted. For instance, the absence of miscues could be taken to indicate a good cognitive match, but it could also hide the fact that the task was too easy, that no cognitive learning had taken place. This could have resulted in two contrasting affective outcomes: either that the children had gained in confidence in their abilities, or that they had become bored. Conversely, the existence of many miscues might be interpreted as a poor match where the task had been too hard and thereby frustrating. If this were the case, the outcomes might be doubly negative, both cognitively and affectively. However, a large number of miscues could indicate that the task had been too easy, uninteresting or unchallenging, and that the children either had not followed the instructions or had not wanted to be bothered with it.

It is most important to monitor each of these four stages of the match. Many opportunities exist where mismatch can occur and many conflicting interpretations are possible. Hence, monitoring the learning processes is vital so that a reflective teacher can gain a better understanding of the learning experiences of the children.

A recent research report, based on interview, observation and testing in infant schools, has revealed the importance of such a detailed monitoring procedure (Bennett *et al.* 1984). The researchers distinguished between five types of task demands:

Incremental. This introduces new ideas/procedures/skills which are acquired during a task.

Restructuring. This requires children to invent/discover for themselves, thus learning is advanced.

Enrichment. By using familiar ideas/procedures/skills on new problems, learning is applied.

Practice. This reinforces ideas/procedures/skills which are assumed to be already known.

Revision. This requires skills which have not been used for some time.

The study found that 60 per cent of tasks set in language and maths were intended as short-term practice, 25 per cent were 'incremental', 6 per cent were enrichment, 6 per cent were intended as long-term revision and only 1 per cent were intended as restructuring.

The very high figure of tasks set for practice needs to be considered carefully. What were these children learning, cognitively or affectively? Practice tasks may be useful in confirming knowledge or skills, but one would have to consider at what point might such tasks cease to increase confidence and cause frustration? Interestingly, the percentage of practice tasks was even higher when examined in terms of how the tasks were perceived and performed by the children. This was particularly so for high-ability children, who were often set tasks intended as incremental or enrichment, but which, in fact, involved yet more practice. Three reasons were suggested for this: that the children were already familiar with the knowledge or skills demanded by the tasks; that tasks were not well planned to meet the teacher's aims; and that tasks were not clearly explained, with the result that children misunderstood them.

In describing each of these types of task, a reflective teacher should consider that tasks of each type are necessary if cognitive and affective learning is to develop positively and surely. For increases in learning do not necessarily occur in a smooth, ever-upward fashion. If learning develops in irregular bursts, then occasional plateaux may also be experienced and needed.

PRACTICAL ACTIVITY 6.8

Aim: To examine tasks in terms of their learning demands.

Method: Analyse the demands of each task set during the day by using the grid below:

Task Type

	Incremental (new skills acquired in task)	Restructuring (known skills advanced in task)	Enrichment (known skills applied in task)	Practice (known skills assumed in task)	Revision (known skills reactivated in task)
Task no. 1 2 3 4 5					

Having analysed the tasks, then ask the children for their views (using terms which they would recognize) about which kind of tasks they thought they were doing.

Follow-up: From this evidence, what can you deduce about the match or mis-match in the classroom? Can you identify the reasons for it? What can you do about it?

A reflective teacher needs to monitor the match closely to try to ensure the best balance between boredom with too easy tasks, frustration with tasks that are too hard, comfort from consolidation tasks and excitement from a task that is challenging but not too daunting.

3 IMPLEMENTING THE CURRICULUM: CONTINUITY AND COHESION

Having considered the issues of identifying, selecting and monitoring our curriculum planning and provision, in the short term, it is now necessary to consider two additional issues.

The first is 'continuity': the long-term planning of consecutive opportunities which focus on a chosen combination of knowledge, concepts, skills or attitudes, so that children can have chances to develop these continually. Hopefully, continuity is integrally related to progression, when understandings are deepened and extended. Unfortunately, this may not always be the case, for new activities may revise and reinforce learning that has already taken place, but without extending it further. Continuity also involves sequencing, particularly in the long term.

The second issue is 'cohesion': links between concurrent tasks, which could support developments taking place in the various tasks by approaching them 'from a different angle' and by drawing learning points together from the broader basis of the whole curriculum. Such linkages may help to balance the curriculum and may well contribute to continuity, as well as to progression.

3.1 The 'basics' and the 'other' curriculum

Two main alternative strategies for achieving continuity and/or cohesion are revealed by the relative emphasis, within the curriculum, that is given to separate 'subjects' and to integrated 'experiences'. Considerable official support, through the Plowden Report (Central Advisory Council on Education 1967), was given to integrated approaches, so that they became a distinctive feature of the primary school ideology. However, before examining integrated approaches in more detail, it is as well to consider just how pervasive these approaches are.

Alexander (1984) suggests that, whatever is said about the primary curriculum, the evidence from research and from the professional literature shows that a 'two-curriculum syndrome' is in operation. The two curricula that he has in mind are those of the 'basics' (reading, writing and mathematics) and those of the rest, the 'other' curriculum. He argues that the rhetoric of child-centred education, which is associated with an integrated form of curriculum organization, has prevented teachers from facing the fact that the basics in the curriculum have often been taught in a relatively discrete and almost subject-based way. It is only with regard to the other, less central, areas of the curriculum that attempts to establish integration have really been made. Table 6.2 shows Alexander's analysis of the major dimensions of the 'two curricula'.

Alexander's model provides both challenges and insights when considering the curriculum. It could be used as a way of analysing the balance in the form of curriculum organization which exists in a class or school. Once again it highlights the necessity for reflective teachers to consider their purpose and strategies actively in planning the curriculum.

The issues of continuity and cohesion are highlighted by this distinction between the two curricula. For example, most primary schools now have a written maths policy. This usually means a carefully devised list of different mathematical concepts and skills which each child should acquire, in which sequence and with which resources. Often such a policy is closely linked to a published maths scheme. Many schools also have a language policy. This often includes handwriting, reading (sometimes linked to a particular scheme) and writing (covering writing for different purposes and different audiences). There may also be some consideration of listening and speaking and the inclusion of suggestions for comprehension, spelling, grammar and study skills. Fewer schools, however, have policies for aspects of the 'other' curriculum.

3.2 The 'collected' curriculum

Although a commitment to various forms of 'integrated' curriculum has been prevalent in primary-school ideology, it is by no means universally accepted, nor, as we have seen, is it always put into practice. An alternative to the integrated curriculum is one which maintains high subject boundaries and thus maintains distinctions between subjects.

Table 6.2 *Dimensions for analysing the primary curriculum*

Status/priority

High————Low
Major time allocation————Minor time allocation
Mandatory————Dispensable

Justification/ideology

Social relevance————Self-actualization
Societal————Individual
Utilitarian————Child-centred

View of knowledge

Received————Reflexive
Rationalist————Empiricist
Positive————Negative, anti-knowledge

Organizational characteristics

Subject differentiation————Undifferentiated
Extensive codification of knowledge and————Little or no codification
skills
Explicit progression of knowledge and————Little or no explicit progression
skills

Evaluation

Pre-ordinate/'objective'————Responsive/'subjective'

Pedagogy

Teacher-directed————Child-initiated

Outcome

Progressive acquisition of knowledge and————Learning experiences random and circular
skills
High level of 'match' between learning————Low level of match
experiences and child's abilities

Professional training and resources

High priority in initial training————Low priority in initial training
Well-developed teacher technology of————Limited teacher technology
schemes and materials
Relatively high INSET commitment————Relatively low INSET commitment
by teachers and LEAs   by teachers and LEAs

(from Alexander 1984, p. 76)

The resulting curriculum, therefore, is a collection of separate subjects. There may be relatively little cohesion between them, though there may be continuity within each separate subject.

A rationale for a 'collected' curriculum, which is sometimes deployed, is that each element is based on logical structures of knowledge which are believed to be unique to that subject or 'form of knowledge' (Hirst and Peters 1970). Such philosophical arguments can be used to justify a subject-based, collected curriculum but, strictly speaking, this is a distortion of Hirst and Peters' position. Hirst (1975) does not advocate that high subject boundaries are necessarily appropriate for primary schools. Nor does he identify traditional school subjects as being directly linked to 'forms of knowledge'.

However, such an approach to curriculum also supports the need for balance within the 'collected' curriculum, for to ignore any form of knowledge is believed to deny certain basic ways of rational development. It is argued that the curriculum should, therefore, not focus on particular 'subjects', but provide courses in particular ways of thinking. One of the reasons put forward to justify such an approach is the recognition that the precise boundaries of knowledge are constantly changing. Therefore, the priority should properly be given to modes of thought rather than subject content.

Perhaps the root of the 'subjects' which are often considered to form the traditional curriculum can more properly be found in the high status which is still attributed by some social groups to the formal, classical education of public and grammar schools. After all, this has been reflected in many aspects of examination structures within the education system.

3.3 The 'integrated curriculum'

Many different types of arguments for the desirability of an integrated curriculum have been proffered. The first which we will consider is based on the idea that children need an active involvement in their learning experiences. Proponents of this approach argue that, although adults play a vital role in helping to create understandings, children must understand, in their own ways, for learning to take place (Dearden 1968). Hence, for adults to impose subject boundaries is considered to be meaningless to a child.

Another argument is that new 'subjects' have emerged which are interdisciplinary and conceptually linked (Pring 1976), for example, environmental studies. Although this example is still located within one form of knowledge, other issues for study have also been identified which cross boundaries. For example, aspects of health education require us to make social, moral as well as scientific responses. This form of integration has been highlighted in some Schools Council projects, for example, *Science 5–13* (Harlen 1975) and *Place, Time and Society, 8–11* (Blyth 1975).

A third suggestion that underpins the notion of an integrated curriculum is that, if the subject boundaries are reduced, it is possible to lessen the dominance of subject content as a curriculum goal. Thus, having lessened the emphasis on particular subject knowledge, a higher priority can be given to general processes, skills and attitudes.

Having noted some of the thinking behind the idea of an 'integrated' curriculum, it is now time to examine the various ways in which it can be put into practice. Integrated parts of the curriculum can be conceptualized in a variety of ways:

Concept based. This might take the form of a study of change and continuity in 'Our Town'. A series of activities may be planned which could easily be identified with associated humanities subjects, such as history and geography. A number of different skills could also be developed, including observation and drawing of buildings, mapping the town and doing a survey of current amenities. This kind of approach is sometimes identified as social, environmental or local studies.

Interest based. This might start from a class visit to a place of interest, or from some event that arouses interest in the children. For example, a child's remark about 'milk growing in bottles' may spark off an interest in dairying and food in general. A series of activities may develop which can be identified with a wide range of subject areas, or forms of knowledge, which are all loosely linked by the theme of food (e.g. where milk comes from; which foods are good for us and why; how to grow runner beans; from which countries our foods come; the cultural and religious significance of certain foods; and also some cooking activities, including weighing, timing and pricing). Such a mixture of activities is sometimes known as 'thematic work' or 'topic work'.

Problem based. This kind of work is often very specific and intended for a shorter period of time. A child may ask, or be set a task, to make a lighthouse with a flashing light. This would involve exploring with batteries and bulbs, then designing and constructing a working model. Such a specific task may be referred to as a 'project' in some schools, though this term is also used for individual, book-based researches.

Although approaches are sometimes combined, these distinctions do highlight two aspects of integration: how closely 'subjects' are intermeshed and how many 'subjects' are intermingled. The greater the integration, the greater portion of the day is usually devoted to the integrated curriculum. Thus, a fully integrated curriculum may result in children spending the whole day following topics of interest, through which knowledge, concepts, skills and attitudes can be developed in a meaningful context.

A reflective teacher needs to distinguish between the various purposes and practices related to an integrated curriculum so as to be able to assess which approach will suit their children most appropriately. Many of the organizational issues will be taken up again in the next chapter, when we consider the coherence between learning aims and teaching strategies. In this chapter, therefore, we suggest Practical Activity 6.9 to help us to analyse the curriculum, as recorded, and to consider the degree of continuity and cohesion that has been provided.

PRACTICAL ACTIVITY 6.9

Aim: To find out about the degree of continuity and cohesion in children's learning experiences in the 'other' curriculum.

Method: Note down the titles of the different topics undertaken during previous terms/years. Then list the activities which have been involved. It is a good idea to ask the children what they remember of previous topics, as well as the teachers. The areas of agreement, and the gaps, may reveal interesting insights about teachers' plans and children's responses.

Follow-up: Consider the extent of the continuity and cohesion, in terms of knowledge content. Has the continuity been of a 'step-by-step' nature; a 'spiral' nature (returning to the same area of knowledge/concepts/skills but, hopefully, at a greater depth); or of a 'spasmodic' nature (with leaps or gaps and the risk that children may feel they have 'done' a lot, but because it was fragmented and discontinuous, they may not know what they have achieved and where it has 'got them')?

Despite the official approval given for so long to the notion of an integrated curriculum, there have also been criticisms of this approach, which have been intensifying in recent years. It is suggested that organizational devices, such as topic work, often lead to a lack of 'rigour' because of a lack of specific attention to the cohesive structures of the various types of knowledge concepts, skills and attitudes which 'should be' involved in the curriculum of primary schools. It is also suggested that an integrated approach frequently leads to repetition and lack of continuity of learning in the topics which are covered. There is, perhaps, a frequent lack of the kind of planning between staff which could lead to continuity and progression throughout the school. There is also evidence that many children, working in classes where integrated approaches are adopted, do experience a disconnected series of learning challenges which lacks cohesion (DES 1978a).

Proposals have been put forward for introducing teachers who have particular subject expertise into primary schools. These, it is suggested, could act as 'consultants' who would help to develop curricular provision in each area. They would offer advice and give support to colleagues. Such 'consultants' might be able to develop greater continuity of curricular experiences and ensure progression throughout the school (Campbell 1985). However, it is not necessarily the case that a more subject-based approach will guarantee a 'better' curriculum. Indeed the subject-based curriculum itself has been a source of much fragmentation and repetition. Further, because of the distinctions between subjects, such an approach can reduce cohesion. Similarly, it is apparent that an integrated curriculum does not inevitably lead to discontinuities in learning experiences. Although difficult, it is quite possible to analyse, plan and monitor an integrated curriculum rigorously.

CONCLUSION

Having reviewed some of the key features of a 'collected' and an 'integrated' curriculum, reflective teachers will need to question the assumptions of both of these key approaches to the curriculum and decide which is more consistent with their own value-position. The two approaches appear to support opposite views on the best starting-point for initiating learning. The integrated approach starts with the children and tries to lead them into a wider understanding of their world, whereas the collected approach starts with areas of knowledge and encourages children to apply such knowledge to themselves and their environment. The integrated approach tends to assume that children will create their own understandings as they interact with their environment; the collected approach suggests that children should be introduced to existing knowledge and that they will later make it their own.

There are also differences between the two approaches in terms of continuity and cohesion. In the integrated curriculum, there is considerable cohesion between areas of experience, though there is a danger that, unless carefully analysed and monitored, there may not be continuity over the whole primary school life of the child. In the collected curriculum, however, there may be little cohesion between areas of learning, though perhaps strong cohesion within each. There may also be greater continuity over the period of schooling, which may be because the framework is pre-planned according to proposed logical structures, rather than responding to child-centred points of interest or to situations as they arise.

In practice, it seems that in many primary schools, the 'basic' curriculum (particularly maths) is often based on a 'collected' approach, sequential, step-by-step and pre-planned, while the 'other' curriculum is more integrated. We would suggest that neither approach necessarily has more rigour than the other as a means of promoting learning. As with so much in education, a lot depends on the understanding and skill of teachers.

NOTES FOR FURTHER READING

There are a number of books which offer overviews of the primary school curriculum.
The following book contains an analysis of primary-school ideology and of its application within the curriculum:

Alexander, R. (1984) *Primary Teaching*. London: Holt, Rinehart & Winston.

The next book adopts a 'process' approach to the curriculum and offers an examination of alternative views of knowledge:

Blenkin, G. M. and Kelly, A. V. (1981) *The Primary Curriculum*. London: Harper & Row.

For a thoughtful book, which includes a stimulating discussion of 'an enabling curriculum', see:

Blyth, W. A. L. (1984) *Development, Experience and Curriculum in Primary Education*. London: Croom Helm.

The following book contains a useful review of curricular issues, in particular the role of postholders in 'collegiate primary schools':

Campbell, J. (1985) *Developing the Primary School Curriculum*. London: Holt, Rinehart & Winston.

For a sustained critique of 'traditionalist' views of the curriculum and of many recent developments, see:

Kelly, A. V. (1986) *Knowledge and the Curriculum*. London: Harper & Row.

It would be useful to look at some of the current documents that are emerging from the DES and, in particular, HMI. For example:

DES (1985) *The Curriculum From 5–16* (HMI discussion document). London: HMSO.

The following provides survey evidence about classroom practices:

DES (1978) *Primary Education in England: a Survey by HMI*. London: HMSO.

Other relevant documents are:

DES (1980) *A View of the Curriculum*. London: HMSO.
Schools Council (1983) *Primary Practice*. London: Methuen.

Three useful books which contain sections illustrating a wide range of views on the curriculum are:

Barnes, D. (1982) *Practical Curriculum Study*. London: Routledge & Kegan Paul.
Golby, M., Greenwald, J. and West, R. (eds.) (1975) *Curriculum Design*. London: Croom Helm.
Horton, T. and Raggit, P. (eds.) (1982) *Challenge and Change in the Curriculum*. London: Croom Helm.

The following books are written by authors who illustrate different approaches to the curriculum. The first two particularly emphasize the social and political context which influences the curriculum. The third provides a developmental view; while the fourth contains a useful review of the hidden curriculum:

Lawton, D. (1980) *The Politics of the School Curriculum*. London: Routledge & Kegan Paul.
Whitty, G. (1985) *Sociology and School Knowledge*. London: Methuen.
Egan, K. (1979) *Educational Development*. Oxford: Oxford University Press.
Meighan, R. (1981) *A Sociology of Educating*. London: Holt, Rinehart & Winston.

Awareness about bias in classroom materials has been increased by growing public discussion of the issues. Evidence of this can be found in:

Dixon, B. (1977) *Catching Them Young: Sex, Race and Class in Children's Fiction*. London: Pluto Press.
Lobban, G. (1975) Sex roles in reading schemes, *Forum*, **16**, (2), 57–60.
Stinton, J. (1979) *Racism and Sexism in Children's Books*. London: Writers & Readers.
Zimmet, S. G. and Hoffman, M. (1980) *Print and Prejudice*. London: Hodder & Stoughton.

Three books already listed also contain useful discussions of key issues in planning a curriculum: Blenkin and Kelly (1981), DES (1985a) and Schools Council (1983). The latter two also focus on the concepts of continuity and cohesion. For further details about analysing curriculum tasks, see:

Blyth, A. (1975) *Time, Place and Society 8–13*. London: Collins.
Ennever, L. (1972) *With Objectives in Mind: Guide to Science 5–13*. London: Macdonald Educational.

Harlen, W. (1977) *Match and Mismatch*, Vol. 1: Raising Questions; Vol. 2: Finding Answers. London: Oliver & Boyd.

Harlen, W. (1985) *Primary Science: Taking the Plunge*. London: Heinemann.

The next book is important for the observational data collected, which helps to build up a picture of primary practice, and also for the analysis of task types offered:

Bennett, N. *et al.* (1984) *The Quality of Pupil Learning Experiences*. London: Lawrence Erlbaum Associates.

The following are examples of writers who are critical of aspects of child-centred approaches and who offer frameworks in which they can be examined:

Anthony, W. (1979) Progressive learning theories: the evidence, in Bernbaum, G. (ed.) *Schooling in Decline*. London: Macmillan.

Bantock, G. H. (1980) *Dilemmas of the Curriculum*. Oxford: Martin Robertson.

The next group of books suggest ways of making the integrated curriculum work through careful analysis and planning. The first, in particular, provides a general theoretical framework and the remainder offer additional practical suggestions:

Avann, P. (ed.) (1985) *Teaching Information Skills in the Primary School*. London: Edward Arnold.

Gunning, D., Gunning, S. and Wilson, J. (1981) *Topic Teaching in the Primary School*. London: Croom Helm.

Walters, D. (1982) *Primary School Projects*. London: Heinemann.

Chapter 7

How Are We Organizing the Classroom?

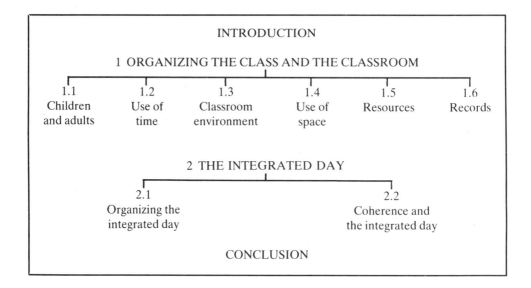

INTRODUCTION

1 ORGANIZING THE CLASS AND THE CLASSROOM

| 1.1 | 1.2 | 1.3 | 1.4 | 1.5 | 1.6 |
| Children and adults | Use of time | Classroom environment | Use of space | Resources | Records |

2 THE INTEGRATED DAY

| 2.1 | 2.2 |
| Organizing the integrated day | Coherence and the integrated day |

CONCLUSION

INTRODUCTION

Organization is vital in implementing values, aims, intended forms of relationships and curriculum plans. It is the last of the main factors which contribute to the 'planning' and 'provision' stages of the reflective-teacher cycle outlined in Chapter 1.

By organization, we mean the way in which the class and classroom is structured to facilitate teaching and learning. For such teaching and learning to succeed, classroom organization must relate to values, aims, relationships and curriculum plans as a whole.

If coherence can be achieved, then the teacher and the children should benefit from having a common framework within which to work. The strength of such a framework will derive from its internal consistency: the mutual reinforcement of its elements, and its legitimacy (the mutual agreement between the teacher and the children). Because of the interdependent nature of organizational elements, it is important to remember that change made in any one aspect is likely to affect other aspects.

However, organizational structure does not mean rigidity, for if the rules and routines of the classroom are clear and agreed, a good organization can free the teacher to teach and the learner to learn (Bennett *et al.* 1984). In particular, it should give the teacher more time to diagnose children's learning difficulties; to design an appropriate match of task to child; and to teach, rather than having to spend time on 'housekeeping' aspects of routine classroom life (Hilsum and Cane 1971; Galton, Simon and Croll 1980).

Six organizational issues are listed below and each will be discussed in detail in section 1 of this chapter:

1. The way in which children and adults are organized
2. The use of time
3. The use of the classroom environment for display
4. The use of classroom space
5. The use of resources
6. The use of records for monitoring classroom organization

Section 2 will examine additional organizational issues related to the 'integrated' day. We will use this for two purposes. First, it will provide a case study to illustrate the importance of coherence between organizational strategies and values, aims and curriculum plans. Second, we believe it is important to try to clarify some of the misconceptions about the integrated day as a form of classroom practice. It is commonly referred to in the rhetoric of primary school ideology, but is variously employed in reality.

1 ORGANIZING THE CLASS AND THE CLASSROOM

1.1 Children and adults

The people in a classroom need to be organized in ways which are most appropriate for supporting the learning activities which have been planned. Obviously, this involves children but, in many classes, it also involves adults, such as ancillary staff. There is also an increasing degree of involvement by parents in classrooms. We will begin by focusing on the children.

The first basic decision to be made about the children concerns the desired balance between individual work, classwork and groupwork. This must be made with regard to both pedagogical and practical considerations. The pedagogical ones include the general aims of the teacher, as well as any particular objectives for the task and children. Practical factors include the number of children, the size of the room and the availability of resources—factors which will be discussed in more detail below.

Some of the different forms of grouping and their purposes are:

Individualization. This is thought to be particularly useful for developing children's ability to work independently and autonomously.

Classwork. This may be useful for starting and ending the day, for giving out administrative instructions, introducing and reviewing work, and for many activities which build a feeling of belonging to a class (e.g. through discussions, story, singing, music, dance and games).

Groupwork. This is often recommended for developing social and language skills which are necessary for collaborative work, where the children need to listen to and learn from each other, or for activities requiring brainstorming to develop some alternative ideas for a problem-solving or creative task (e.g. designing a machine, drama/role-play).

Each of these ways of organizing the children has its advantages and rationale, but each also has its particular limitations. For example, a teacher who relies heavily on individualization may find that similar teaching points have to be explained on many separate occasions to different children. Individualization also often results in a lot of movement in the classroom, with either the teacher moving around the classroom seeing each child in turn, or the children moving from their chairs and queueing at the teacher's desk. This emphasis on working with each individual separately inevitably means that only a limited amount of time can be spent with any one child. Even then, it has been shown that most of this time is spent in monitoring each child's work, rather than in developing their understanding (Galton, Simon and Croll 1980).

Teachers using whole-class organizational procedures tend to spend more time in discussion with the class. Such opportunities may give the teacher a chance to demonstrate discussion techniques, encourage collaborative learning and stimulate children's thinking by exploring ideas, asking more 'probing' questions, sharing common problems and encouraging children to join in trying to solve them. However, if classwork is used too extensively, it may pose a severe strain on both the teacher and the listener, for it is very difficult to match the instruction appropriately to each child's different needs without sufficient individual consultation.

'Groups' are likely to exist in some form in every classroom. However, their form and function may vary considerably. Five main types of groups can be identified:

Task-planning groups. The teacher may have a group of children in mind when setting or allocating a task, though the group may not sit or work together.

Teaching groups. Groups can also be used for 'group-teaching' purposes, where the teacher instructs a group of children who are at the same stage of doing the same task, at the same time. This may be followed by the children working individually. Such a system can be an economical use of teacher instruction time and, possibly, of resources.

Seating groups. This is the most common form of grouping, where a number of children sit together around a table, usually in a four or six. Such an arrangement is flexible. It allows children to work individually, to socialize when appropriate, and can be used as the basis for other forms of groupwork.

Joint-learning groups. This is where a group of children work on related activities. The outcome may be a set of linked, individual pieces where the task has been shared out.

Collaborative groups. This is a more developed form of 'groupwork', where work is done together and the outcome is a combined product, perhaps in the form of a model or play.

Although groups are very commonly found for planning and seating purposes, and sometimes for teaching purposes, very little groupwork of the joint or collaborative types has been found (DES 1978a; Galton, Simon and Croll 1980). Teachers have identified a number of problems which they associate with groupwork and, therefore, consider to be disadvantages (Tann 1981). First, many teachers appear concerned about motivating the children and helping them to recognize that being in a group is for the purposes of work rather than a chance to chat and just 'have fun'. Secondly, the monitoring of groupwork can pose problems, especially if it is intended that the group should work collaboratively on its own without a teacher. Thirdly, the management of groups, in terms of such issues as who should be in the group, how many children and where they should work, may pose difficulties which have to be overcome.

Identifying criteria by which groups may be formed may help to clarify some of these issues (Kerry and Sands 1982). Possible criteria may include:

Age groups. These are occasionally used as a convenient way of grouping for some activities. They are much less useful as a basis for specific teaching points because of the inevitable spread of achievement, interests and needs.

Achievement groups. These are useful for economically setting up specific and well-matched tasks. They are divisive if used as permanent way of grouping.

Interest groups. It is important to enable children with shared interests to work together. These have possible social advantages when children are of different ability, sex, race or social class.

Friendship groups. These are popular with children and provide opportunities for social development. An awareness of the needs of any isolate and marginal children is necessary, as is some attention to the possibility that friendship groups can set up divisive status hierarchies among the children, or reinforce stereotypes about gender/race.

Convenience groups. These are often used for organizational purposes, but they are sometimes an unconscious source of unnecessary divisiveness (e.g. girls/boys).

As with decisions about the balance between different general strategies for organizing the children, if groupwork is to be used, a degree of balance is necessary in the use of particular types of groups. Each has a different purpose and specific potential and, therefore, its own place in the primary classroom.

PRACTICAL ACTIVITY 7.1

Aim: To decide the most appropriate type and size of grouping for the activities planned.

Method: We suggest that notes on the size of groupings are made on the most appropriate cell of a matrix of types such as the one given below:

Activity	Individual work	Whole-class work	Groupwork				
			Random grouping	Age grouping	Achievement grouping	Interest grouping	Friendship grouping
Storytime							
Measuring activities							
Dismissal							
Topic work							
Claywork							
Drama							

Follow-up: The benefit of this sort of analysis is in the increased sensitivity to the unique potential of each type of learning situation. This should help in greater coherence between the learning aims, the social context and organizational strategy.

The second very important category of people who are increasingly to be found in primary-school classrooms are adults, particularly parents. While this is a developing trend, it still is the case that less than half of British primary schools involve parents in the classroom (Stierer 1985).

A wide range of patterns of parental involvement exist. Three basic types can be distinguished:

Parents as clients: receiving the services of the teacher, but maintaining a discrete separation of parent and teacher responsibilities (e.g. where involvement is through formal 'parents' evenings' and other 'managed' school events).

Parents as resources: providing a range of help, for example:
- parental activity in support of the school, as in PTA fundraising schemes outside school-time
- parents working in school on non-educational activities, such as helping to duplicate or mend books
- parents involved with educational activities, such as helping children in the library, hearing reading
- parents teaching with small groups, such as in cooking and sewing
- parents teaching in the classroom, such as in the art area, or with general learning activities

Parents as partners: recognized as an equal partner in each child's all-round development (e.g. discussing the curriculum and each child's response; having open access to the classroom and regular informal contacts with teachers).

It seems that both parents and teachers, and perhaps the children, have mixed feelings on the subject (Cullingford 1985). For instance, some parents may feel anxious and uneasy about working in a school. This may be because of their own 'bad' experiences of school, or because they do not feel they have anything to offer the 'expert' teacher. Parents may be unsure about how to relate to children in the school situation, particularly if their own child is in the class to which they are attached. Because of this, parents are unlikely to take initiatives in the classroom unless these are suggested and endorsed by the teacher. Further, parents are often only available for short and specific periods of the day. They are volunteers and have many other responsibilities and do not, therefore, always find it easy to fit into school routines. However, other parents feel unwilling to participate in classroom activities for quite different reasons. Some would maintain that it is the teacher's job to do the teaching, so they should be allowed to get on with it. Others may feel that if they tried to help the child, at home or at school, they may do things in different ways to the teacher's approach, which might only confuse the child. Although we have talked of 'parents', we are, in general, referring to non-working mothers, for very few working fathers or mothers can participate in school life because of working hours.

There are also mixed feelings among teachers. Some welcome the opportunity to create a stronger partnership between home and school so that both can work together in the interests of the children. Others, however, feel that having adults in the classroom could undermine their status in the eyes of the parents, should anything go wrong. Some also believe that parental involvement reduces the likelihood of getting support for better staff–pupil ratios if 'volunteer' help, in the form of parents, is readily available. Further, because only some parents are both available and willing (for the reasons mentioned above), parental help may become a socially divisive factor, giving still greater advantages to the already advantaged middle-class children whose parents are more likely to participate in such schemes.

Despite some well-documented educational benefits of the involvement of parents, there is also considerable scope for the wastage of their time and their talents. In addition, there is scope for misunderstandings and anxieties to emerge. Perhaps two basic things need to be done. The first is to find time for adequate discussion with parents to find out what they have to offer and to help them relax in the school environment. The second is to think carefully about how parents can be most educationally productive when they are in the classroom. In studies of 'room management', it is suggested that the quality of classroom teaching is greatly enhanced if all the adults in a classroom plan together, so that they understand and carry out specific activities in a coordinated and coherent fashion (Thomas 1985). Parental partnership in the classroom needs careful organization to use the time and talents of parents to the full. A related range of organization issues could be applied to ancillary helpers.

PRACTICAL ACTIVITY 7.2

Aim: To prepare for having parents or ancillary assistants working in the classroom.

Method: A pro forma, such as the one below, could be used to prepare for a session with parental involvement, to monitor it and to get the parents' feedback.

Initial discussion with parent about involvement ☐

    Parent's feeling about involvement ....
    Parent's strengths ....
    Interests ....
    Availability ....
    Any possible problems ....

Educational activities and objectives for sessions
    1. ....
    2. ....
    3. ....

Best contribution for parent ....

....

Specific discussion about parent's contribution with parent ☐

The aim, and parent's degree of responsibility, is agreed ☐

Comments ....

The session in action ☐

Comments on how it went ....

....

Follow-up discussion with parent ☐

Notes on feedback ....

....

Follow-up: It is unlikely that this activity would be carried out for every session involving parents, but it is very valuable when starting off a new partnership for classroom work with a parent. It is also useful on an occasional basis to heighten awareness and to check that benefits are being maximized.

1.2 Use of time

The way in which time is used in a classroom is very important. Studies, such as that by Hilsum and Cane (1971), have shown that actual instruction only took up approximately a quarter of the teacher's time; organizational matters, such as planning and marking, absorbed almost half; while the remaining quarter was used in non-educational, routine activities. Thus, it was clear that a great deal of time in primary-school classrooms was spent on mundane, 'housekeeping' issues. Similar results were found by the ORACLE project (Galton, Simon and Croll 1980). Taking this issue a little further, Bennett (1979) identified two considerations about time which were particularly significant to the children's progress. These were the time which is actually made available for 'curriculum activity' and the time spent in 'active' learning.

It is important to remember that 'active learning', as opposed to just 'busy work', is a qualitative category, not just a quantitative one. 'Active learning' is linked to further factors, such as motivation, stimulus and concentration. There is also evidence to suggest that, in order to maintain 'active' learning, appropriate variety in activities is needed.

We thus have three aspects to consider in the use of time:

● time available for curriculum activity
● time spent in active learning
● stimulus and variety in activities over time

The first of these, time available for curriculum activity, is relatively easy to document.

PRACTICAL ACTIVITY 7.3

Aim: To record the time available for curricular activity.

Method: The time available for curricular activities is the time remaining in each teaching/learning session, once it has properly started, excluding interruptions and up to 'tidying-up' time. All that is necessary here is to use a notebook and a watch to record the actual time available for activities throughout a school-day.

Follow-up: Assuming that a fairly representative day has been chosen, it may provide a salutary experience to multiply the total for the day by the total number of school-days in the year, excluding holidays, 'occasional days' and election days if the school will be closed, etc. Similarly, it may prove interesting to analyse the proportion of time spent on each area of the curriculum.

The second of the issues identified above was the time spent on active learning. This is affected by a wide range of factors. Thus, while the time spent on active learning can be assessed at any point (see Practical Activity 7.4), it may also be seen as providing summative information: a product of the overall organization, relationships and teaching which are provided for the children.

However, the time in a classroom which is spent on active learning is clearly related to a number of organizational strategies. The most obvious of these concerns are the routine procedures which are developed: for example, those which help to avoid queues and bottle-necks. These help to manage the pressure which might otherwise be placed on the teacher by the children and contribute to producing a positive, structured classroom environment. Checklist 7.1 may be helpful in considering these.

CHECKLIST 7.1

Aim: To consider classroom organizational routines.

Purpose of routine procedure	Procedure	Evaluation of procedure	Possible improvement
Entry in morning			
Registration			
Dinner-money collection			
Introduction to activities			
Playtime			
Dinner-time			
Assembly			
Changing for PE			
Going to the toilet			
Procedure for getting help in class			
Procedures for using resources			
Getting work marked			
Knowing which task to move on to			
Tidying up			
Exit at end of day			

PRACTICAL ACTIVITY 7.4

Aim: To monitor an individual child to estimate active learning time.

Method: Watch a chosen child during a teaching/learning session. Judge the times at which:

1. The child is 'on task' (i.e. actively engaged in the given task).

2. The child is doing other necessary activities related to do the task (e.g. sharpening pencils, fetching equipment).

3. When the child is 'off task'. Calculate the amount of active learning time.

Follow-up: Are there any changes in organizational strategies which could help to maximize active learning time?

The third aspect, stimulus and variety of tasks over time, is one to which Kounin (1970) drew attention when arguing that teachers should avoid 'satiation' (i.e. letting the children get bored by monotony in activities). For instance, it is very easy to fall into the trap through an over-reliance on published materials, such as maths schemes, reading and spelling workshops, or through the setting of other repetitive individualized activities. Resources in the form of schemes are convenient. They appear to offer a secure curricular basis in which progression and coherence have been systematically considered and they are often strongly marketed by publishers. However, over-reliance on schemes can have a narrowing effect on the curriculum and lead to satiation and boredom. For instance, considerable amounts of child activity will inevitably be directed through print, there is a tendency to require written recording and a hierarchical structure is often inbuilt. All these aspects impose a relatively depersonalized and technical control on the children. Indeed, it has been argued that the preponderance of such routine activities in some schools may produce a docile work-force, rather than develop children whose creativity and critical thinking have been stirred (Apple 1982b).

PRACTICAL ACTIVITY 7.5

Aim: To evaluate the stimulus and variety of tasks and activities.

Method:
1. This could be done by an observer who focuses on a particular child for a day. All activities should be recorded in terms of their motivational appeal, explicit purpose and what the child was required to do (write, draw, listen, watch, move, sing, etc.).

2. Alternatively, tasks could be monitored, by the teacher, for a longer period.

3. Some questions which might be asked could include:
    (a) Is there a planned highlight for each day?
    (b) Are there long sequences of seatwork?
    (c) Is there a reasonable degree of variety between active and passive tasks?
    (d) Is there a reasonable degree of variety between children working alone, in small groups, as a whole class?

Follow-up: Consider the findings from this exercise and, preferably with a colleague, try to deduce the reasons for any patterns you identify. What could you do to improve the results?

1.3 Classroom environment
Research by ecological psychologists (for example, Barker 1978; Bronfenbrenner 1979) has pointed to the importance of the quality of the environment and its influence on behaviour. Such research reinforces the view, which is commonly expressed by practitioners, that the environment in a primary-school classroom should be aesthetically pleasing; should stimulate children's interests; should set high standards in the display and presentation of children's work; and should be created in such a way that it is practical to maintain.

Reflective teachers may also aim to structure the environment so that opportunities are taken to reinforce their overall purposes. They should be able to develop their classroom environment by considering the questions in Checklist 7.2.

CHECKLIST 7.2

Aim: To examine the classroom environment.

1. *Design.* What are the main design features of the room and how do they affect its aesthetic feel?

2. *Possibilities.* What are the possibilities for display (in two and in three dimensions?) on walls, on windows, on flat surfaces, off the ceiling? What are the possibilities for plants or animals? Is work displayed in an aural medium (e.g. tape), as well as a visual one? Is it mobile or static?

3. *Purposes.* Do the displays stimulate and inform? Do they provide opportunities for children to interact with them, for example, by posing questions; inviting their participation in a quiz or make-your-own adventure; offering alternative viewpoints to consider; encouraging the children to touch/smell/taste, as well as look and listen? Further, do displays only show finished products or do they also reveal processes, which might be used for discussion, sharing problems, giving mutual support and advice?

4. *Quality.* Is the standard of mounting, writing and display such that it shows that the children's work is valued? Does it provide a model which children may apply to their own work?

5. *Practicality.* Is the classroom environment as practical as it can be to maintain? How often is it necessary to change displays? Do the children mount their own displays? Can children help with classroom jobs, such as watering plants and feeding pets?

1.4 Use of space

PRACTICAL ACTIVITY 7.6

Aim: To produce a classroom plan.

Method: A simple plan should be made of the fixed points in the classroom—walls, windows, doors, sinks, pegs, etc. If squared paper is used, it is relatively easy to produce a plan to scale. A plan which is not to scale will not be of much use. Major existing items of furniture should be represented on card and to the same scale as the classroom plan.

Follow-up: Careful analysis is needed of the space requirements of each activity and of each activity in relation to the others. So, for example, it is important to note if 'messy' or 'noisy' activities will interfere with 'quieter' ones. Also, consider the relationship of the activity area and the accessibility of the resources for each activity. Finally, it is necessary to relate the location of the activities to the likely movement of the children, so that crowding or bottle-necks can be anticipated. This may need to be done on a session-by-session basis, and by first considering the most commonly occurring sessions. The children can help in this activity, and thereby become more aware of the need for careful use of space.

Space in a classroom is always limited; yet what space there is must be utilized in such a way that the wide-ranging activities which form essential elements of the primary-school curriculum can occur without major disruptions. This requires a considerable amount of thought. A first step is to produce a planning tool, such as a classroom plan (see Practical Activity 7.6 above), with which the existing constraints and the possibilities of the room and furniture can be explored.

1.5 Resources

A good supply of appropriate resources is essential, given that most primary-school teachers believe that children learn best through direct experience and practical work. In some ways, this aspect of organization is a straightforward matter, but it, too, requires careful thought and attention to detail. For instance, it is all too easy to discover that the clay has dried out or the paint is not mixed, when a group of children come to use them.

Four possible criteria which might be considered when organizing resources are:

Appropriateness. What resources are needed to support the learning processes which are expected to take place?

Availability. What resources are available? What is in the classroom, the school, the locality libraries, teacher centres? Are there cost, time or transport factors to be considered?

Storage. How are classroom resources stored? Which should be under teacher control? Which should be openly available to the children? Are they clearly labelled and safely stored?

Maintenance. What maintenance is required? Is there a system for seeing that this is done?

PRACTICAL ACTIVITY 7.7

Aim: To plan the resources to support learning activities.

Method: Identify the aim for each activity, then consider the resources which are required, using the four criteria listed in section 1.5 as a starting-point: appropriateness, availability, storage, maintenance.

Follow-up: Analysing the need and use of resources in this fashion could lead to their more rational and practical deployment.

1.6 Records

There are two basic types of record which teachers have to keep: organizational and educational. We deal with organizational records here and with educational records in Chapter 4.

By organizational records, we simply mean those records which are necessary to ensure the smooth running of the school and classroom. These range from the attendance and dinner registers, which are extremely important for the administration of the school, to such things as records of group membership for various activities, timetables for use of shared school facilities (for example, the hall) and records of resource maintenance or loan periods.

PRACTICAL ACTIVITY 7.8

Aim: To trace procedures for doing the registers.

Method: Try to follow the administrative chain in a school. This typically takes a form as suggested below:

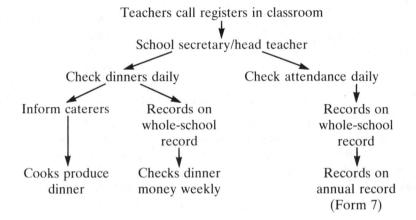

Ask the school secretary, the cook and the head teacher to explain the importance of accurate and promptly available registers.

Follow-up: This activity may be helpful in understanding the tension that can sometimes be created when registers are kept poorly and in grasping the significance of the information which derives from them.

Records for classroom organization also have to be kept. The detail of these records—and who will be initially responsible for keeping them, the child or the teacher—often depends on the extent to which the school day is 'integrated'. A teacher may keep a simple list to show which children are expected to do what activity and in which order. This information may be kept in a teacher's record book, be written on a blackboard, or displayed on a wall chart indicating children's names and tasks. Alternatively, it may be the child who plans the task (Hohmann *et al.* 1979) or who draws up a 'contract' with the teacher indicating the work intended to be covered. Whatever system is chosen, it is most important that a record system should be quick and easy for the teacher to refer to, and for anyone else who may have to take over the class in an emergency.

2 THE INTEGRATED DAY

In this chapter we have focused so far on the organizational means by which we could put our plans into practice. Clearly, to implement them fully, we have to develop organizational strategies which are coherent with each other and with our aims. We noted in Chapter 6 that the notion of an 'integrated curriculum' was prevalent in contemporary primary-school ideology, although it was far from prevalent in practice. A similar situation exists with the notion of an 'integrated day', which refers to an organizational pattern intended to match child-centred aims. The two terms do not always go together: an integrated day can exist without an integrated curriculum, although an integrated curriculum would be unlikely to occur without an integrated day. In this section we will examine the concept of an 'integrated day' in terms of its organizational features and its coherence with curriculum goals.

2.1 Organizing the integrated day

The concept of an 'integrated day' became popular in the late 1960s and early 1970s in response to the perceived need to develop particular forms of organization which were coherent with child-centred pedagogic aims. However, just as there are many interpretations of the 'integrated curriculum', the 'integrated day' is similarly used to refer to a wide range of differing organizational practices.

Some of the main organizational aspects of the 'integrated day' are listed below:

1. Organizational aspects at the school level
(a) *Integration of age groups:* e.g. organizing children into 'vertically grouped' classes, which refers to the practice of combining more than one year group into a single class. For instance, 5- to 7-year-olds or 7- to 9-year-olds may be grouped together. This is sometimes done out of necessity in small schools, but it is also deliberately chosen by teachers who believe that there are positive advantages in such integration.

The possible advantages include:
- older children can help the younger ones to settle
- opportunities exist for children to develop responsibility
- stable, long-term learning situations provide greater continuity for the children and give the teacher a better chance to understand the children, which could lead to a better match of tasks to children.

Possible disadvantages include:
- the wider range of ages may make whole-class activities difficult (e.g. PE, story-time)
- the need for a wide range of resources and tasks may pose storing and planning difficulties
- younger and less able children could feel overawed by the older or brighter children
- the wide range of age and achievement demands very careful monitoring by the teacher to ensure an adequate matching of task and child

(b) *The integration of teaching responsibilities:* e.g. in open-plan schools where team-teaching is used. This is a form of organization where more than one class, or home/base unit, works in large shared areas with more than one teacher. In such open situations, cooperation is essential to co-ordinate activities and to avoid simultaneous demands on resources. Teachers may also plan their curriculum jointly and, in this sense, integrate their planning and provision. Again, advantages and disadvantages coexist in such a system.

Advantages could include:
- being able to give each other greater support
- being able to pool and develop ideas
- being able to make use of each other's specialisms

- being able to share tasks (e.g. story-time) and give each other time to do other jobs (e.g. mounting children's work)

Disadvantages could include:
- extra time may be needed to have the necessary meetings to plan and co-ordinate planning and provision
- the possibility that teachers have different values or aims
- reduced opportunities may exist for flexibility in tasks, to match individual children or to introduce changes in activities spontaneously

2. Organizational aspects at the classroom level
(a) *The integration of space and curriculum activities:* in infant classrooms, specialist areas of space, such as art, sand/water, library/reading corners, are usually incorporated into one classroom area.

Possible advantages could include:
- the teacher can oversee the children across all curriculum activities
- the children can move freely and easily between the curriculum activities without waiting for set times

Possible disadvantages could be:
- the wide range of demands on the teacher's expertise
- the possible hazards and distractions, particularly from the 'noisy' or 'messy' activities

In junior classrooms, specialist areas are also often incorporated within the classroom, though activities (such as cooking or woodwork) and sometimes practical science are removed from the classroom. This may be because of the scarcity of resources or a school policy for central location.

(b) *The integration of teaching sessions:* i.e. the minimal use of timetabling, which is perhaps the main hallmark of the integrated day.

Advantages are seen as:
- flexibility for the children to choose how much time to spend on an activity, and in which order, thus encouraging greater responsibility for their own work
- an increase in the children's intrinsic motivation to learn, resulting from the greater control over and involvement in their own learning

Disadvantages relate to:
- the difficulty of monitoring who is doing what in a busy classroom
- the probably greater range of resources required, which in turn makes more demands on teachers to 'manage' them, thus making it harder to find time to 'teach'

A number of different organizational practices have been developed to try to achieve a smoothly operating integrated day. For instance, a teacher may devise a number of tasks which the children may do on a rotation basis. Or, children may be given tasks to complete during a day, in the order of their own choice, on a quota basis. The tasks may be displayed as a constant reminder in either pictorial codes or writing. Older children may extend this and negotiate with the teacher on a range of tasks that need to be completed over the period of a whole week, and which can be chosen in any order. Even very young children can be encouraged to take some responsibility in deciding the tasks and in planning when and how they should be completed. This has been demonstrated by the High Scope nursery project (Hohmann *et al.* 1979), where children are asked to 'plan', 'do' and then 'review' their activities.

The main rationale for having an integrated day, at the classroom level, is that it allows children to follow their own interests and to be in control of their own learning (see Rowland 1984). Hence, it can serve as a motivational device by freeing children from the constraints of starting and finishing tasks according to organizational requirements, and by allowing them to follow their own pattern of learning. It is, therefore, an integral part of child-centred approaches to learning and must be considered in the light of the discussion of the values and assumptions embedded in such approaches.

The practical implementation of the integrated day is often characterized by organizing a number of different tasks to occur simultaneously. However, the existence of multiple, simultaneous activities does not necessarily mean that an integrated day, in the sense of enabling children to exercise more control over their own learning, is in operation. An alternative rationale for having multiple, simultaneous activities is that it is a managerial device for making maximum use of minimal resources.

One of the reasons for the diversity in interpreting the concept of the integrated day may lie in the fact that 'integration' became a 'symbolic' word in the early 1970s, through its close association with child-centredness (Moran 1971). It has come to represent individualism: a fluid open-ended curriculum based on children's interests, delegation of responsibility to the children and the belief in children as active, intrinsically motivated learners.

2.2 Coherence and the integrated day

As reflective teachers, we need to analyse the degree of coherence between the values underlying our curriculum planning and the organizational strategies which are adopted when we try to implement those plans.

As an example of this, we can consider the relationship between the possible forms of an 'integrated curriculum' and an 'integrated day'. A number of key dimensions can be distinguished to help in analysing the learning contexts which the children experience. Table 7.1 distinguishes seven aspects which can be used to consider the ways in which the 'other' curriculum is implemented (Alexander 1984, see Chapter 6). Two of these key aspects relate to the curriculum and the remaining five relate to its organizational implementation. Table 7.1 provides a starting-point for analysing these features and for analysing underlying aims. It could, therefore, be useful in helping us to examine the degree of coherence between our curriculum, organization and aims. The table does not represent polar opposites, but dimensions which distinguish between 'traditional' and 'progressive' practice, remembering that these terms alone are rather simplistic.

For example, if a child is working on an individual project, the context allows for developing autonomy and independence. Conversely, if children are working in a group or whole-class situation, the context allows for the development of a wide range of collaborative social skills. On the other hand, a teacher-directed context may be more suitable for children who have not yet learned the necessary skills and attitudes for working independently. However, the learning opportunities are immense if children are placed in a position where they can plan collaboratively and take responsibility not just for their own efforts, but for the whole class. Further, using each kind of resource is valuable, if it is feasible. Each kind of resource imposes its own organizational demands. The same applies to the different audiences. Finally, recording can provide valuable evidence to help us monitor the continuity, cohesion and coherence of the learning and teaching experiences of the class.

Table 7.1 *Characteristics of integrated-curriculum practice*

Place in the curriculum	'basics' in morning 'other' in afternoon ←——→ fully integrated throughout the day
Content focus	single/combined subject ←——→ multi-disciplinary
Organization	whole class doing similar work ←——→ groups doing related work ←——→ individuals have own 'projects'
Resources	secondary sources (book-based) ←——→ audio-visual, e.g. TV 'Watch' programme (vicarious 'visits' and orally presented information) ←——→ primary sources, first-hand experience (and experiments)
Control	teacher-directed ←——→ teacher and child(ren) negotiate ←——→ child decides own project unaided, or children evolve group/class study
Audience	for teacher to assess ←——→ for class to share ←——→ for others to respond, e.g. parents, community
Records	none ←——→ list of titles ←——→ outlines or 'webs' kept centrally ←——→ 'log' kept by child; parent, teacher commenting on likes/dislikes, evaluating hard/easy, suggesting reinforcement/extension/new direction

---

PRACTICAL ACTIVITY 7.9

Aim: To identify learning objectives which are coherent with each of the positions on the seven dimensions in Table 7.1.

Method: Using Table 7.1, identify the possible learning aims which could be associated with each of the labelled positions on each dimension. You could do this in terms of skills and attitudes.

Follow-up: Which of these learning aims are consistent with your own aims, as identified in Practical Activity 4.4? Which organizational practices would, therefore, be coherent with your own aims?

PRACTICAL ACTIVITY 7.10

Aim: To analyse 'topic' work in terms of the seven dimensions in Table 7.1.

Method: Review the activities contributing to current topic work.

Follow-up: How much variety of approaches is experienced by the children? Is there comprehensive and coherent coverage of alternative approaches, so that the strengths of each can be exploited? In the light of this examination, what decisions need to be made about the next 'topic'?

Some teachers always implement their curriculum plans in a similar way (e.g. at the extreme left of each dimension, or the extreme right). Others may adopt positions at different points of each of the seven dimensions, but always remain with that same combination. Yet others may deliberately vary the combinations to exploit the strengths and minimize the weaknesses of each different combination.

Because different positions along each of the seven dimensions are coherent with particular learning aims, there is no single 'best way'. In order to provide opportunities for learning a wide range of skills, attitudes, knowledge and concepts, organizational practice must vary so that it can match a wide range of aims and thus help to ensure coherence.

CONCLUSION

In this chapter we have discussed some of the key aspects of organizational planning and the need for consistency between them. We have also emphasized the importance of coherence between classroom organization and underlying aims and values. It is now time to turn to the issue of managing the implementation of those plans in action.

NOTES ON FURTHER READING

Organization is a very complex area and particular circumstances vary in different classrooms. Nevertheless, some general books with sound practical advice are listed below. The last two are particularly relevant to younger children.

Bassey, M. (1978) *Practical Classroom Organization*. London: Ward Lock Educational.
Dean, J. (1983) *Organizing Learning in the Primary School Classroom*. London: Croom Helm.
Waterhouse, P. (1983) *Managing the Learning Process*. London: McGraw-Hill.
Hohmann, M., Banet, B. and Weikart, D. (1979) *Young Children in Action*. Ypsilanti, Michigan: High Scope Educational Research Foundation.
Taylor, J. (1983) *Organization and Integration in the First School*. London: Unwin.

For a good review of research on classroom organization, see:

Boydell, D. (1978) *The Primary Teacher in Action*. London: Open Books.

The above books are especially good on organizing children. Bassey also includes case studies of working with other teachers. The following books focus on issues relating to parents in the classroom, many of which are relevant to working with other adults.

Cyster, R., Clift, P. S. and Battle, S. (1980) *Parental Involvement in Primary Schools*. Slough: NFER.
Lang, R. (1986) *Developing Parental Involvement in Primary Schools*. London: Macmillan.
Topping, K. and Wolfendale, S. (1985) *Parental Involvement in Children's Reading*. London: Croom Helm.

On classroom display, see:

Dean, J. (1973) *Display*. London: Evans.
Phelps, R. (1969) *Display in the Classroom*. Oxford: Blackwell.

Ideas for record-keeping appear in many different 'subject'-based books. However, for a very wide range of suggested ways for 'keeping track', see:

Clift, P., Weiner, G. and Wilson, E. (1981) *Record Keeping in the Primary School*. London: Macmillan.

Many of the above books have suggestions on the integrated day as it has become such an important part of primary-school practice. The following books focus on the concept of the integrated day and also discuss some of the practicalities.

Allen, I. *et al.* (1975) *Working an Integrated Day*. London: Ward Lock.
Walton, J. (ed.) (1971) *The Integrated Day: Theory and Practice*. London: Ward Lock.

Chapter 8

How Are We Managing and Coping? Considering Teachers' and Children's Strategies

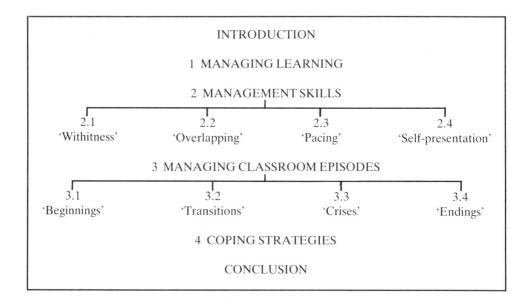

INTRODUCTION

1 MANAGING LEARNING

2 MANAGEMENT SKILLS

2.1	2.2	2.3	2.4
'Withitness'	'Overlapping'	'Pacing'	'Self-presentation'

3 MANAGING CLASSROOM EPISODES

3.1	3.2	3.3	3.4
'Beginnings'	'Transitions'	'Crises'	'Endings'

4 COPING STRATEGIES

CONCLUSION

INTRODUCTION

Having considered the issues involved in organizing a class, we now move it into the 'action' part of the reflective teaching cycle. This chapter begins with a consideration of classroom management. This includes considering how to manage and cope with learning itself and with learning situations.

These are issues of perennial concern to teachers because of the numbers of children in a typical classroom. As Jackson (1968) indicated, this means that, in a sense, the teacher is always dealing with a 'crowd'. Control of that crowd must, therefore, be a priority. It is a well-documented finding that, for many student teachers in particular, this concern initially displaces almost all other aims as they take on the challenge of coping with the class. Nevertheless, it is a legitimate concern and is an issue about which it is important to develop both skills and judgement.

However, the focus of attention should arguably be directed at the prevention of managerial problems, so that crises are avoided. To a considerable extent, this depends on the thoroughness of the planning for teaching/learning sessions that has been undertaken. Earlier chapters have suggested some areas that require prior reflection: such as the need to be clear about our values, aims and commitments, and consideration of relationships, curriculum and organization. For instance, if the curriculum is appropriate and our organization coherent with our aims, discipline is less likely to emerge as a problem.

This chapter has been structured in four sections. The first focuses on planning a specific learning session. The second discusses some key management skills. The third considers some of the most regularly occurring classroom episodes which require management. Section four analyses some of the coping strategies which both teachers and children may develop.

1 MANAGING LEARNING

Classroom learning sessions are central activities for teachers and learners. These have to be planned carefully and put into action sensitively. Reflective teachers are likely to have already considered their general aims, curriculum forecasts and organizational strategies. They may also have been collecting information about their children so that specific objectives can be identified. Against this background, a particular learning session may be planned.

When planning a learning session, a number of questions need to be considered:

Context
1. What are the present capabilities of the children?
2. How and when will planning be done: by a teacher before the session; with a group/whole class at the start of a session?
3. Are there any constraints imposed by simultaneous demands from other teachers or events (e.g. timetabling of hall)?
4. With which audiences will the learning be shared: a teacher, other adults, the class, the school during Assembly, or parents at an 'open evening'?

Objectives
5. What are the specific objectives, in terms of: learning elements (skills, attitudes, concepts and knowledge) and learning domains (intellectual, social, moral, physical-motor and aesthetic domains)?

Action
6. What learning opportunities will be provided for the selected objectives to be developed?
7. What organizational strategies will be required in terms of: people (individual, group, class), time (part, whole or more than session), place (classroom, library, grounds, etc.), resources (for information, e.g. telephone, books, stamps for letter-writing; for investigation, e.g. artefacts, minibus, specimen containers; for presentation, e.g. paper, paste, scissors, material)?
8. How will the session start, develop and end?
9. What will the teacher be doing at each of these stages and what range of things will the children be doing?

Evaluation
10. How will the progress of the session and the progress of the children be monitored and recorded?
11. How will such information be analysed and used?

PRACTICAL ACTIVITY 8.1

Aim: To consider the planning of a learning session, in terms of context, objectives, action and evaluation.

Method: Draft responses to each of the sections listed above. In this way, you should be able to produce an outline sketch of what will happen during the session.

1. Context . . .
2. Objectives . . .
3. Action . . .
4. Evaluation . . .

Follow-up: This process should help you to anticipate potential management problems, so that you can avoid many of them. By being prepared, you will be more likely to be able to encourage and extend the children's learning by appropriate questioning and explaining. It should also be possible to diagnose difficulties and spot opportunities for development, and to motivate, manage, maintain and monitor learning successfully.

Having analysed one learning session in this way, it is, of course, important to look at other sessions so that the links between them can be considered. For example, it would be useful to check for:

- appropriate range of learning elements (skills, attitudes, concepts and knowledge)
- appropriate levels of task demand (revision, incremental, restructuring, enrichment or practice)
- appropriate experience of areas of knowledge
- appropriate differentiation and progression
- appropriate continuity and cohesion
- appropriate coherence between aims, objectives and organizational practices

2 MANAGEMENT SKILLS

Having considered how a learning session might be planned, we will now look at four important management skills which relate to the maintenance and development of such sessions in action: 'withitness', 'overlapping', 'pacing' and 'self-presentation'.

2.1 'Withitness'
This is a term coined by Kounin (1970) to describe the ability to be aware of the wide variety of things which are simultaneously going on in a classroom. This is a constant challenge for any teacher and can be a particular strain for a new teacher until this skill is acquired.

Teachers who are 'withit' have 'eyes in the back of their heads'. They are able to anticipate and to see where help is needed. They are able to nip trouble in the bud. They are skilful at scanning the class while helping individuals and they position themselves accordingly. They are alert; they can pre-empt disturbance; and they can act fast. They can sense the way a class is responding and can act to maintain a positive atmosphere.

2.2 'Overlapping'

This is another of Kounin's terms and describes the skill of being able to do more than one thing at the same time. This can be related to withitness if, for example, a problem emerges concerning occasions when giving sustained help to a particular child results in relatively neglecting the rest of the class. In addition, overlapping is also an important and separate skill in its own right. Most teachers work under such pressure that they have to think about and do more than one thing at a time. Decisions have to be made very rapidly. Jackson (1968) calculated that over a thousand interpersonal exchanges a day typically take place between each teacher and the children in their care. For these reasons, reflecting, anticipating and making rapid judgements are very much a necessary part of any teacher's skills.

2.3 'Pacing'

Pacing a teaching–learning session is another important skill. It involves making appropriate judgements about the timing and phasing of the various activities and parts of a session and then taking suitable actions. At the simplest level, there is the practical judgement to be made at the end of a session about when to switch into a 'tidying-up phase'—it is very easy to get involved in activities, forget about the clock and suddenly to find that it is play-time. More complex educational judgements are necessary in relation to learning activities and the various phases of a typical session. For instance, the activities have to be introduced: this is often an initial 'motivational phase' where the children's interest is stimulated. This motivation also has to be maintained. Sessions then often enter an 'incubation and development phase' in which children think about the activities, explore ideas and then tackle tasks. From time to time, there may be a need for a 'restructuring phase', where objectives and procedures may need to be clarified further. Finally, there may be a 'review phase' for reinforcing good effort or for reflecting on overall progress.

Judgements about pacing—about when to make a new initiative—depend crucially on being sensitive to how children are responding to activities. If they are immersed and productively engaged, then one might decide to extend a phase or run the activity into the next session. If the children seem to be becoming bored, frustrated or listless, then it is usually wise to retain the initiative, to restructure or review the activity or to move on to something new. If the children are becoming too 'high', excited and distracted, then it may be useful to review and maybe redirect them into an activity which calms them down by re-channelling their energies.

2.4 Self-presentation

The last of the four management skills which we have identified is self-presentation, for how to 'present' oneself to children is also a matter for skill and judgement. Teachers who are able to project themselves so that children expect them to be 'in charge' have a valuable ability. There is a very large element of self-confidence in this and student teachers, in particular, may sometimes find it difficult to enact the change from the student role to the teacher role. Perhaps this is not surprising, for a huge change in rights and responsibilities is involved. The first essential, then, is to believe in oneself as a teacher.

A second range of issues concerned with self-presentation is more skill based. Here non-verbal cues are important. Self-presentation relates to such things as gesture, posture, movement, position in the room, facial expression, etc. These will be actively interpreted by children. The intended impression might be one of sureness, of confidence and competence. The reflective teacher will need to consider how non-verbal cues can help to convey such attributes.

A further very important skill is voice control. A teacher's use of voice can be highly sophisticated and effective. Changing the pitch, volume, projection and the intensity of meaning can communicate different aspects about self. If anyone's voice is to be used in this way, then it will require some training and time to develop. Teachers, like singers and actors, can learn to use their diaphragm to project a 'chest voice', to breathe more deeply and speak more slowly in order that their voice and their message is carried more effectively. Developing voice control is also an important asset in telling and reading stories, which may involve having to present many different characters. In the first instance, it may be a good idea to try out different 'voices'—privately and far enough away from others that a 'big' voice does not disturb anyone else! Although tape recorders never seem flattering, recording a practice story-telling can be a useful way of seeing how much appropriate voice variety is developing.

A fourth and more general area of skill which is involved in how teachers present and project themselves is that of 'acting', as though on a stage. In this sense, it is the ability to convey what we mean by 'being a teacher', so that expectations are clear and relationships can be negotiated. Acting is also an enormous strength for teachers for one other particular reason. When one is acting, one is partially detached from the role. It is possible to observe oneself, to analyse, reflect and plan. Acting, in other words, is controlled behaviour which is partially distanced from self. In the situations of vulnerability which sometimes arise in classrooms, this can be a great asset.

The skills which we have been reviewing above need to be put in a context. They are simply skills and have no substantive content or merit in their own right. A self-confident performer who lacks purpose and gets practical matters wrong (for example, who has ill-defined objectives, mixes up children's names, plans sessions badly, loses books, acts unfairly) will not be able to manage a class. A teacher has to be competent as well as skilled and must understand the ends of education as well as the means.

PRACTICAL ACTIVITY 8.2

Aim: To gather data about one's management skills and judgement.

Method:
1. Ask a colleague to observe a session which you take and to make notes on the way in which you manage the children. Your colleague could watch out for examples of appropriate withitness, overlapping, pacing and self-presentation (or chances missed). Discuss the session together afterwards.

2. Set up a video camera to record a session which you take. Analyse the play-back in terms of the criteria above.

Follow-up: Such analysis should increase self-awareness of management skills. Try to identify possible improvements which could be made. This can be practised and improved upon.

---

3 MANAGING CLASSROOM EPISODES

'Flow' is an important summary criterion which can be used to describe classroom management. By 'flow' we mean the degree of continuity and coherence which is achieved. It implies a steady, continuous movement in a particular direction. Thus, the

CHECKLIST 8.1

Aim: To consider how we get the children's attention and keep it.

1. How do we call for attention? Is a recognized signal used (e.g. standing in the front, clapping hands)?

2. How do we know if we have got their attention? Have they stopped what they were doing? Are they looking? Are they listening?

3. Has the speaker maximized conditions for listening? Are the listeners facing the speaker (so those who hear little can see facial expressions)? Is it quiet (so those who hear 'too much' have fewer distractions)?

suggestion is that we, as teachers, should aim to develop a coherent sense of purpose within our classes; should organize our classrooms in ways which are consistent with those purposes; and should manage the children, phases and events so that educational objectives are cumulatively reinforced. We would suggest that, if this can be done, then energy, interest and enthusiasm in learning are likely to be focused productively.

Achieving such a flow of activities requires a high degree of awareness, sensitivity and skill and it is sometimes the case that events seem to conspire to produce jerky, fragmented, incoherent sequences of activities which lack momentum.

There are four classroom episodes which pose particular management challenges to the flow of sessions. These are 'beginnings' of sessions; 'transitions' between phases of sessions or between sessions themselves; 'crises' and 'endings' of sessions. We will discuss each in turn.

3.1 'Beginnings'
The beginnings of a session are often seen as important because of the way in which they set a tone. The aim is usually to introduce and interest the children in the planned activities; to provide them with a clear indication of what they are expected to do; and to structure the activity in practical organizational terms.

CHECKLIST 8.2

Aim: To consider how the children are stimulated at the start of the session.

Some possibilities are:
- Capitalizing on their interests and own experience (e.g. someone who has a wobbly tooth or a filling)

- Challenging them to investigate, interpret (e.g. survey of number of new teeth or fillings in the class)

- Channelling their curiosity: artefacts, models, posters, stories, videos (e.g. dentist leaflets, jaw bones)

1. Which kind of stimulation is used most?

2. How often are alternatives tried?

3. What has been most/least successful—why and when?

4. How have we judged 'successful'?

CHECKLIST 8.3

Aim: To consider how the children are orientated so that they know exactly what is expected of them.

1. Do they know why they are doing this activity?

2. Do they know what they are going to learn from it?

3. Do they know if any follow-up is expected?

4. Do they know on what criteria it is to be assessed?

5. Do they know what they are going to do with completed work?

6. Do they know which activity they are to go on to next?

3.2 'Transitions'

'Transitions' are a regular cause of control difficulties, particularly for student teachers. This often arises when expectations about behaviour concerning one activity are left behind and those of the new one have yet to be established. In these circumstances, a skilled teacher is likely to take an initiative early and to structure the transition carefully.

For example, it would be a challenging prospect if a whole range of creative, literacy and maths activities were in full flow when it was realized PE in the hall was timetabled. We would suggest that it is important to break down a transition such as this into discrete stages. The skill lies in anticipating problems before they arise; in pre-structuring the next phase; and in interesting the children in the next phase so that they are drawn through to it. These principles apply to any transition.

CHECKLIST 8.4

Aim: To monitor a transition.

1. Did I give an early warning of the transition?

2. Did I give clear instructions for leaving existing work?

3. Did I give the children clear instructions for the transition and for any movement that was necessary?

4. Did I arouse the children's interest in the next phase?

3.3 'Crises'

A classroom 'crisis' is obviously an immediate source of disruption to the flow of a session. Crises can come in many forms, from a child being sick or cutting a finger, to children or perhaps a parent challenging the teacher's authority and judgement. Despite the wide-ranging issues which are raised, there are three fairly simple principles which can be applied from the classroom-management point of view.

The first principle is to minimize disturbance. Neither a child who is ill or hurt, nor a parent or child who is upset can be given the attention which they require by a teacher who has continuing classroom responsibilities. Help from the school secretary, an ancillary helper or the head teacher should be called in either to deal with the problem or to relieve the class teacher so that he or she can deal with it. In this way, disturbance to the classroom flow can be minimized and those in need of undivided attention can receive it. Of course, a student teacher usually has a full-time teacher upon whom to call.

The second principle for handling a crisis is to maximize reassurance. Children can be upset when something unexpected happens and it may well be appropriate to reassert the security of their classroom routines and expectations. Therefore, a degree of caution in the choice of activities for a suitable period might be wise.

The third principle which is appropriate when a crisis arises concerns oneself and pausing for sufficient thought. Obviously, this depends on what has happened and some events require immediate action. However, if it is possible to gain time to think about the issues outside the heat of the moment, then it may produce more authoritative and constructive decisions.

PRACTICAL ACTIVITY 8.3

Aim: To monitor responses to a classroom crisis.

Method: After a crisis has arisen, a diary-type account of it and of how it was handled could be written. This might describe the event, and also reflect the feelings which were experienced as the events unfolded. It would be valuable to encourage children to make a similar description and reflection after the event, so that you can gain an insight into why they behaved as they did. The following questions might be asked:

1. Did I minimize disturbance?
2. Did I maximize reassurance?
3. Did I gain time to produce a considered response?
4. Did I give a positive indication of what was expected?

Follow-up: Having examined your view and the children's views, it would probably be helpful to discuss the event and the accounts with a friend or colleague.

Although, hopefully, crises will be rare, there may be other sorts of behavioural problems which can upset the 'flow' of a session. However, by constant monitoring and being 'withit', it is usually possible to anticipate undesirable behaviour which threatens the 'working consensus' and to 'nip it in the bud'. Nevertheless, difficulties are bound to occur from time to time and prudent teachers should think through possible strategies in advance, so that they can act confidently in managing such situations. A range of strategies exist which might be used to meet a range of possible incidents:

Strategies to pre-empt general misbehaviour
1. Make sure each child knows what to do and how to do it
2. Show approval of appropriate work or behaviour
3. Be supportive of any problems encountered

Strategies to respond to misbehaviour
1. Ignore it if it only occurs once

2. If repeated:
    2.1 Make eye contact
    2.2 Move towards the child
    2.3 Invite the child to participate—ask a question or encourage a comment

3. If persistent, in addition to the responses above:
    3.1 Name the child firmly and positively
    3.2 Move to the child
    3.3 Stop the action
    3.4 Briefly identify the inappropriate behaviour
    3.5 Clearly state the desired behaviour
    3.6 Remind the child of the relevant rules and classroom understandings
    3.7 If necessary, isolate the child—avoid a contagious spread, a public clash and an 'audience' which can provoke 'showing-off'

4. After the event:
    4.1 Encourage the child to identify what had been wrong, thus sharing responsibility with the child
    4.2 Invite the child to draw up a 'contract' of what the child and the teacher will do and with which tangible rewards
    4.3 Modify behaviour by withdrawal of privileges and by providing opportunities to earn praise

Other, major on-going problems can also exist in any classroom. These may be associated with an individual child who has particular difficulties. In such instances, it is important to analyse the behaviour and try to identify the possible causes before any positive action can be taken.

Conditions. When exactly does the disruption occur?
* is it random or regular?
* is it always the same child?
* is it always regarding the same task?
* is it always with the same teacher?

Characteristics. What exactly happens?
* is it a verbal reaction?
* is it a physical reaction?

Consequences. What are the effects?
* on the child, the teacher?
* on the class, the school?
* do they join in, ignore, retaliate?

Such major, persistent problems are best discussed with other colleagues and a common strategy worked out. This might also involve the parents and the whole class, if necessary, so that a consistent approach can be adopted.

Whether a problem is associated with an individual child or most of the class, a consistent approach is essential and would, hopefully, provide security for the children as well as support for the teacher. It must be remembered that children respond to situations and experiences. We, as teachers, structure such experiences. Thus, if children respond problematically, we must reflect on the experiences we provide.

A final, regularly occurring type of event or phase which influences the flow of classroom life concerns the endings of sessions.

3.4 'Endings'
Ending a session is a further management issue and four aspects will be reviewed. The first is a very practical one. At the end of any session, equipment must be put away and the classroom must be tidied up, ready for future sessions. The second aspect relates to discipline and control. Children can sometimes get a little 'high' at the end of a session when they look forward excitedly to whatever follows. This, combined with the chores of tidying up, can require a degree of awareness and firmness from the teacher. The procedures which are called for here are similar to those for transitions. The two other aspects involved in ending sessions have more explicit and positive educational potential. One of these concerns the excellent opportunities which arise for reviewing educational progress and achievements; for reinforcing good work; and for contextualizing activities which have been completed. This is complemented by the opportunities which also arise for asserting the membership of the class as a communal group. Shared experiences, team-work and cooperation can be celebrated and reinforced through enjoying poetry, singing, games, stories, etc. Thus, there are lots of very productive opportunities at the ends of sessions, and even an odd space of unexpected time, perhaps waiting for a bell, can be used constructively.

Overall, a carefully thought out and well-executed ending to a session will contribute to the flow of activities by providing an ordered exit, by reinforcing learning and by building up the sense of 'belonging' within the class as a whole.

CHECKLIST 8.5

Aim: To monitor the end of a session.

1. Did I give early warning of the end of the session?

2. Did I give clear instructions for tidying up?

3. Did I reinforce those instructions and monitor the tidying up?

4. Did I take opportunities to reinforce the educational achievements, efforts and progress made?

5. Did I take opportunities to build up the sense of the class as a community?

6. Did I praise the children for what they did well?

7. Did I provide for an ordered exit from the room?

---

4 COPING STRATEGIES

The previous sections of this chapter have considered classroom management exclusively from the point of view of the teacher's judgements and actions. However, classroom management is a more complex issue than this implies, for the obvious reason that it applies to an interactive situation between the teacher and children. The process of managing and coping is thus one of active judgement and decision-making on both sides.

The concept of coping strategy is useful here (Woods 1977; Hargreaves 1978; Pollard 1982). It refers to the strategies which people adopt in response to their circumstances, as a means of sustaining their sense of self. The issues of classroom management, control and survival are all included in this concept. For a teacher, a major question might be, 'How do I cope in my classroom with large numbers of children, limited space and resources and a wide range of expectations bearing on me?' For a child, a prominent question might be, 'How do I cope in the classroom when I am on my own among so many other children, having to do certain things, with the teacher judging my work and when my parents and friends expect certain things of me?'

The answer, to both questions, is that action is likely to be strategic (i.e. based on judgements which are made about actions which will best serve each person's interests in particular situations). A great many different examples of teacher and child strategies have been identified. Among these are the child strategies listed below:

Open negotiation—collaborative participation
  • discussing, reasoning, initiating
  • sharing a joke

Seeking recognition/reassurance
  • fake involvement
  • acting

Drifting—relying on routines for cover
  • pleasing the teacher
  • docility/resignation
  • right answerism

Evasion—apathy
  • time-stealing
  • re-doing work

Withdrawal—avoidance
  • minimizing effort

Rebellion—aggression
  • messing around
  • 'winding up' the teacher

PRACTICAL ACTIVITY 8.4

Aim: To reflect on the range of coping strategies which children use in the classroom.

Method: Observe a small group of children in a classroom (either in your own class or a colleague's). Afterwards, you could discuss some of the events with the children to gain insights into their interpretation of events, rather than just to rely on your own.

Follow-up: Understanding children's coping strategies can help us to be more sensitive to their needs when we make managerial decisions.

Such strategies can be identified by observation and interviews with children. They may well strike a chord with personal experiences of being a pupil or, indeed, cause reflection on children who have been taught. Such strategies are a means by which children 'manage' in the classroom.

Some common types of teacher strategies which have been identified include the following:

Open negotiation—mutual collaboration
- discussion and explaining
- sharing a joke

Distancing—avoiding confrontation
- enforcing rigid routines
- ritualizing

'Routinization'
- keeping them busy
- repetition
- moderating demands

Manipulation
- using reward/punishment
- flattery
- personal appeals

Domination/charisma
- relying on personal charisma
- intellectual 'showing off'

Coercion
- sarcasm
- threatening
- hitting

PRACTICAL ACTIVITY 8.5

Aim: To reflect on the coping strategies which we use when teaching.

Method: This issue can be tackled by a combination of personal diary records together with the comments and observations of a colleague. Alternatively, a video-recording of a session, followed by analysis, could also be a way of collecting information about our own coping strategies.

Follow-up: Having identified the range of strategies and the types most frequently used, the questions of their appropriateness and educational effectiveness can begin to be answered.

It is important to note the interactive context of the classroom; since the actions of teachers and children have an immediate effect on each other, a mesh of teacher-and-child strategies tends to develop. This, of course, is closely related to the form of relationships and to the 'working consensus' which has been negotiated (see Chapter 5). One way of conceptualizing this mesh of strategies is indicated in Figure 8.1.

Teacher strategies			Child strategies
Unilateral strategies	Strategies within the working consensus		Unilateral strategies
domination coercion	open negotiation distancing . . . . seeking recognition routinization . . . . drifting manipulation . . . . evasion		withdrawal rebellion

Figure 8.1 To show the interrelationships between teacher and child strategies

The significant implication of this model of interaction is that the actions of the children are clearly related to the actions of the teacher. It suggests that, if difficulties arise in connection with classroom management, it is not sufficient just to review the 'awkward characteristics' of the children, for this simply passes all responsibility on to them and generates negative ideas about them. It is also necessary to analyse the situation interactively and to consider our responsibilities as teachers.

CONCLUSION

This chapter has examined aspects of management which help to establish and sustain conditions for successful learning. These questions of management are matters of great concern to teachers, as is the question of how teachers and children learn to cope with each other and with learning situations. These are challenges with which most of us soon become more familiar and gradually grow in confidence and competence. Direct experience is often felt to be irreplaceable in developing competence, but there is also much to be said for sharing ideas, problems and successes through discussion with colleagues.

NOTES ON FURTHER READING

For a book which provides many insights into classroom management, and which has become a classic, see:

Kounin, J. S. (1970) *Discipline and Group Management in Classrooms* New York: Holt, Rinehart & Winston.

A book which provides a wide-ranging review of issues and approaches to classroom management in primary schools is:

Roberts, T. (1983) *Child Management in the Primary School*. London: Allen & Unwin.

and also:

Docking, J. M. (1980) *Control and Discipline in Schools*. London: Harper & Row.
Fontana, D. (1986) *Classroom Control*. London: Methuen.
Good, T. and Brophy, J. (1978) *Looking in Classrooms*. New York: Harper & Row.

Another concise discussion of the major issues, and with a good section on teacher stress and how to cope with it, is provided by:

Laslett, R. and Smith, C. (1984) *Effective Classroom Management*. London: Croom Helm.

For an up-to-date account of alternative ways of analysing disruptive behaviour, see:

Tattum, D. P. (ed.) (1986) *The Management of Disruptive Pupil Behaviour in Schools*. Chichester: Wiley.

A recent empirical study of the issue, though based on secondary teachers, is:

Corrie, M., Haystead, J. and Zaklukiewicz, S. (1982) *Classroom Management Strategies*. Edinburgh: Scottish Council for Research in Education.

An analysis of teacher and child coping strategies in the primary school can be found in:

Pollard, A. (1985) *The Social World of the Primary School*. London: Holt, Rinehart & Winston.

Chapter 9

How Are We Communicating in the Classroom? Considering Classroom Interaction

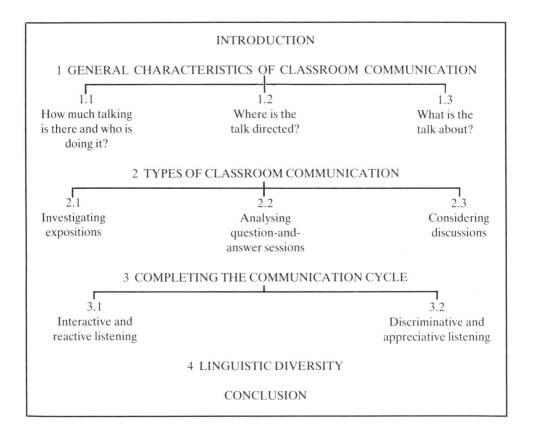

INTRODUCTION

1 GENERAL CHARACTERISTICS OF CLASSROOM COMMUNICATION

1.1
How much talking
is there and who is
doing it?

1.2
Where is the
talk directed?

1.3
What is the
talk about?

2 TYPES OF CLASSROOM COMMUNICATION

2.1
Investigating
expositions

2.2
Analysing
question-and-
answer sessions

2.3
Considering
discussions

3 COMPLETING THE COMMUNICATION CYCLE

3.1
Interactive and
reactive listening

3.2
Discriminative and
appreciative listening

4 LINGUISTIC DIVERSITY

CONCLUSION

INTRODUCTION

So far, in Part 2, we have examined the perspectives and expectations of children and teachers; their relationships; the ways in which knowledge, concepts, skills and attitudes are planned and presented through the curriculum; and the manner in which classrooms can be organized and managed. All of these aspects facilitate the learning which we hope will be taking place in the classroom. It is now time to turn directly to teaching and learning processes. Fundamental to these processes is the language through which teaching and learning is mediated. The Bullock Report (DES 1975), which supported the crucial role of language in learning, suggested that all teachers were 'language teachers'. In accepting the centrality of language, this chapter focuses on the nature of communication, and on how it might affect teachers, children and learning.

Four main teaching approaches can be identified. First, teachers can demonstrate, or show children how to do certain tasks. Second, they can be didactic, or tell children the how and why of specific activities. Or, third, they can leave children to discover and explore experiences for themselves. Fourth, most teachers would probably engage in some discussion about the task—to clarify what each task was; why it was important; how it might be approached; and to check that its purpose was understood, as well as to explore any problems that might be experienced. Often, all these approaches are combined, with different emphasis according to specific activities, particular individuals and special circumstances at that time. However, discussion is particularly important because it is central to exchanging views and understandings. We would argue, therefore, that it is at the heart of a reflective teaching–learning process.

Most of our teaching and learning is achieved through some form of communication. In schools, although communication may be partially accomplished in non-verbal ways, the most important media are talking, listening, writing and reading. However, despite the fact that most of the time spent in classrooms is spent in trying to communicate, such efforts are not always successful.

Communicating is a complicated business, for it involves three sets of skills. It involves people and, therefore, requires social skills as well as the more obvious language skills. In addition, since communication is about something, it also requires cognitive skills: knowing something about the subject under consideration and being able to think about and process what others are trying to communicate to us. Alongside these skills, it is also important to consider the attitudes of the participants and the context itself, for these are also likely to add meanings to the encounter.

Further, it is important to remember that, in classroom situations, teachers and children will each play the parts of both speakers and listeners. Hence, all the participants need to acquire knowledge, skills and attitudes appropriate to both talking and listening.

Finally, we have to note the para-verbal and non-verbal features of oral language which also contribute to the effectiveness of how we communicate. Apart from what we say, a great deal is conveyed by how we say it. Thus, tone of voice, pace, pitch and how we project our voice are all part of the communication process. Meanings which we convey by these para-verbal features are open to misinterpretation, particularly by those from different cultures and backgrounds. In addition, there are non-verbal aspects, such as looks, gestures and the ways in which we move, which accompany what we say. These can sometimes extend our meanings, but they can also confuse or even contradict what we say.

Having identified the importance of oral communication in this introduction, the chapter develops with a general review of the characteristics of classroom communication. This is followed by a focus on particular types of classroom 'talk' and then by a consideration of the demands made on 'listening'.

1 GENERAL CHARACTERISTICS OF CLASSROOM COMMUNICATION

Any observer in a primary classroom cannot fail to notice the amount of talking—and listening—that occurs. If we examine this talk closely, a number of characteristics can be identified. These can provide important clues about the quality of the teaching–learning process.

PRACTICAL ACTIVITY 9.1

Aim: To investigate the time spent in talking and listening in a classroom.

Method: Tape-record (or better still video-record) part of a teaching session (e.g. 15 minutes). Remember that unless radio microphones are worn, it may be difficult to hear what is said against the background classroom bustle. In a whole-class situation, mostly the teacher's voice is heard. In a small-group situation, all the participants can usually be heard on the average cassette recorder.

Focal points for consideration:
1. How much talking is there and who is doing it?
   - Calculate total amount of time spent on teacher talk.
   - Calculate time spent by children talking to teacher, and to each other. Are there any differences between boys/girls, able/less able, etc.?

2. Where is the talk directed?
   - Calculate the number of times the teacher is spoken to, by whom, why?
   - Calculate how often different children are spoken to, by whom, why?

3. What is the talk about?
   - Calculate the amount of time spent on social/personal chat.
   - Calculate the amount of talk spent setting up the task, and supervising the work.
   - Calculate the amount of time spent on discussing the main points, or substantive content, of the task.

Follow-up: Information of this kind can highlight the pattern of talk in our own classroom. It can often reveal aspects which surprise us, because it is so difficult to be aware of how much we talk, to whom and why, while we are engrossed in the process of teaching itself. Having identified the pattern of talk, we need to decide whether what we do is consistent with our aims.

1.1 How much talking is there and who is doing it?
Research in America suggested that two-thirds of the teaching sessions studied were usually spent in talk and two-thirds of that talking was done by the teacher (Flanders 1970). Since then, investigations in British primary schools have shown similar figures (Galton, Simon and Croll 1980; Bennett *et al.* 1984).

1.2 Where is the talk directed?
The findings of the largest recent investigation into classroom talk, the ORACLE research, showed that approximately 80 per cent of teachers' time, in junior-school classrooms, was spent in talk between the teacher and children: 56 per cent with individuals; 15 per cent with the whole class; 7 per cent with groups (Galton, Simon and Croll 1980). Apart from the size of the 'audience' with whom the teacher is communicating, it is also significant to consider how the teacher's time is distributed between the children, between girls and boys, and between children of different abilities or different needs. Some research suggests that boys often receive a greater share of a teacher's attention, both positive and negative (Clarricoates 1981; Spender and Sarah 1980), and that children of different ethnic origins receive different types of attention (Galton

1986). The impact of integrating children with special needs has also been studied (Croll and Moses 1985).

1.3 What is the talk about?

The ORACLE study showed that the highest percentage of teacher talk was generally devoted to supervising tasks set, rather than to talking about the substantive content of those tasks (Galton, Simon and Croll 1980). Most of this talk was in the form of statements of fact. Very little time indeed was spent in asking questions which required children to think for themselves in any kind of open-ended, problem-solving capacity. In general, teacher talk seemed to be largely concerned with the smooth running and management of the classroom and the practice of engaging the children in challenging discussion was rare.

As reflective teachers, it is important to review these findings and consider their significance. For example, what might be the effects on the children? What impressions might children gain about learning and about their own role in the learning process? What kinds of attitudes towards learning might children acquire? What types of learning are likely to take place?

To begin to answer such questions, a reflective teacher is likely to want to collect data rather than rely on subjective impressions. Tape recording can be a useful technique for collecting certain kinds of data on classroom talk, though an alternative way of collecting information about particular aspects of teacher talk is to devise checklists. These can be helpful both as a guide when preparing a session, or as a framework within which to reflect afterwards. A third approach is to devise a schedule of specific categories of behaviour. For example, three categories could be used, such as when the teacher asks a question, explains a task, or tells off a child. Each time one of the listed behaviours is noted, it can be 'marked up', using a tally system.

2 TYPES OF CLASSROOM COMMUNICATION

There are three particularly common communicative situations which occur in the classroom. These are:

'Expositions': where the speaker describes, informs, instructs, or explains

'Question-and-answer' exchanges: often for testing and checking purposes, where there is often one right answer (i.e. a 'closed' situation)

'Discussions': where the participants (whole class or small group) explore ideas and feelings together (i.e. an 'open' situation)

Each of these situations has features in common, as well as features which are unique to itself. For example, since every communicative situation is at least a two-way process, we need to consider the speakers as well as the listeners. In an 'exposition' situation, the listeners are not likely to participate verbally. Nevertheless, the speaker should be aware of the listeners and watch the listeners for signs of understanding or otherwise, so that adjustments can be made. The listeners must listen, must be able to react and show if understanding has taken place, or, if not, must be able to ask for clarification. In addition, the listeners may also want to respond more actively. Hence 'expositions' can sometimes become 'discussions'. In such situations, the roles of speaker and listener may change rapidly. The listeners will have to respond to the speaker and formulate their own ideas, but they must also wait their turn so that their ideas are added at an appropriate time. Hence, in a discussion situation of this kind, considerable linguistic, social and cognitive demands are made.

Each situation, in fact, calls for particular types of awareness about the rules of the 'communication game' and, in order to participate productively, the 'rules' must be clear and each participant must understand and accept those rules. Learning to speak and to listen are thus very important skills. Neither skill can be considered 'passive', for they both take place in an interactive situation.

We now turn to examine the first of the three main types of communicative situations that we find in the classroom: exposition.

2.1 Investigating expositions

Often the first task in each teaching session is to stimulate the children and to structure activities. This is just as pertinent to whole-class sessions as to group or individual work. Expositions, therefore, are a common aspect of any teacher's talk. They are less regularly tasks for the children, though they do occur when children 'report back' on an activity, or 'tell their news'. In any such situation, the opening 'moves' are very important in setting the tone of the session.

A number of different aspects of exposition might be considered:

1. Getting attention
2. Motivating the listeners
3. Orientating, so that expectations about the session are clear
4. Constructing and delivering the exposition itself

The first three of these aspects have already been discussed in the previous chapter (section 3.1). Therefore, we suggest some checklists to help to focus our attention on a further aspect concerning expositions (i.e. constructing and delivering expositions).

CHECKLIST 9.1

Aim: To investigate aspects in the construction and delivery of expositions.

When the speaker delivers the exposition:
- is eye contact sustained, to hold attention and give interim feedback?

- is an interesting, lively tone of voice used?

- is the pace varied; are pauses used (not hesitations)?

- is the exposition varied by encouraging orderly participation?

- are alternative media used (visual/aural)?

- are variations made in the level of cognitive demand, size of the conceptual steps, and length of the concentration span required?

- is a written or illustrated record of key points provided as a guide if listeners need memory aids?

CHECKLIST 9.2

Aim: To examine how an exposition is constructed.

Are the instructions/directions/descriptions/explanations clear, concise and coherent?

Has the speaker:

1. Planned what is going to be said?

2. Stated the outline structure of the exposition? ('advance organizers', e.g. 'We are going to find out . . .')

3. Selected the key points: identified and made explicit the relevance of each and their relationship to each other? ('There are four things we need to think about, . . . because . . .')

4. Sequenced key points appropriately?

5. Used short, simple sentences: explained specialist vocabulary, if it needs to be used, given concrete examples (or asked the listeners)?

6. Signalled when a new point is made? ('Now let's look at . . .', 'The third thing to look out for is . . .')

7. Summarized key points, or got the listeners to summarize them?

8. Sought feedback to check understanding (at each point, if necessary)?

2.2 Analysing question-and-answer techniques

Teachers, and children, use questions for a wide range of purposes and they can be seen as a vital tool for teaching and learning. They account for a high proportion of teacher talk. Asking questions provides immediate feedback on how participants are thinking and on what they know. They are, therefore, seen as essential means of helping us to understand learning processes. Listening to the 'answers', and not pre-judging them, is an important way of learning about a learner.

Particular aspects about questions which might be reviewed are:

1. The purpose, or function, of questions
2. The form in which questions are asked
3. The ways in which responses are handled

Each of these aspects are now considered in further detail.

The purpose, or function, of questions

Questions can be grouped in many different ways. However, two main categories commonly occur. The first is psycho-social questions: those which centre on relationships between children or between a teacher and the children. The second category is 'pedagogic' questions: those which relate to more specifically educational concerns, and to the teaching and learning of skills, attitudes, concepts and knowledge.

CHECKLIST 9.3

Aim: To provide a framework for analysing classroom questions.

Purposes of psycho-social questions:
- to encourage shy members to integrate by participating
  (e.g. 'Jan, you've got a little kitten too, haven't you?')

- to show interest in and value for group members
  (e.g. 'You had a good idea, Norita. Will you tell us?')

- to develop respect for each others' views
  (e.g. 'What do you think you would have done?')

- to assert control
  (e.g. 'Wayne, what are you up to?')

- to implement routines and procedures
  (e.g. 'Ahmed, what did I tell you to do next?)

Purposes of pedagogical questions:
1. Closed questions (low-level cognitive demand)
   - to recall information: for testing, consideration or feedback (e.g. 'Where is Ethiopia?')

   - to give on-the-spot solution: application of known rule to new variables (e.g. 'What is 28 divided by 4?')

   - to encourage analysis by describing, comparing or classifying (e.g. 'What's the difference between . . .?')

2. Open questions (high-level cognitive demand)
   - to explore information and ideas with no set 'answer' (reasoning/ interpreting, hypothesizing/speculating, imagining/inventing) (e.g. 'How do you think the hero would feel if . . .?')

   - to encourage synthesis of information and ideas by focusing on contradictions, discrepancies, different sources of evidence (e.g. 'What do you think really happened . . .?')

   - to encourage evaluations, decision-making, and judgements (e.g. 'Would it be fair if . . .?')

   - to encourage the transfer of ideas and application of knowledge (e.g. 'Is what we've found out useful . . .?')

The form of questions

Among the most important issues associated with classroom questioning techniques is the form in which the question is posed in relation to its purpose.

The form of a question can have very diverse effects. For example, a question can be posed in such a way as to invite a monosyllabic answer (e.g. Question: 'Did you like the book?' Answer: 'Yes/No'). What effects would such a question have if the aim were to develop a discussion? Conversely, would this be any more appropriate in a testing situation? For example, Question: 'Has potato got starch in it?' Answer: 'Yes/No'.

Another form is the 'direct' question, which is short and simple in construction and has a single specified focus. For instance, 'How did the Vikings make their boats?', to which the answer may be lengthy, though straightforward and factual; or 'What makes a good book?' to which the answer may also be lengthy, but consisting of opinions and ideas which may be complex to articulate. Very different effects might result from using a 'direct' question compared to one which invites a monosyllabic response. A reflective teacher would need to consider whether such a form would be appropriate if the aim were to encourage exploration, evaluation, or to focus contributions on a particular suggestion.

A third form of question is the 'indirect' question. This is a long, composite question which may include a number of different leads. Again, such a question can be very useful in some situations, but inappropriate in others. For example, 'indirect' questions can offer a number of different suggestions which might help in opening out a discussion and in providing a range of possible leads to explore. It would be less suitable in a testing situation, as the focus of the question would be relatively unclear. It could also be confusing to a child who found it hard to take everything in and who therefore got lost.

The ways in which responses are handled
A third aspect of questioning, that of handling responses, is also important to consider. A key issue is how long to pause and wait for and answer. Very often we wait only one or two seconds before either repeating a question, re-phrasing it, re-directing it to another child, or extending it.

Having got a response, teachers have many alternative strategies which can be used. We can reject the response, modify, ignore, pass over, correct, or accept it. We can also hold it with others for general consideration when many suggestions have been given, offer it for others to comment upon, extend it, invite a child to develop it, or respond with praise. With such a range of strategies, a reflective teacher might usefully consider what the effects would be for different children in different situations.

Practical Activities 9.2 and 9.3 suggest ways of examining question-and-answer sessions with regard to asking the questions and handling the responses.

PRACTICAL ACTIVITY 9.2

Aim: To investigate 'question-and-answer' exchanges: first focus, teacher asking questions.

Method: Either tape-record a teaching session or, by agreement, observe a colleague.

Choose three five-minute periods in a teaching session (e.g. beginning/middle/end) and write down the questions the teacher asks during each period.

In addition, it may be possible to code the audience to whom the questions were addressed (e.g. B=boy, Bb=group of boys, G=girl, Gg=group of girls, Mg=mixed group, C=class).

The questions could be classified using Checklist 9.3.

Follow-up: Classifying questions should highlight the variety and level of the cognitive demands that were made. It is then possible to consider whether what we do matches our intentions, and if not what changes could be made.

If the audience has been noted, it is also possible to analyse the distribution of questions and to consider any implications.

The activity could be repeated to analyse children's questions.

PRACTICAL ACTIVITY 9.3

Aim: To investigate 'question-and-answer' exchanges: second focus, teacher's handling of children's responses.

Method: Choose three five-minute periods during a teaching session (e.g. beginning/middle/end) and record how the teacher handles the responses during each period.
   The responses can be classified using the list of strategies discussed in the section above.

Follow-up: Analysing the data may help reflection upon the teacher's intentions, and whether they were fulfilled. What effects can be identified resulting from the ways in which responses were handled?

Apart from monitoring the level and variety of types of questions, it is also important to remember that a listener may not perceive a question in the same way as the person who asks it. For example, a teacher may ask an apparently closed question, intended to check understanding, but to a child who does not know the answer, the question may seem very open. In addition, there are rules and conventions which guide this kind of classroom interaction. For example, a question directed to a child may appear perfectly acceptable, but may, if directed to the teacher without altering para-verbal and non-verbal features, be regarded as 'cheeky'.

Such discrepancies between how a question is intended and how it is received raise some important issues about the classification of questions. This is a difficulty which is both theoretical (in terms of identifying and defining 'types' of questions), as well as practical (in terms of recognizing and interpreting intention and, therefore, responding appropriately).

2.3 Considering discussions
In addition to 'expositions' and 'question-and-answer' sessions, there are also many 'discussion' situations to be found in classrooms. Encouragement to increase the use of discussion opportunities has come from two different sources. Since the 1960s the National Association of Teachers of English, among many others, have been demonstrating the benefits of allowing children to make 'knowledge their own' by discussing among themselves, on their own terms, in their own language (Barnes, Britton and Rosen 1969; Ede and Wilkinson 1980). This encouragement, which was coming from the grass roots, was endorsed by the Bullock Report (DES 1975) and further supported by HMI (DES 1978a, 1985a). However, despite the considerable interest being shown and the claims being made, much less has been said about how to help children improve their discussion skills and how teachers can best contribute.

Whether a discussion is between the whole class with the teacher present or within a small-group discussion without the teacher, a number of particular issues often arise:

1. What are the range of roles participants might play?
2. What do the participants learn, including those that do not participate?
3. How do different kinds of tasks, group size and composition affect group processes?
4. How can we use discussion to develop and monitor the participants' discussion skills?

Each of these will be discussed in turn.

Roles

Early work in this field highlighted the often inhibiting effect of the teacher's presence on a group discussion. This was because groups often began to try to guess what was in the teacher's mind and to try to 'answer' rather than 'discuss' (Barnes, Britton and Rosen 1969). Without a teacher, groups learnt to take responsibility for their own learning. Other research has shown that even infants can take on the additional roles which are usually denied to them in either a whole-class situation or if the teacher is present in the group—particularly the roles of instigator and chairperson (Prisk 1987; Tann and Armitage 1986). To collaborate orally in a group requires different skills from individual, written, classroom tasks. Hence, small discussion groups provide a unique forum where children with different skills can come to the fore.

Group learning

As was mentioned earlier, learning to discuss is a complex activity, requiring linguistic, cognitive and social skills. Particular attitudes need to be encouraged so that children listen, value and respond to each other's contributions. Oral discussion of ideas and opinions needs to be valued as learning in the same way as reading and writing. Further, children need to value the fact that learning can be achieved collaboratively and not just in an individualized (sometimes competitive) fashion; that sharing ideas is a valuable form of learning rather than a form of cheating.

   Social skills are also a vital ingredient of successful groupwork. For example, children need to learn how to reject an idea but not the person, by responding with 'Yes, but . . .', rather than with an outright rejection, or by offering a reasoned modification or alternative proposal rather than a contrary assertion. (See also section 3.1 of this chapter on interactive and reactive listening, and further turn-taking skills.)

Group tasks, size and composition

An important contributory factor to successful group activity is the nature of the task itself. It is necessary to decide whether a task would be done best by an individual or by a group. If groupwork is intended, it is important that there is a genuine need for the group to work together. This, of course, depends on the purpose of the task and on the way it is set. Groups can be very suitable for a number of kinds of tasks, as the following examples show:

Buzz groups can be used to stimulate ideas and generate alternatives at the beginning of an activity.

Groups can be used for problem-solving where the goal is a single product resulting from collaboration (e.g. a play, model-making and practical measuring or recording, where more than two hands are needed to use equipment).

Groups can also be used as a forum in which ideas and views can be shared and explored (e.g. a response to a poem or a debate on a contentious issue), where understanding could be enhanced through a positive exchange of views. In this case, the end-product may be a single oral report of the common issues, a tabulated review of pros and cons or of differences of opinion. Alternatively, individual responses to a collective experience could be made. These could be written, put on tape, or conveyed through a poster. A forum can also be used to share and discuss common problems that have arisen during an activity, or to show and evaluate work at the end of an activity.

Hence, the reflective teacher needs to examine how group processes may be affected by both the kind of problem that each task itself poses, and by the form of product that is chosen.

Another feature to consider about groupwork is the size of groups, for it is important that this is related to the tasks being tackled. Large groups may be more suitable for buzz groups, where lots of ideas are wanted, provided members are willing to participate. In contrast, a problem-solving group needs to come to a decision which can be collectively implemented, so a smaller group of say five or six may be more suitable. The more people involved, the harder it may be to get agreement. Forums for personal or contentious issues may need to be conducted in a supportive atmosphere where threat and vulnerability is minimized. In such cases, small intimate groups are usually more appropriate.

Furthermore, it is most important that group members are compatible. While some activities may be best suited to groups based on children of similar ability, for other activities children of mixed ability, but similar interest, may be more suited. After all, it

---

PRACTICAL ACTIVITY 9.4

Aim: To analyse the dynamics of group discussions.

Method: Tape-record (or video) a group discussion. General features can be monitored on the following schedule. Additional detailed analysis can be carried out using Checklists 9.1 and 9.2 above.

Group characteristics	Comments
1. Composition of the group (e.g. size, sex, ability)	
2. Seating arrangement (draw diagram)	
3. Was there a leader, or scribe?	
4. Was this challenged?	
5. Did anyone not participate? (how did the others respond?)	
6. In what ways did the group collaborate?	
7. Was help needed/requested?	
8. What intervention was given?	
9. In what ways was the task successful?	
10. Did the group feel satisfied?	

Follow-up: Information gained from such schedules can help in the analysis of group interaction. It can help in understanding the roles of the members and whether these change if the composition of the group changes. Devising our own schedule can make us more aware of what we are aiming at. It also provides a framework for action to develop the potential of the group.

is being able to work well together as a group that is a major priority here. The question of whether to base group composition on the same or mixed sex, or on friendships, will depend on teacher judgements of the personalities of the children in each class. Nevertheless, a reflective teacher needs to be alert to cliques which might exist; to isolated children whom no one may want in their group; or to group divisions which may tend to form, based on sexist or racist assumptions. As teachers, we still have a responsibility to make a judgement whether to allocate children to ensure the mix which we may believe is appropriate, or to give children free choice in forming their own groups.

Developing and monitoring discussion skills
Several phases have been identified in successful groupwork which can be used as a

---

CHECKLIST 9.4

Aim: To examine discussion skills.

A reflective teacher may find it useful to consider the following points:

1. Do the participants take turns or do they frequently talk over or interrupt?

   Do they invite contributions, re-direct contributions for further comments, give encouragement?

   Do they listen to each other? Are they willing to learn from each other (i.e. respond and react to each other's contributions)?

   Or do they indulge in 'parallel' talk (i.e. continue their own line of thinking)?

   Does conflict emerge or is harmony maintained (at all costs)?
   - are the ideas disputed?
   - is the speaker attacked?

   Is conflict positively handled?
   - by modifying statements, rather than just reasserting them?
   - by examining the assumptions, rather than leaving them implicit?
   - by explaining/accounting for the claim, rather than ignoring the challenge?

2. Do they elaborate, rather than answer in monosyllables?
   - by giving details of events, people, feelings?
   - by providing reasons, explanations, examples?

   Do they extend ideas, rather than let ambiguity go unchallenged?
   - by asking for specific information?
   - by asking for clarification?

   Do they explore suggestions?
   - by asking for alternatives?
   - by speculating, imagining and hypothesizing?

   Do they evaluate?
   - by pooling ideas and suspending judgement before making choices?

CHECKLIST 9.5

Aim: To consider strategies for intervening in discussions.

A reflective teacher might consider to what extent the following strategies, drawn from Tough (1981), could prove useful in monitoring discussions, and whether children should also learn to operate them.

1. Setting the task
   - giving instructions
   - establishing expectations of performance

2. Setting the scene
   - giving an overview of the task itself
   - providing main idea, general perspective

3. Encouragement/enabling
   - showing acceptance of contributions
   - showing interest to invite participation

4. Opening out/exploration
   - using probing questions for wider exploration, finding alternative ways

5. Clarification
   - seeking examples/explanations to improve/check understanding

6. Closing in/focusing
   - using questions to focus/develop aspects
   - establishing relevance/priorities/choices

7. Reorientating
   - re-directing discussion if 'stuck'
   - specific focusing on overlooked aspect

8. Informing
   - giving a point of information or giving instructions concerning method/ approach

9. Reviewing/reflecting
   - encouraging review, consensus-testing, summarizing

10. Evaluating
    - of conclusions, and of the discussion itself and its effectiveness

framework in monitoring progress. First, children need to be encouraged to spend time orientating themselves to the other members of the group. They need time to listen to each other and to explore the demands and boundaries of the particular task. Second, during the development phase, the participants must learn to share ideas and extend suggestions and give time for the ideas to incubate. Although the number of contributions at this stage may be an indication of exploration and collaboration, it is the nature of the interactions which is of greatest importance to the quality of discussion. In the third, conclusion phase, the quality of group interaction, together with the quality of the ideas themselves, should be evident. This should be apparent when the final 'product' is shared with the rest of the class.

Checklists 9.4 and 9.5 offer a framework for monitoring discussion strategies.

A major component of developing discussion skills is encouraging the participants to monitor themselves. While the more socially and linguistically competent children may well 'pick things up', and therefore learn to discuss by discussing, many may benefit from more specific support. Hence, discussion about discussing can make an important contribution to developing discussion skills. At the end of a discussion, a group can be asked if it thought it had been a 'good' discussion and if so, what had made it good. The children could be encouraged to consider their discussion and identify useful strategies using their own terms. These can then be compared to those in Checklists 9.4 and 9.5.

Teachers can do a number of things to help develop discussion skills. For example, they can model the strategies themselves during discussions. They can identify and praise those strategies which children use. They can motivate children to want to contribute. Also, they need to manage the classroom so that opportunities for discussion can be supported. Finally, teachers need to monitor discussions with the children and to record their progress and problems.

3 COMPLETING THE COMMUNICATION CYCLE

If communication is a two-way process, we have dwelt long enough on the speaker, or 'initiator'. It is also necessary for teachers and children to be competent listeners, or 'receivers'. However, we have already noted how the position of 'initiator' is usually taken by the teacher and that the role of 'receiver' is more often than not assigned to the children. Estimates of the amount of time children spend listening are difficult to establish. However, the ORACLE findings suggested that for 40 per cent of their day, individual children were not interacting at all, but working silently. They were only interacting with the teacher for 12 per cent of the day, most of which was spent in listening. The remainder was spent in interacting with their peers—both listening, talking and sharing activities. The average teacher, however, spent 80 per cent of the day interacting with different children, and doing most of the talking!

It is possible to identify different types of listening situations within classrooms, which serve specific purposes and impose particular demands. These purposes can be categorized in the following way:

1. 'Interactive' listening (i.e. during a discussion, where the role of speaker and listener changes rapidly).

2. 'Reactive' listening (i.e. where listeners follow an 'exposition'). For example, a set of instructions may be given which children are then expected to act upon, or an extended input of information may be provided, which the listeners are expected to be able to 'take in', possibly 'take notes' on, and then respond to. In reactive and interactive listening, the emphasis is on following the meaning of the speakers. Differences are often in the degree of formality and the status of the speaker *vis-à-vis* listeners.

3. 'Discriminative' listening (i.e. where listeners have to discriminate between and identify sounds rather than meaning). For example, phonic sounds for spelling or reading purposes, or environmental/musical sounds.

4. 'Appreciative' listening (i.e. where listeners listen for aesthetic pleasure, perhaps to musical or environmental sounds; to the rhythm or sounds of words in poems and fairy stories; or to other languages or accents).

It is useful to distinguish between these different types of listening so that we can be aware of the demands we make upon ourselves and the children. For example, how often do we allow appreciative listening, requiring perhaps a receptive level of listening? Do we convey how we want the children to listen actively in such a situation? How often do we demand extended attention, in a reactive situation, so that we hear someone out, follow a line of argument, consider a large amount of information, before moving into discussions?

PRACTICAL ACTIVITY 9.5

Aim: To analyse listening demands in the classroom.

Method: During a session, a day or a week, try to note down how much time a teacher or children spend:

1. on each of the four types of listening mentioned above
2. in each of the four contexts indicated below

The results could be recorded on a matrix for each session/day.

Types of listening (purposes)	Contexts for listening			
	Where (informal to formal)	To whom (known to unknown)	What (familiar to unfamiliar)	For how long
Interactive				
Reactive				
Discriminative				
Appreciative				

Follow-up: Having collected the data, it is then possible to estimate how different a teacher's experience is from the children's (and whether the children's experiences are very different). It is also possible to reflect upon the range and balance of experiences and to decide on their implications.

As reflective teachers, we may want to be aware of the different demands that each type of listening makes. We also need to consider how many different listening contexts are experienced and how this might affect our listening and that of children (Dickson 1981). Practical Activity 9.5 suggests some possible criteria which a reflective teacher may wish to review.

3.1 Interactive and reactive listening

Active listeners in an interactive situation have to be able to develop the social skills necessary to show when they want to participate. This 'bidding' skill is again one which develops gradually as children grow older (Willes 1983). A reflective teacher may want to consider the different ways in which people try to bid for their turn to speak: for example, whether it is by raising a hand; sitting more upright and forwards; or by starting to move their lips. Some individuals will not have acquired any such skills and thus find it very hard to draw attention to the fact that they want to join in. Others may find it hard to notice tentative moves by group members and therefore may not 'let others in'.

As listeners, one of the most important skills is to be able to provide feedback to a speaker; in particular, to show whether they understand or not. Children often fail to show whether they have heard a statement, much less whether they have understood it. As listeners, we are usually so busy trying to follow the verbal flow as it emerges, bit by bit, that it is quite hard to reflect on the whole to see if it 'makes sense'. Research has shown (Dickson 1981) that younger children usually blame themselves if they don't understand: they fail to realize that the message itself might be at fault and that it could be altered and improved. Even if they do recognize that there was ambiguity, it may be difficult for them to identify what was ambiguous. It may, therefore, be difficult for them to ask an appropriate question. Further, if a listener can identify and can ask for clarification, it is then the task of the speaker to be able to rephrase or elaborate. If this is required of a young child, most find it very difficult and tend to repeat what was originally said. Hence, the skill of asking questions in an active, interactive situation is one that has to be encouraged and developed.

Finally, we turn to the phenomenon of learning the art of 'right answerism', which has been noted as a feature of many classrooms (French and MacLure 1983; Mehan 1974). This refers to the art of learning to 'guess what's in a teacher's mind', to understand cues and know what is expected. As reflective teachers, we need to consider whether this is a phenomenon in our class, and whether it is desirable. For instance, does a lot of questioning occur because we have not made ourselves clear? Why are the children so keen to get the answer 'right'? Do we mostly set up situations where we ask testing questions which have one right answer? How often do we create opportunities for exploring issues, where questions are genuinely aimed at finding out individual views and experiences: a situation in which every response can be valued?

Classroom situations, however, are often evaluative (Jackson 1968) and the social and linguistic 'rules' are very different from those in domestic conversation. Adults, in the learning context of a classroom, frequently ask children what they are doing or how they did something, in order to discover the children's thinking or feelings, and to check on their understanding. If, in a domestic conversation, the same number or kind of questions were asked of children, or of other adults, it would be inappropriate or even offensive. In school, most children soon learn to accept such questioning and know what is expected. However, the legitimacy of such questioning is particular to the 'culture' of a school environment. As reflective teachers, we need to be aware of the difficulties some children may have in adapting to such a 'culture', particularly those children who feel uneasy with the language of school, or who come from very different linguistic and cultural backgrounds.

3.2 Discriminative and appreciative listening

These kinds of listening are different from interactive and reactive listening, both in their purpose and in the skills demanded. Discriminative listening requires greater attention to detail and is usually undertaken in short, concentrated periods of activity. It is also used to diagnose hearing capacities, the physical/neurological prerequisite for all normal communication. Appreciative listening requires less attention to the detail of distinct sounds, or to understanding general meanings. It is an opportunity to respond and empathize, often physically as well as emotionally.

PRACTICAL ACTIVITY 9.6

Aim: To appraise the listening skills of individuals.

Method: Record, or observe, a range of individuals (including the teacher) during normal teaching–learning situations in a classroom.
   Note the types of listening called for and the contexts. Also, note the children's behaviours that might indicate that they heard, understood, or responded. For example, did they: look at the speaker, or look around; appear to follow, answer/questions, offer suggestions; show awareness of others' needs, take turns?

Follow-up: By watching individuals closely, it is possible to pin-point more precisely any particular difficulty a child might have, and whether it is general or specific to certain types of listening or contexts.

---

4 LINGUISTIC DIVERSITY

Attitudes to language have changed dramatically in the last twenty years. For instance, there is much less consensus about *the* way to talk or write. This has occurred partly because of changes in two separate spheres. First, there has been a change in our understanding of the efficiency, as means of communication, of different styles of language. Early work by Labov (1973) identified the grammars of Black teenagers in New York and argued that their language was not 'deficient', 'sloppy' or sub-standard. He suggested that their grammars were 'different' and just as regularly rule-bound as more socially accepted forms of standard English. Secondly, there has been a change in the social acceptability of a wider range of different styles of language. This has meant that the notion of 'appropriateness' has increasingly come to be used (i.e. that different kinds of language are suitable for different purposes, audiences and situations). This is a contrast to the notion of 'accuracy', as an absolute standard to be used to judge all language situations.
   Within classroom contexts, this has led to two further developments. The first of these is support for the importance of accepting a child's language because it is part of accepting the child and thereby strengthening a positive self-image. This, in turn, leads into the broader issue of acceptability of language varieties. The use of non-standard English has for long had negative social consequences, of a discriminatory nature. Now, however, there is greater acceptance that variation in language style should not be equated with language deficit, intellectual deficiency or social disadvantage (Edwards 1983; Stubbs and Hillier 1983).

PRACTICAL ACTIVITY 9.7

Aim: To highlight some of our own responses to language varieties.

Method: Use the results of this provocative rating scale for discussion with the results that colleagues obtain.

	I tend to agree				I tend to disagree
1. Dialects are ungrammatical forms of English	1	2	3	4	5
2. In general, middle-class children speak better than working-class ones	1	2	3	4	5
3. The first task for all children in Britain is to learn good English	1	2	3	4	5
4. Dropping your 'Hs' is sloppy and creates a bad impression	1	2	3	4	5
5. Poor grammar and spelling should be corrected	1	2	3	4	5
6. It is confusing for young children to speak two languages in school	1	2	3	4	5
7. We should not use expressions like 'black mark' as they illustrate racist language	1	2	3	4	5
8. We should always try to use books which show different people as equals	1	2	3	4	5
9. Books with class or race stereotypes can be used with care	1	2	3	4	5

Follow-up: It is very important for us to be aware of and to question our own views of the language we use and the language of which we do or do not approve. Similarly the language and values which are evident in the books which we use need to be carefully considered in terms of how children may be affected by them, what they will learn of others and how they will view themselves.

CONCLUSION

This chapter has raised a large number of issues relating to the communication which takes place within teaching–learning situations. Communication has been viewed as a key component of classroom life and, therefore, as an important influence on the learning which might take place. It is now time to consider that learning itself and how reflective teachers might analyse and then respond to it.

NOTES FOR FURTHER READING

The first two books discuss many of the theoretical and practical issues involved in collecting and interpreting 'talk'. Adelman contains case studies of classroom talk, from nursery to lower secondary; while Edwards and Westgate focus on methods for investigating language.

Adelman, C. (ed.) (1981) *Uttering, Muttering*. London: Grant McIntyre.
Edwards, A. D. and Westgate, P. G. (1987) *Investigating Classroom Talk*. London: Falmer Press.

The next two books are outcomes of separate research projects based on observation in infant, junior and secondary schools. Both contain a wealth of detail on a wide number of issues, as well as those raised in this chapter.

Bennett, N. *et al.* (1984) *The Quality of Pupil Learning Experiences.* London: Lawrence Erlbaum Associates.

Galton, M., Simon, B. and Croll, P. (1980) *Inside the Primary Classroom.* London: Routledge & Kegan Paul.

Although based on secondary practice, the analysis provided in the following book gives an insight into classroom communication more generally—and reasons for its tendency to fail.

Hull, R. (1985) *The Language Gap.* London: Methuen.

The next book provides a very clear overview of classroom talk.

Richards, J. (1979) *Classroom Language: What Sort?* London: George Allen & Unwin.

For a selection of interesting research reports on classroom communication, see:

Stubbs, M. and Hillier, H. (eds.) (1983) *Readings on Language and Classrooms.* London: Methuen.

The following book provides detailed suggestions on ways of monitoring many aspects of teacher talk. Although it is primarily designed for teachers in further or higher education, it is likely to be useful to all teachers.

Brown, G. A. (1978) *Lecturing and Explaining.* London: Methuen.

The next three books provide interesting insights into teachers' language strategies, ways of identifying them and how to improve them.

Kerry, T. (1982) *Effective Questioning.* London: Macmillan.
Sutton, C. (ed.) (1981) *Communicating in the Classroom.* London: Hodder & Stoughton.
Wragg, E. C. (ed.) (1984) *Classroom Teaching Skills.* London: Croom Helm.

Much has been written about children's discussions. The following work covers the whole primary age-range: from nursery and infant (Tough; Ede and Wilkinson; Tann and Armitage; Prisk) through to junior (Tann) and middle-school/lower secondary (Phillips; Gormon; Barnes, Britton and Rosen).

Barnes, D., Britton, J. and Rosen, H. (1969) *Language, the Learner and the School.* Harmondsworth: Penguin.
Ede, J. and Wilkinson, J. (1980) *Talking, Listening and Learning.* London: Longman.
Phillips, T., Beyond lip-service: discourse development after the age of nine, and Gorman, T. Language assessment and language teaching: innovation and interaction, both in Wells, G. and Nicholls, J. (eds.) (1985) *Language and Learning: an Interactional Perspective.* London: Falmer Press.
Prisk, D. M. (1987) Letting them get on with it—a study of unsupervised group talk in an infant school, in Pollard, A. (ed.) *Children and their Primary Schools.* London: Falmer Press.
Tann, S. (1981) Grouping and groupwork, in Simon, B. and Willcocks, J. (eds.) *Research and Practice in The Primary School.* London: Routledge & Kegan Paul.
Tann, S. and Armitage, M. (1986) Time for talk, *Reading,* **20** (3), 184–89.
Tough, J. (1976) *Listening to Children Talking.* Schools Council.

The following books provide an introduction to some social and linguistic aspects of listening skills. The first is research based and the next two are more practical.

Dickson, W. P. (ed.) (1982) *Oral Communication in Children.* New York: Academic Press.
South-West Herts. Teachers' Centre (1982) *Children Don't Listen.* Watford: Herts. LEA.
Willes, M. (1983) *Children into Pupils.* London: Routledge & Kegan Paul.

The last group of books contains useful chapters on linguistic variety:

Edwards, V. (1983) *Language in the Multicultural Classroom.* London: Batsford.
Saunders, M. (1982) *Multicultural Teaching.* Maidenhead: McGraw-Hill.
Tough, J. (1985) *Talk Two: Children using English as a Second Language.* London: Ward Lock.

Chapter 10

What Are We Achieving?
Considering Learning Processes, Social
Consequences and Classroom Policies

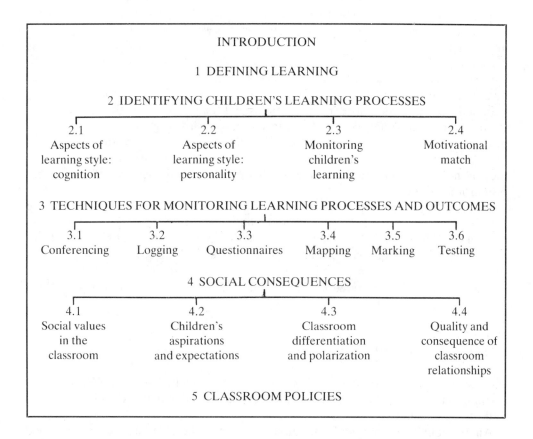

INTRODUCTION

1 DEFINING LEARNING

2 IDENTIFYING CHILDREN'S LEARNING PROCESSES

2.1	2.2	2.3	2.4
Aspects of learning style: cognition	Aspects of learning style: personality	Monitoring children's learning	Motivational match

3 TECHNIQUES FOR MONITORING LEARNING PROCESSES AND OUTCOMES

3.1	3.2	3.3	3.4	3.5	3.6
Conferencing	Logging	Questionnaires	Mapping	Marking	Testing

4 SOCIAL CONSEQUENCES

4.1	4.2	4.3	4.4
Social values in the classroom	Children's aspirations and expectations	Classroom differentiation and polarization	Quality and consequence of classroom relationships

5 CLASSROOM POLICIES

INTRODUCTION

In this chapter, which is the last in this part of the book, we focus on evaluation and reflection. In doing so, we highlight two major themes which are associated with the educational product of classroom practice. The first concerns children's learning as such, for clearly this is of paramount concern to teachers. Attention can sometimes get drawn towards 'teaching' in ways which almost seem to detach it from 'learning'. It is for this reason that we focus on learning in this chapter and include techniques for monitoring learning outcomes. The second theme is that of social consequences, for a reflective teacher is one who is concerned with social justice as well as learning efficiency. We, therefore, suggest some ways of monitoring our practice and outcomes regarding this issue. Finally, we discuss the formation of social policies to guide our classroom decision-making.

1 DEFINING LEARNING

In trying to reflect upon what we are achieving in our classroom, it is important to clarify what we mean by learning. Learning can be considered as the processes by which skills, attitudes, knowledge and concepts are acquired and understood, applied and used, or advanced and extended. However, learning should not be confused with mere completion of tasks, for children may complete a task and 'get it wrong'. Indeed, they may also complete a task 'correctly', but have 'learnt' nothing.

Children may also learn something other than that which the teacher intended. Such unintended learning could be most productive, even a more appropriate match of their current needs. Conversely, children might learn things which could cause them problems later (e.g. incorrect letter formation skills, inefficient subtraction procedures or inaccurate information).

In addition, children may acquire attitudes and feelings towards themselves, their learning and each other. Successful learning may result in gains in confidence, in pleasure and in a sense of achievement, but failure may result in low self-esteem, apathy, aggression or avoidance. For example, children might learn how to avoid work they do not like by pacing themselves so that preferred activities always take longer proportions of time.

A final aspect of children's learning, which needs to be considered when analysing learning processes and outcomes, is that of children's learning style. This refers to the ways in which activities and challenges are typically approached, explored and tackled. An individual's learning style can be seen as the product of both cognitive and personality factors. These are considered in section 2 of this chapter, together with issues relating to the medium through which learning takes place and the question of motivation.

2 IDENTIFYING CHILDREN'S LEARNING PROCESSES

A 'learning style' can be described as the way an individual typically approaches a learning situation and it derives from a mix between an individual's cognitive processes and their personality.

An individual's 'learning style' has often emerged by the age of 6 and has been found to have considerable stability throughout the years of compulsory education. Children do, however, also acquire the ability to adopt specific cognitive strategies, or particular techniques for particular tasks. These may modify the 'style' so that it becomes more flexible and mature.

It has been suggested that there is no 'best' style, though certain styles have been found to be more suitable for particular tasks or situations. Learning styles can be a significant factor in matching processes, for, as teachers, our own learning styles may affect the way we present tasks and activities. Where there is a mismatch of teacher-style and learner-style, then learning may become adversely affected (Entwistle 1981).

A number of factors have been identified which appear to affect how we respond to tasks in particular learning situations. These include such factors as time (whether it is limited or unlimited) and social factors (whether a task is done alone or in a group).

Awareness of such variations could help us to identify features of an individual's learning style and could help us to notice how individuals learn best and, therefore, how they can be helped.

2.1 Aspects of learning style: cognition

While there is, not surprisingly, no clear agreement on the precise nature of different 'learning styles', a number of key dimensions have been identified. Such dimensions can sharpen our analysis, but they should not be taken to imply value judgements.

Among the dimensions which have been conceptualized are the following:

1. Wholist/serialist (Kagan and Kogan 1970; Pask 1976): from wholists who like to get a quick grasp of a whole, general picture before filling in details; to serialists who prefer to methodically and analytically build up a picture bit by bit. (A weakness of the wholist may be a tendency to overgeneralize and simplify; whereas the serialist may focus on separate details and miss the significance of inter-relationships or of the whole.)

2. Field-dependent/field-independent (Witkin *et al.* 1977): from field-dependents who use a general context, or their experience, to interpret or solve a problem; to field-independents who analyse a stimulus, identify and manipulate a problem's components. (A weakness of a field-dependent is to be trapped by previous experience and to focus on similarities while ignoring the differences; whereas a field-independent may not put experience to practical use, and thus may 're-invent the wheel'.)

3. Scanning/focusing (Bruner, Goodnow and Austin 1956): from scanners who make an initial general hypothesis and then judge subsequent events or information by whether they fit or not; to focusers who choose component variables and test each one before arriving at a final conclusion. (A weakness of scanning may be an unwillingness to drop an original hypothesis, even if some facts do not fit; whereas the focusing approach can be very slow and laborious.)

4. Divergent/convergent (Torrance 1962): from divergers who use inspirational flair and imagination; to convergers who wish to find the 'right' answer and prefer closed situations. (A weakness of divergers is the possibility of an erratic approach without perseverance; whereas convergers may be thorough, but unimaginative and perhaps blind to alternative and new ways of tackling old problems.)

2.2 Aspects of learning style: personality

While the above characteristics distinguish cognitive aspects of learning style, there are also personality dimensions which are associated with how we learn. The most frequently identified are:

1. Impulsivity/reflexivity (Kagan *et al.* 1964): from impulsives who rush at a task without stopping to think first; to reflexives who like to chew it over, sometimes endlessly.

2. Extroversion/introversion (Eysenck and Cookson 1969): from extroverts who are outgoing and gregarious, sometimes over-dependent on stimulus or security from a group; to introverts who are more 'private' and may prefer to keep themselves to themselves, who sometimes do not have the necessary skills to make friends.

3. Anxiety/adjustment (Finlayson 1970; Fransson 1977): from those who are anxious about work, their relationships with children or about teachers; to those who are accepting or satisfied with these aspects.

4. Vacillation/perseverance (Brookover and Thomas 1965): from those with short concentration spans, who are changeable in their application to work, sometimes giving up quickly; to those who have long concentration spans, great staying-power, who sometimes 'stick at' a task long after they should have asked for help.

5. Competitiveness/collaborativeness (Johnson and Johnson 1975): from those who measure their achievement against others and may find it hard to share efforts with others; to those who work well with others, sometimes relying on them too much and who are unwilling to work independently.

Such dimensions, although not precise, may be helpful in interpreting the results of observations and discussions with children about learning processes. They may, for instance, help us to understand distinctions between a child who is slow to respond, who may be reflexive and considered in approach, and a child who is slow to understand. Similarly, we might reflect upon the significance of the difference between a child who does not join in, who may be shy and 'private'—a loner—and a child who cannot join in because he or she does not know how to—lonely.

PRACTICAL ACTIVITY 10.1

Aim: To analyse individual children's learning styles.

Method:
1. Observe individual children when working in a range of situations (i.e. different types of tasks, different time demands, different social contexts). Note their behaviour carefully for a set time-span. Later, review the notes in the light of the cognitive and personality dimensions listed above. Build up a profile on individuals to assist in diagnosing their learning style.

2. Try to monitor yourself in a similar range of situations, and thereby identify aspects of your own style.

Follow-up: Use this information to review the match between task and child, and to consider the relationship between your own teaching style and children's learning styles. From these insights, it may be possible to develop alternative stategies and approaches suited to particular tasks, so that a range of strategies are available to you.

A particular application of the possible significance of learning style has been suggested by Kagan (1965) and Roberts (1986). They argue that differences in learning style may have important implications in learning to read. An individual may employ a global, visual approach (e.g. look–say); or rely on the whole context (e.g. language experience); or adopt a reflexive, analytic approach using their knowledge of aural/oral aspects of language (e.g. phonetic approach).

PRACTICAL ACTIVITY 10.2

Aim: To analyse our own responses to different learning styles.

Method: Tape-record, take diary notes, or ask a colleague to observe your teaching during selected sessions. Monitor the way you 'help' children.

Follow-up: Review the range of 'help' that you offer. Try to distinguish reasons for the variety and assess whether the action taken did 'help'. Then use the information to analyse your response to others. For example:

1. Do you seem to prefer some learning styles to others, or to respond differently?

2. Do you expect different kinds of learning behaviour from boys and girls? Do you reward them differently?

3. Do you provide different kinds of tasks and opportunities for each of these styles to develop, or do you tend to prepare tasks in your own style?

What are the implications of the answers to such questions?

However, to be able to make any use of such suggested applications of the concept of learning styles, it is necessary to be able to identify and monitor some of the learning processes which children use.

2.3 Monitoring children's learning

Teachers invest considerable amounts of time in assessing the quality of the end-product of children's work and in judging how 'well' it has been done. As busy teachers, and as parents viewing work which has been displayed, there is a tendency to focus on end-products. This is often relatively easier, for children's work frequently takes a tangible form (e.g. a piece of writing, a model, a display). However, consideration of products has a major drawback in that it is often difficult to tell how they were produced or what thinking and learning was involved. One has little evidence of 'process'.

The difficulty of managing to gain access to such processes may be one of the reasons why HMI concluded that two-thirds of tasks set in primary classrooms were either too easy or too hard for the pupils (DES 1978a). Because it is difficult in a busy classroom to work out how particular tasks are tackled, it is easy to misinterpret causes of misunderstandings.

One way forward here is by creating more time for discussion, for talking about tasks can serve as an excellent way of encouraging children to show their 'workings' and to reveal their thinking. However, as we saw in the previous chapter, the language used in school is, itself, not without problems. Indeed, Donaldson (1978) suggested that part of the mismatch problem is due to task expectations which are ineffectively communicated. She maintained that teachers tend to overestimate children's language skills, but underestimate their cognitive skills. Thus, children often understand the gist of what is said, because of the way it is communicated and because of clues from the context in which the talking takes place, even though they may often not fully understand the actual language used. The facts that so many school activities are conducted through language and that so many tasks are divorced from 'real' contexts are not always helpful to children. We also have to remember that, when it comes to explaining retrospectively how they set about a particular task, some children may have difficulties. In such circumstances, the dangers of misinterpretation by a busy teacher are considerable.

A second approach to monitoring the processes of children's learning is to watch the way they work. To do this it is necessary to make time to stand back and observe a child or a group and, if possible, to take notes. Such observation, combined with discussion, can provide valuable insights into individual learning styles.

Some psychological research on learning processes has tended to conceive learning as a linear sequence of cognitive steps. Models of learning were often derived from laboratory experiments on subjects (often adults) performing set tasks (often closed and logical). However, recent action–research studies (Armstrong 1980; Rowland 1984) have favoured observing children exploring open-ended and creative tasks, in normal classroom settings. Learning in these situations often seems highly complex and is difficult to interpret—perhaps because it is happening in leaps and sideways steps, or not at all, rather than in a neat sequence.

Armstrong (1980) argued that the 'intellectual life' of play was one of the few opportunities for children to exercise autonomy, to formulate ideas, to experiment and evaluate for themselves. He also found children motivated by the delight and excited speculation which they experienced in the 'romance of exploration' with different media and activities. His close observations of individual children gave insights into how young children learn through struggling to use the traditions of, for example, literature, art or science to understand their own experiences. Such 'appropriation' of knowledge enabled them to examine, extend and express their growing understanding in a very conscious way, stimulated by their discovery of 'the mind's germinal power' for self-development (Armstrong 1980, p. 207).

Similarly, Rowland (1987) has argued that children need to feel in control of their learning in order to fully engage in it. He suggests that a teacher should seek to understand and support the children *as* they develop their own understandings. Rowland calls this an 'interpretive' approach and sees it in marked contrast to both a 'didactic' approach and one which leaves children to 'discover' for themselves. It is, however, an approach which makes heavy demands on a teacher's sensitivity in monitoring children's learning and in offering appropriate guidance.

Apart from the cognitive and personality dimensions of learning style, children may show different preferences for the medium in which they like to work (e.g. aural/oral, reading/writing, visual/tactile and motor/movement). These also need to be monitored, for the ease with which we can learn in different media is an important factor in choosing the way we wish to learn and to demonstrate what we have learnt. Some may prefer to engage in open discussion; while others may prefer to reach their understandings privately through reading. Furthermore, if a book is chosen, its written style may also affect the ease with which we can learn (Entwistle 1981). For example, some may prefer a discursive, narrative style; while others may prefer clearly sequenced, step-by-step text.

Differences in how well individuals understand what they read or hear have also been noted. There is some evidence to suggest that at least 40 per cent of primary children tend to be 'visualizers' rather than 'verbalizers'. For instance, 'visualizers' can translate what they read or hear into their 'mind's eye' or into pictures/diagrams. Those who can do this are more likely to have acted upon the information. However, 'verbalizers' rely on retelling the text, often with good recall, but with less likelihood of acting upon the text and making it their own (Beech 1985).

Finally, as teachers, we need to be very aware of the different tasks set and the ways in which we appraise them, for we may find we penalize some learning styles. For example, how many of our assignments are open, closed, or multiple choice? How many are timed, or open ended? How many are oral, written, graphic, or dramatic? How many are tests of what has been mastered? How many are applications of knowledge and skills to novel, creative situations? How might such differences affect children with particular learning styles?

PRACTICAL ACTIVITY 10.3

Aim: To analyse tasks in relation to learning styles.

Method: Make a grid.

1. List different types of tasks/assignments on the left-hand side (e.g. open/ closed/multiple choice, timed/untimed, oral/written/graphic/dramatic, mastery/creative).

2. List different learning styles (cognitive and personality dimensions) across the top.

3. Fill in the grid to indicate which types of tasks are likely to suit (or not to suit) which learning styles.

Follow-up: The conclusions that we draw from this activity could be useful in helping to understand the different ways in which children tackle classroom tasks. They could help us to anticipate the range of difficulties children might experience.

2.4 Motivational match

So far in this chapter, we have considered the relationship between learning styles and tasks. While this is clearly important, it is also essential to consider motivational aspects of learning, for an activity which fails to stimulate or, at least, interest children is unlikely to be productive, however well intentioned and carefully planned it may be.

Motivation is highly subjective and is likely to be related to children's perceptions of themselves, teachers and schooling. On the other hand, it can also be affected by very specific, immediate moods and situations.

Children's positive motivation towards learning is important not only for maximizing learning outcomes, but because of the disruptive effects which children who are poorly motivated can produce. A reflective teacher thus needs to consider the meaning and worthwhileness which an activity is likely to have for children, as well as its potential for developing learning.

Being able to motivate children is thus basic to the smooth running of the classroom and to effective learning. However, no teacher can be certain of how children will respond to a particular activity. Hence, developing a motivational match requires sensitivity to the children, flexibility, spontaneity and imagination.

Motivation can stem from a wide range of factors, from positive interest to negative fear. The most commonly identified types of motivation are:

Intrinsic: when inherent qualities of an activity are appreciated.

Collective: where pleasure derives from sharing work with friends, the class, school or family.

Extrinsic: based on achieving involvement through the use of such devices as stars, house points or the privilege of showing work to the head teacher.

Coerced compliance: where children carry out tasks to avoid punishments.

A teacher can influence the type of motivation which is likely to develop and attitudes towards learning by the ways in which activities are set up and by the nature of the activities themselves. However, no teacher can actually know for certain how children will respond to a planned activity. Thus, being attuned to children's motivation also often calls for flexibility and imagination.

PRACTICAL ACTIVITY 10.4

Aim: To review the motivational qualities of a series of classroom activities.

Method: Consider one teaching/learning session and list the requirements which were made of selected children. This might be done by asking a colleague to observe, or by interpreting a tape recording. From the perspective of each of the selected children, make a judgement of the type of motivation which you feel influenced their actions. Record your judgements.

   If possible, discuss the session with the children involved and record their accounts.

Follow-up: By comparing teacher judgements and children's accounts, it should be possible to obtain many insights which could help in developing more appropriate approaches to motivating children in the future.

---

3 TECHNIQUES FOR MONITORING LEARNING PROCESSES AND OUTCOMES

In choosing a range of techniques for monitoring different learning outcomes within a classroom, it may be helpful to consider them as a corollary to the monitoring already suggested for curriculum activities and for aspects of classroom organization and management, for they are all interrelated. They also represent a development of techniques for investigating classrooms which were outlined in Chapter 3. We review six techniques below: the first three of which are particularly useful because they can provide insights into both cognitive and affective aspects of children's learning.

3.1 Conferencing
This is a term used to describe an extended discussion between a teacher and child. Conferencing is similar to conducting an informal interview. Such a session offers an opportunity for a teacher and child to come to a mutual understanding of the nature of work in progress and to discuss what has been found to be enjoyable/not enjoyable or easy/challenging/hard. It also provides a chance to discuss any difficulties which are being experienced and to plan future activities. Such discussions should allow a teacher and child to talk about the activities and their feelings towards them. Conferencing can contribute greatly to an openly negotiated working consensus (see Chapter 5).

   Such in-depth discussions could pose management problems for a teacher: the main problems being how to fit in all the necessary discussions, and what the rest of the class does while the teacher is thus engaged. The length of discussion is likely, of course, to vary with the needs of the child. However, a teacher using conferencing would have to plan to set aside a certain amount of time, perhaps at a set period each day, when the class knows that the teacher should not be disturbed, if at all possible. In many situations, discussions with a group would be appropriate, though it is important that the group context does not inhibit some individuals within the group. This procedure can be used with even very young children. For instance, a 'review session' is an essential part of the High Scope programme used in some nursery schools.

3.2 Logging

Logging refers to a system whereby the children write down their reflections of their learning experiences, rather than rely on oral discussion as the main mode of expression. It is particularly useful, for example, for children doing self-directed topic work. They can use a log-book to comment on their on-going progress, to keep the teacher 'in touch' without posing the management problems of conferencing and even to ask for help or resources.

A written log can take many forms. It might include the child's original plan of intended work, and the reason for doing it. It might also include a description of what was done, whether any changes were made and why. It could include an analysis of what knowledge or skills had been employed; which were reinforced; which were acquired; and which extended. The child could then go on to comment on what had been enjoyed, or not enjoyed, and what had been worthwhile, or not. Finally, a log could include the children's view of what they would like to move on to next. Such a self-analysis requires considerable sophisticated self-reflection from a child. It may be something which, at first, is found difficult, but, by attempting such an analysis, a child may become more aware of his or her progress and of his or her strengths and weaknesses.

An important extension of logging is the opportunity it can also provide for parents and teachers to add comments and respond to issues which are raised. In this way, a growth of mutual understanding may be possible.

3.3 Questionnaires

This third technique is a more formalized way of collecting information on children's perceptions. Questionnaires can be used most profitably for evaluative purposes at the end of a unit of work. They encourage children to reflect on their recent learning experiences and to comment on them by answering specific questions to focus their response. These questions can be open-ended (e.g. What did you like about . . .?), or closed (e.g. questions with given multiple choice or Yes/No answers). The answers may be required as written sentences, by ticking boxes, or by ringing a word/number on a rating scale (e.g. hard/quite hard/just right/easy, or from 'exciting' 5–4–3–2–1 'boring'). For younger children, scales have been devised which require the child to colour the face which shows how they feel in response to a statement which is read out by the teacher: the faces range from happy to neutral, bored, worried or angry.

The next set of techniques for monitoring learning outcomes focuses more extensively on the cognitive aspects.

3.4 Mapping

The term 'mapping' denotes a procedure which requires children to 'map' out what they have learnt and how it appears to 'fit' together (Ghaye 1984). Children might be helped to draw a web or flow chart to show what they have been learning. Such a chart would, eventually, represent the ideas, concepts and knowledge that the children have been using during a particular unit of work, as perceived by the child. The procedure might begin by listing aspects of the topic which were covered (e.g. baby teeth and big teeth, dentist, wobbly teeth, bad teeth, fluoride, healthy food, toothbrush, etc.). The children can then map the relationships which they perceive between the different items, using key words, phrases or sentences to explain how they see any links (see Figure 10.1, for example). This provides a clear indication and record of what they have understood. It could then provide a basis for teacher and child to talk over understandings and misunderstandings.

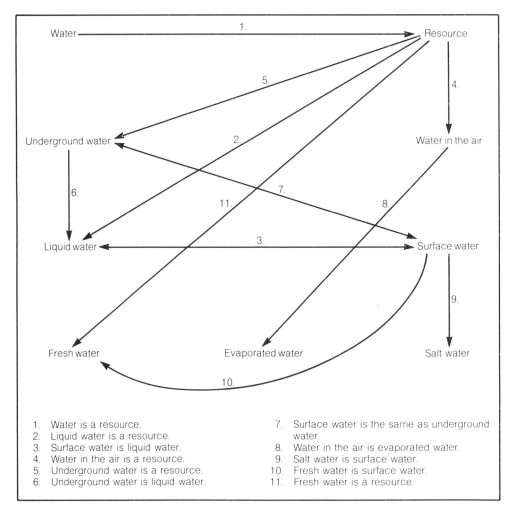

1. Water is a resource.
2. Liquid water is a resource.
3. Surface water is liquid water.
4. Water in the air is a resource.
5. Underground water is a resource.
6. Underground water is liquid water.
7. Surface water is the same as underground water.
8. Water in the air is evaporated water.
9. Salt water is surface water.
10. Fresh water is surface water.
11. Fresh water is a resource.

Figure 10.1 A concept map by an eleven-year-old, indicating his or her understanding of a topic on water (from Ghaye 1984).

3.5 Marking

The most common way for teachers to monitor children's learning is to 'mark' work which has been completed. This can be anything from a verbal comment (e.g. 'What an exciting story!'), to setting spelling corrections at the end of an exercise, or a grade/mark. This form of monitoring is often done by the teacher in the absence of the children concerned, so that there is no opportunity to talk with them and find out more about how they set about the task. Such monitoring is more evaluatory than diagnostic, in contrast to the preceding examples of monitoring. It focuses exclusively on the product and is, therefore, a monitoring technique which has a limited function.

Marking can, however, be used in conjunction with other forms of monitoring. For instance, diagnosis of a process of learning, through discussion, could have taken place earlier. It is often used in conjunction with observation, occurring as a teacher circulates around the room, and also through discussions.

When marking, it is important to consider each piece of work as part of a sequence. It is only by comparing each example with previous work that it is possible to assess whether any learning has taken place and what significance to attach to any mistakes. If such mistakes, or 'miscues', are analysed carefully, they may provide valuable clues to possible learning difficulties. For instance, it is revealing to note whether 'miscues' are consistent or one-off. If a pattern emerges, then a future teaching/learning point has been identified. Such diagnostic marking can provide useful information on which to base subsequent discussion, or be used when making judgements about devising future tasks.

3.6 Testing

Tests can also be used for a range of different purposes and are distinguishable by a number of criteria:

Teacher tests/published tests. Those which teachers devise themselves and are directly related to what has been taught, compared with published tests which are intended to be applicable generally to a wide range of situations.

Criterion/norm tests. Those tests which use specific items to identify aspects of individual children's competence compared to tests which are used to compare individuals in terms of 'normal' expectations of achievement.

Diagnostic/prognostic. Those which aim to identify what the child can/cannot do now, compared with tests designed to highlight future potential (e.g. IQ/11+ tests).

Open/closed. Those which have questions to which there is room for imagination and creativity, compared with tests to which there is one right answer.

Teachers often devise their own tests for particular diagnostic purposes to help them achieve the best cognitive match which is possible. Such tests could be used to discriminate between children's achievements, or used to assess a teacher's effectiveness in implementing specified learning objectives. Mastery tests are often used in athletics, swimming and gymnastics and are popular with some children. Awards are made for achievement in a carefully planned series of tests.

Published tests are often used in schools to obtain comparative academic scores for children. Such tests may potentially be compared with national norms and thus used to review the attainments of children, teachers or schools. Whatever type of test is used, it is most important for a reflective teacher to try to identify its strengths and weaknesses and the assumptions about learning which underly it. For example, what does a 'reading' test 'count' as reading; upon which theory of learning to read is it based; is it culturally neutral; is it successful in what it aims to do? Above all, does a test gather valid data so that it really measures what it is supposed to, and can the test be reliably used so that data collected is consistent?

PRACTICAL ACTIVITY 10.5

Aim: To evaluate different monitoring techniques.

Method: Make a 6×2 table, with each of the six monitoring techniques listed on the left, and two adjacent columns for the 'pros' and 'cons' of each. Fill in the table, bearing in mind:
- Why monitor in this way?
- For whom is this monitoring being done?
- What can be most appropriately monitored in this way?
- How often might this technique be used?
- In what situations can this technique be used?
- How can the results be interpreted?
- Are there any unforeseen effects of such monitoring?
- Are the techniques valid and free from cultural/political bias?

Follow-up: Having made your own decisions about the 'pros' and 'cons' of different monitoring techniques, you should now be in a position to choose which techniques you will use for various purposes, and which contexts. This should help you to devise a flexible and powerful set of techniques to help you monitor processes and products within your classroom.

---

4 SOCIAL CONSEQUENCES

The concept of reflective teaching, as we discussed in Chapter 1, encompasses a consideration of the social consequences of educational processes. It also involves us in identifying our degree of responsibility for their consequences.

In Chapter 2, we introduced a model of the relationships between individuals and society which was based on the notion of a dialectical process. This suggested the existence of a continuous interplay of social forces: history and constraint with individual action, biography and creativity.

The significance of the idea of a dialectical process of social change is that it should cause us to look at our daily actions in the classroom and to consider their possible social consequences for the future. In this view, 'society' does not develop exclusively 'somewhere else', controlled by indeterminate powers—by 'them'. Future developments are partially in our own hands and we can make our own small, but unique, contribution.

4.1 Social values in the classroom

As teachers, the consequences of our actions may show in the perspectives, attitudes and behaviour of children whom we influence. Indeed, to 'socialize' children into the 'values of society' has often been seen as part of a teacher's role (Dreeben 1968; Parsons 1959; see also Chapter 4).

Another way of conceptualizing the social consequences of teachers' actions is to see them as being part of the 'hidden curriculum'. As we saw in Chapter 6, the hidden curriculum is formed from tacit assumptions and practices which, nevertheless, convey messages and expectations to children. Some sociologists have suggested that the hidden curriculum is directly concerned with producing social conformity. For instance, Bowles and Gintis (1976) argued that schools are geared to inducing passivity and the acceptance of authority. They were seen to be concerned with the quantity and quality of work, irrespective of its purpose or meaningfulness, and there was said to be a 'correspondence' between the social relationships of work-places and those of schools. The suggestion which follows is that children who attend such schools may come to accept future positions in society which 'seem appropriate' to their social class, gender and race. Their future opportunities and rights as individuals might thus be narrowed by school practices. Dale (1977) suggested that processes of social reproduction have always existed within the education system. Whereas in Victorian times they were relatively explicit in the official curriculum, now, he argues, it is the 'form' of schooling which is important—the 'hidden curriculum'.

An example of this may be helpful. Pollard (1985) collected examples of teachers' talk—instructions, comments, questions. They were analysed to reveal three clusters of values:

1. Relating to productivity and efficiency at school-work:
   - Effort (e.g. Let's make a really big effort today)
   - Perseverance (e.g. Try a bit longer)
   - Neatness (e.g. That's a nice page)
   - Regularity (e.g. Is that your best work?)
   - Speed (e.g. Has anyone finished yet?)

2. Relating to behaviour and social relationships:
   - Self-control (e.g. Stop being silly)
   - Obedience (e.g. Did you hear what I said?)
   - Politeness (e.g. That's not a very nice thing to do)
   - Quietness (e.g. Silence, now)
   - Truth (e.g. Let's have it straight now)
   - Respect for authority (e.g. Hands up if you want something)

3. Relating to individualism and competitiveness:
   - Achievement (e.g. Have you got that right?)
   - Individualism (e.g. Do it yourself)
   - Hierarchy (e.g. Who got ten out of ten?)
   - Self-reliance (e.g. Go and find out)

The existence of such values in schools may seem appropriate to some. They can be seen as serving to support the current social and economic system, which sets out to achieve high levels of both economic productivity and of individual competition. At the class-room level, though, such values may simply be seen as supporting teachers' concerns with discipline and control. They may thus 'make sense' at two levels, the macro and micro.

In contrast, other values, though not absent, may be found less frequently: for inst-ance, collaboration, criticism, divergence, informality, directness, spontaneity, ex-pressiveness, respect for others. Arguably, one might expect to find more of such values in classrooms than in fact occur, given the nature of child-centred, primary-school ideology.

The projection of values of some sort is inevitable in a classroom, but this should be carefully monitored as a necessary part of reflective teaching and a procedure for this is suggested in Practical Activity 10.6.

PRACTICAL ACTIVITY 10.6

Aim: To gather indications of the social values which form part of the hidden curriculum.

Method: A tape recording, or use of an observer taking field-notes, could be used to note the instructions, guidance, exhortations, reinforcement, reprimands and condemnations which are used when working with children.

These could be sorted into those to do with 'work' and those to do with 'behaviour'. An analysis of the underlying values could be carried out.

A further development would be to sort statements by the characteristics of the people to whom they were directed: by sex, race, social class, etc.

Follow-up: Reflective teachers might consider how results from evidence of this kind relates to their own educational values (see Practical Activity 4.3).

4.2 Children's aspirations and expectations

A very important factor influencing children's futures concerns their present self-confidence and aspirations. How do children see the possibilities which are open to them—be they boys or girls, middle class or children of unskilled workers, and whatever the colour of their skin?

Issues of this sort were made prominent some years ago by McClelland (1963). He argued that it was possible to identify various levels of 'achievement motivation' among different social groups and societies, and that this was related to rates of economic development. It may be so. But it is perhaps even more important to consider the issue in terms of social justice for the individuals concerned, particularly in education systems which aspire to open, democratic ideals. What, then, are the parameters of expectations of girls in our classes, or of black children? What are our responsibilities?

PRACTICAL ACTIVITY 10.7

Aim: To obtain indications of children's aspirations and expectations regarding their future lives.

Method: The essential element here is to ask children to compare. First, they should be asked to say what they would like to be or do as adults. Second, they should be asked to say what they actually expect to do or be. If there are differences, they can be asked to consider the reasons for them.

Drawings, discussion or writing may be appropriate, depending on the age of the children.

Follow-up: Such an exercise cannot actually 'prove' anything but it can provide a reflective teacher with vivid and indicative data on children's perception of their futures. Data can be sorted out and provoke reflection on the provision of role models and the nature of social expectations in school.

The issues of teachers stereotyping and of children's views of each other are relevant here (see Chapter 4), as is a consideration of curriculum provision (see Chapter 6). An additional factor is the role models which teachers provide through their own actions and lives. Such issues are under a degree of teacher control and it is, therefore, reasonable for us to expect to take responsibility for them. Many other powerful factors, such as the influence of the family, media and some aspects of popular culture, are likely to be more intractable.

In Practical Activity 10.7, we suggest ways of monitoring the overall effect of such influences in terms of children's aspirations. We also suggest distinguishing aspirations from actual expectations and gathering data on that too, as a means of facilitating children's own awareness of social issues.

4.3 Classroom differentiation and polarization

We use 'differentiation' here to refer to classroom processes which increase distinctions between children and which are largely under teacher control. For instance, such distinctions might emerge from the use of ability-based groups; of hierarchically organized schemes of work; of 'star' systems for rewarding good behaviour; or from imbalances in the display of children's work; or from teacher's perceptions in their relationship with particular children. We discussed several factors similar to these when considering the concept of the 'incorporative classroom' in Chapter 5.

Differentiation of some kind is unavoidable; indeed, the emphasis which we have placed on matching learning tasks and individual children makes that clear. However, differentiation can have consequences for the way in which people feel that they are valued, and it is this that reflective teachers should consider.

There has been a series of studies of the internal workings of secondary schools (Hargreaves 1967; Lacey 1970; Ball 1981) which has shown how children interpret their experiences of differentiation. There are tendencies for them to identify with or against school, with children who feel that they are 'educational failures' rejecting school values to protect their own pride and self-esteem.

PRACTICAL ACTIVITY 10.8

Aim: To highlight the possible influence of classroom differentiation and polarization processes.

Method: Simple indicators for both differentiation and polarization are required.

1. For differentiation: positions in ability-based groups or on reading/maths schemes can be used to rank individuals or group children into ability quartiles; teacher judgement could also be sought or standardized test scores used, if available.

2. For polarization: patterns revealed by a socio-gram can be used (see Practical Activity 4.12).

These indicators then have to be examined together, for example, by setting out friendship groups and recording the differentiation indicators beside each child's name.

Follow-up: This exercise may suggest ways in which classroom practices by teachers, and children's responses, interact to create or reinforce social and individual differences. If this is so, a reflective teacher would want to consider what, if any, action should be taken.

When children who share a similar position in relation to school success or failure come together as a group, they begin to develop sub-cultures. Such processes can be termed 'polarization', for they involve a reinforcement of the initial differentiation as the children themselves respond to it.

Primary schools are very different from secondary schools, but similar processes may be found. Indeed, one recent study (Pollard 1985) identified three types of friendship groups among 11-year-olds. 'Goodies' were very conformist, fairly able for the most part, but considered rather dull. 'Jokers' liked to 'have a laugh', were very able and got on well with their teachers. 'Gang' group members were willing to disrupt classes, had low levels of academic achievement and were thought of as a nuisance. These types of group were related to processes of differentiation within the school and classrooms and seemed to be leading to further polarization.

Perhaps differentiation and polarization processes are almost inevitable in schools, but this cannot diminish our responsibility as teachers for monitoring them and for acting to minimize any unnecessarily divisive effects. Practical Activity 10.8 is designed to assist in this.

4.4 The quality and consequence of classroom relationships

It is possible to take children's attitude to learning and to school life as an indication of one type of social consequence. In particular, it may contribute to their sense of identity and thus have long-term results.

In Chapter 5, we discussed classroom relationships at length and suggested that teachers and children usually negotiate a 'working consensus'. This represents mutually understood ways of getting along together. From it emerges a range of tacit rules about behaviour and a sense of what is and what is not 'fair'. We suggested that children's actions might range from conforming to rules, to engaging in routine deviance or, by stepping outside the bounds of the 'working consensus', to acting in unilateral and disorderly ways.

If we relate this to the previous discussion of types of groups of children, then we get a particular pattern of parameters of behaviours (see Figure 10.2).

	Actions within the understandings of the working consensus		Actions outside the understandings of the working consensus
	Conformity	Routine deviance	Disorder
Goodies	————→		
Jokers	——————————————→		
Gangs	————————————————————————————→		

Figure 10.2 Parameters of children's actions

Figure 10.2 simplifies great complexities, but it does highlight one social consequence of classroom relationships. In particular, it draws attention to the issues of being fair and offering interesting learning opportunities. If the quality of both interpersonal relationships and curriculum provision is high, then the parameters of children's actions are likely to move to the left on the diagram and differentiation may decrease. If interpersonal relationships are poor and the children feel that injustices are occurring, or if the curriculum is boring or inappropriate, then the parameters of children's actions are likely to move to the right on the diagram. The result is likely to be an increase in disruption, a decrease in learning and the growth of dissatisfaction with school. Overall, differentiation is likely to increase, particularly as the teacher acts to deal with disruptive children.

It is very easy and common to see causes of disruption as being exclusively to do with particular children. Reflection on the quality and pattern of relationships, and of teacher actions in respect of the working consensus, may provide another set of issues for consideration; issues, furthermore, which, to a great extent, are within our own control as teachers.

PRACTICAL ACTIVITY 10.9

Aim: To reflect on the quality and consequences of relationships between teacher and children, over several weeks.

Method: We suggest that a diary is kept. In this diary, feelings and observations can be recorded regarding the responses and behaviour of children who have different dispositions to school. Perhaps 'goody', 'joker' or 'gang' children might be tentatively identified.

The diary might be analysed to see how our own feelings, provision and actions affected the behaviour and responses of the children.

Follow-up: Perhaps the children's behaviour and application to work will be seen to have varied with the quality of educational provision and our own energy and commitment. If this happens, then a reflective teacher may want to consider such things as the nature of deviance and conformity and their own responsibility for them.

---

5 CLASSROOM POLICIES

In this chapter, we have suggested a number of ways in which reflective teachers might monitor their achievements in terms of children's learning and social consequences. Such monitoring may facilitate our own learning and professional development because of the increase in our understanding of classroom life. We would also expect that the detailed data collected would lead to better matching of tasks to children's immediate learning needs and to a sounder basis for negotiating long-term goals to support children's development.

However, there can be difficulties here, for classroom life makes complex demands on teachers. Indeed, Doyle (1977) has suggested that, for student teachers, the complexity and need for rapid decision-making can often be overwhelming. Ways of simplifying such complexities need to be found.

We would suggest that one way of doing this is to try to consciously develop classroom policies. As long-term targets, such policies could inform specific actions and support continuous development. Reflective teachers, who have engaged in the activities in this book, should be in a very good position to think through such policies and to take control of their own classroom actions. It is one more way of ensuring that the cyclical process of reflection, discussed in Chapter 1, moves forward positively.

We will give some examples of issues about which long-term policies might be framed, though obviously many others could be identified.

1. *Listening to children.* As part of the search for understanding the interactive nature of the teaching–learning process, it is clearly important to gain access to children's perceptions. This requires that we are open and receptive listeners. In encouraging children to explain their views, the children are also likely to begin to reflect. This process may help the children to become more aware of themselves as learners and perhaps help them to develop as independent and autonomous members of the class. However, such developments are unlikely unless we consciously and consistently provide the conditions for children to talk and explain their points of view.

2. *Being positive.* It is very easy to respond negatively to children when under pressure. Perhaps taking a policy decision to try to be encouraging, and to seek out good work and reinforce creativity, would provide a check and a guide when responding in potentially difficult situations.

3. *Challenging children.* This relates to the curriculum and to the cognitive and motivational match of tasks. It is hard to provide a stimulating and appropriate curriculum all the time and all too easy to drift into routine work. However, if learning experiences are consciously monitored and reviewed, it may become easier. Indeed, if information about each child's learning processes, perspectives and progress is carefully gathered, it may be possible to sustain a desired degree of breadth and balance, progression and differentiation, continuity and cohesion.

4. *Acting 'fairly'.* This is a very suitable issue for a policy decision, bearing in mind the power of teachers as seen by children. It is a very important issue to children and simply calls for consideration of how they are likely to view a teacher action *before* making it.

Despite such good intentions regarding classroom policies, it is clear that classroom teachers, however reflective, cannot act without feeling the influence of the school in which they work and the society in which they live. For this reason, we conclude the book by moving beyond the classroom and by considering the reflective teacher in the context of schools and society.

NOTES FOR FURTHER READING

For two basic introductions to alternative approaches to children's learning, see:

Child, D. (1981) *Psychology and the Teacher*. London: Holt, Rinehart & Winston.
Fontana, D. (1981) *Psychology for Teachers*. London: Macmillan.

A series of books are available which provide brief, though somewhat dense, reviews of their fields:

Kirby, R. and Radford, J. (1976) *Individual Differences*. London: Methuen.
Peck, D. and Whitlow, D. (1975) *Approaches to Personality Theory*. London: Methuen.
Serpell, R. (1976) *Culture's Influence on Behaviour*. London: Methuen.
Turner, J. (1975) *Cognitive Development*. London: Methuen.

For excellent discussions of children's learning, and in particular critiques and development of Piagetian theory, see:

Donaldson, M. (1978) *Children's Minds*. London: Fontana.
Meadows, S. (ed.) (1983) *Developing Thinking*. London: Methuen.

The following books contain interesting articles relating to individual differences in learning styles, particularly Section 5 in Whitehead (1975) and Section 2 in Entwistle (1985):

Entwistle, N. (ed) (1985) *New Directions in Educational Psychology: Learning and Teaching.* London: Falmer Press.
Entwistle, N. (1981) *Styles of Learning and Teaching.* London: Wiley.
Whitehead, J. (ed.) (1975) *Personality and Learning.* Sevenoaks: Hodder & Stoughton.

Regarding the social consequences of classroom practices in primary schools, more complete treatments can be found in:

Hartley, D. (1985) *Understanding the Primary School.* London: Croom Helm.
King, R. (1978) *All Things Bright and Beautiful.* Chichester: Wiley.
Lubeck, S. (1985) *Sandbox Society.* London: Falmer Press.
Pollard, A. (1985) *The Social World of the Primary School.* London: Holt, Rinehart & Winston.
Sharp, R. and Green, A. (1975) *Education and Social Control.* London: Routledge & Kegan Paul.

For reviews of the field more generally, see:

Delamont, S. (1983) *Interaction in the Classroom.* London: Methuen.
Woods, P. (1983) *Sociology and the School.* London: Routledge & Kegan Paul.

Beyond Classroom Reflection

Chapter 11

Reflective Teaching and the School

INTRODUCTION

1 THE FEEL OF A SCHOOL

2 CURRICULUM, POLICIES AND PRACTICE

3 STRATEGIES FOR INNOVATION

CONCLUSION

INTRODUCTION

In this chapter, we focus on reflective teaching in the context of the whole school. In recent years, there has been a growth of interest in whole-school development, innovation and self-evaluation (Bolam 1982; Hopkins and Wideen 1984; McMahon *et al.* 1984). This stems from a new recognition of the difficulties of bringing about change without team-work and coherent planning at an institutional level. Rodger and Richardson (1985) characterize a 'self-evaluating school' as follows:

> It is the school which is aware of the pressures of accountability being experienced in education yet is concerned to maintain and advance its professionalism, not least in the area of autonomy of decision-making. It is a school which sees itself as having many relationships with its employers, its community and particularly its clients. . . . It is a school in which the staff see themselves as part of a collaborative venture aimed at the purposeful education of children . . . It is a school which also recognizes that it may lack experience and expertise in particular areas and it is therefore prepared to be open to advice and information from outside agencies. It is a school which is prepared to devote precious time and energy to reflective activities . . . Above all, it is the school which has a genuine desire to find out about itself and by so doing to make itself a better place for young children to develop.
>
> (1985, p. 20–21)

This view is consistent with the position which we are advocating in this book, but we have to recognize that not all schools fit the model which Rodger and Richardson suggest. In fact, in many cases the schools in which reflective teachers find themselves may be far more static, 'routinized' and locked into 'taken-for-granted' conventions. This chapter and its associated practical activities are intended first, to assist reflective teachers to gather and analyse information about their school; and second, to decide on appropriate and longer-term strategies for action.

Some sharp ethical and professional issues may be raised by this focus, for it represents a move outside the classroom with the traditional protection of teacher autonomy. For a classroom teacher or a student teacher to investigate and reflect on a whole-school basis could cause difficulties, and we would advise that the practical activities which are suggested might be discussed with the head teacher and appropriate colleagues prior to embarking upon them. Ultimately, though, there can be no side-stepping of the issues, for each individual teacher contributes to and is influenced by the whole school. Further, primary schools are increasingly developing team-based and collegiate approaches and the pace of change means that all schools will need to maximize the use of their reflective, innovative and adaptive resources in the future (Campbell 1985). In this context then, reflective teachers have both a right and a direct responsibility to consider the school context in which they work and should not avoid it. The initial approach, though, should, in our view, be open-minded, seeking to understand perspectives and the contraints which may have influenced the development of policies and practices. Such understanding should provide a sound foundation for acting strategically and with positive value-commitments to influence future developments.

1 THE FEEL OF A SCHOOL

We begin this chapter by discussing the subjective feel of a school: variously termed school climate, school ethos or 'institutional bias'. This is an important initial consideration because of the way in which perspectives, behaviour and action in schools are very

---

PRACTICAL ACTIVITY 11.1

Aim: To describe a school ethos.

Method: Rate the school on the mapping device below (derived from Rodgers and Richardson 1985, p. 52–3.) Ask some colleagues to do the same and discuss the results.

	1	2	3	4	5	
busy						inactive
happy						miserable
purposeful						aimless
relaxed						tense
enthusiastic						apathetic
noisy						quiet
messy						tidy
chaotic						organized
welcoming						formidable
open						closed
disciplined						unruly
confident						insecure

Follow-up: Use of the mapping device, and the conversations with colleagues which follow, should provide a good idea of the subjective feel of the school. An excellent extension would be to ask children, parents or non-teaching staff to carry out the exercise too. They are likely to have different perspectives. All sorts of issues for school practice and provision might follow if particular patterns emerge from the exercise.

often influenced by established conventions, expectations and norms. Such norms usually remain tacit and may easily be taken for granted by people who know a school well. Other people, as relative 'strangers', are likely to be more explicitly aware of them.

'School ethos' and 'school climate' are well-established notions, but their specific origins are rarely identified. However, such concepts are useful for describing how a school feels.

The Practical Activity 11.1 suggests one way in which this might be done.

The sociological concept of 'institutional bias' may take our understanding of this issue a little further. It also refers to subjective meanings, understandings, conventions, habits and routines, but it is linked to an analysis which sees them as having been negotiated over time between all those who are, or have been, involved in the school.

Any school can be seen as an institution to which people bring their perspectives, opinions, skills and enthusiasms. These are used, in interaction with others, to construct understandings about the 'way the school is'. Obviously, the influence of any one individual will depend on his or her degree of status, power, charisma and authority. Thus, while some people will exert considerable influence, perhaps in alliance or association with others, other people, such as students on a school-experience programme, may feel and be highly marginal. Clearly, a head teacher has a particular degree of power to initiate and influence the development of an institutional bias. It is hard to underestimate the influence of head teachers in this respect, and Practical Activity 11.2 suggests two particular ways of developing an understanding of a head teacher's point of view.

PRACTICAL ACTIVITY 11.2

Aim: To understand a head teacher's perspectives and aims for her or his school.

Method: The first method is simply to ask. An interview or series of conversations, perhaps structured around statements of aims which may be contained in a school brochure, will produce a valuable account of the head's perspective and goals.

Second, we would suggest that the head teacher's account is triangulated with some data of actual behaviour. An excellent source of data here are assemblies. Assemblies have symbolic and ritual functions, as well as being used for practical managerial purposes. Because large numbers of children are involved, the control and discipline conventions in the school are likely to be evident and the normative structure of the school and expectations of the head teacher are likely to be made explicit.

Follow-up: This exercise will produce a clearer understanding of the way the key leadership figure in the school conceptualizes goals and attempts to enact them. For reflective teachers, the application of such understanding derives from the way in which it can inform decisions about future action.

Clearly, it is important to understand the views and actions of head teachers, but it is certainly not the case that they are the only influence on an institutional bias. Many other individuals and groups within a school also have power to influence events and contribute to the formation of expectations. For instance, it is likely that the deputy head, post-holders with curricular responsibilities, other teachers, the caretaker and school secretary, will all have some influence. Parents and governors are likely to have a more long-term influence on the nature of the school. The emergence of understandings about the 'way the school is' should thus be seen as a result of negotiation between a number of different and competing influences and interests. It follows that the institutional bias may change and develop over time.

The concept of institutional bias thus leads to an analysis of the micro-politics of schools as a constantly developing and adapting set of negotiated practices and expectations.

PRACTICAL ACTIVITY 11.3

Aim: To describe and analyse the institutional bias of a school.

Method: This is a long-term activity which draws on ethnographic methods. It will take several weeks to do. We suggest that all possible opportunities are taken to listen, observe and understand the perspectives, assumptions and taken-for-granted understandings of the various people who are involved in the school (see also Practical Activity 11.4). Make notes so that these are not forgotten.

Review these notes and look for patterns in the understandings. Consider if the patterns relate to particular groups of people and use this awareness to orientate you in your future observing.

Make comparisons between the views of different people and/or groups. This should help to refine your understanding.

Try to produce a summary analysis. You might distinguish:

1. The main individuals and/or groups and their perspectives.

2. The shared understandings which exist about policy and practice in the school.

3. The degree of agreement with these understandings which exists from individual to individual or group to group.

Follow-up: Through this activity, you should produce a tighter understanding of the institutional bias, of the groups in the school and of the degree of legitimacy of the existing institutional bias. Such understanding is a very useful starting-point for taking a new initiative which is strategically well judged, or simply for 'fitting in' to a school.

Whether or not one is interested in analysing an institutional bias, there are, as was mentioned in Chapter 4, many good reasons for doing everything one can to understand the roles, work-experience and perspectives of other people who work at or are associated with the school. In this, we would include school ancillary helpers, dinner supervisors, catering staff, road-crossing patrol helpers, the school secretary, the school cleaners and caretaker. The contributions which they make to school life often go relatively unnoticed and yet they provide essential services without which no school could operate smoothly. People who work in such jobs have particular concerns, interests and feelings about school and their work and these are well worth exploring directly.

PRACTICAL ACTIVITY 11.4

Aim: To identify the main concerns, interests and feelings of various non-teaching staff regarding school.

Method: We suggest that time is spent with non-teaching staff. In conversation, some issues could be explored, such as the nature of their jobs, the aspects of the job which they like best, the main problems which are encountered and the constraints within which they work: such as time, resources, pay and conditions.

Follow-up: For a reflective teacher who wishes to contribute to and to develop the strength of the whole-school team, establishing such links and an appreciation of other's concerns is important. In its simplest terms, it helps to understand why getting 'chairs up' at the end of each day may be important, why it may be helpful to get the children 'out' for dinner on time and many other small but significant points.

Similar activities could profitably be devised by a student teacher to explore the concerns of the governors and of parents. One simple suggestion here, once data has been collected (as suggested in Practical Activity 11.4), is to focus on the opinions of the various people as they affect the teaching role.

It is possible to distinguish between 'pressures' to do certain things and 'constraints' not to do certain things. For instance, the staff culture or cultures of a school, which are particularly evident in the staffroom, provide very significant examples of this. If a teacher or student teacher is accepted into a staff group, then a considerable source of support and advice is provided. However, there may also be pressure to conform in such things as dress, speech, opinion and practice. Constraints may take the form of a withdrawal of support and a questioning of membership if conformity is not observed.

PRACTICAL ACTIVITY 11.5

Aim: To monitor the support, pressure and constraint which result from relationships with other staff.

Method: One appropriate way to collect data on this is through a private diary over a period of time. Clearly the issue should be borne in mind when making entries. After a period, reflection on the diary and memories of various incidents should make it possible to review the support, pressures and constraints which are perceived.

Follow-up: Bearing in mind one's aims and value-position, it may or may not be a good thing to be drawn into an existing staff culture. Carrying out this exercise may make one more conscious of staff relationships and may provide a basis for actively contributing to future understandings, developments and innovation.

2 CURRICULUM, POLICIES AND PRACTICE

A range of whole-school issues are raised here, for a reflective teacher is likely to be concerned both with the overt, officially stated curriculum and with curricular practices which, while they may remain tacit and hidden in normal teaching and learning processes, still influence the curriculum-as-experienced by children. In addition, a reflective teacher will be concerned with the processes by which policy and practice are evaluated and reviewed.

This suggests a cyclical model for curriculum development, similar to the model for reflective teaching which we suggested in Chapter 1. We will simplify it here into three elements (Figure 11.1) and consider each in turn.

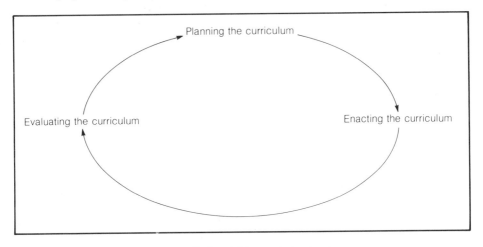

Figure 11.1 A cyclical model for curricular development

The first stage, that of planning, has received considerable attention in the past few years. The 1978 HMI report on primary education (DES 1978a) emphasized the production of curriculum guidelines and the deployment of promoted staff to take responsibility for particular curriculum areas. For instance, they published a table showing the percentage of schools with written guidelines or schemes of work in each subject area (see Table 11.1).

Table 11.1 *The percentage of schools with written documents or schemes of work for each subject*

Subject	% of schools	Subject	% of schools	Subject	% of schools
Mathematics	88	Music	37	Social studies	18
Language	85	History	36	Dance	17
Religious		Geography	35	Health	
education	72	Environmental		education	17
Science	43	studies	34	French	15
Art	42	Games	26	Humanities	9
Craft	41	Swimming	19	Other subjects	17
Gymnastics	38	Drama	18		

(HMI 1978a, p. 40: Table 25)

There are many indications that these percentages are higher today and that more staff have a specifically designated area of curricular responsibility.

In addition, a number of other issues have emerged on which many local education authorities and schools have adopted specific policies. The most obvious here are those concerned with equal opportunities (particularly anti-sexism and multi-culturalism/ anti-racism); on children with special educational needs; and on relationships with parents.

Studying such guidelines and policy documents is an excellent way of understanding the overt plans and intentions which have been officially endorsed by the staff of a school.

PRACTICAL ACTIVITY 11.6

Aim: To study the documentation of the school curriculum and policy in important areas.

Method: There are various possible sources of documentation which may be available:

- school brochures
- internal curriculum and policy statements
- records of staff and governors meetings

The areas in which one might seek information would include:

- the curriculum (such as creative arts, play, maths, science, health education, social studies, religious education, etc.).

- policies which might be expected to permeate (such as equal opportunities (gender, race, social class), language, writing, special educational needs, relations with parents, teaching/learning approaches).

Follow-up: Study of such documents provides immediate insights into the degree of awareness and quality of thinking, as well as the substantive nature of the planning of curriculum and practice in a school. It thus indicates starting-points for further enquiries, for discussions with staff who have particular responsibilities and for policy and curriculum development.

However, the value of guidelines and policy documents is recognized as being as statements of goals, and one would expect some variation when focusing on the second 'enacting' phase of the cyclical model. Indeed, whatever the effort and commitment in schools, as in many other walks of life, there is often a gap between rhetoric and reality, between intention and implementation. Anning (1983) suggested that new head teachers attempting curriculum innovation face a course rather like that of the Grand National. The first jump, the improvement of the school environment, and the second, that of producing new curriculum guidelines, are accomplished smoothly. Beecher's Brook looms when it is realized that actual practice in the classrooms may not be changing as fast and cannot be influenced by aesthetics and policy documents alone. This is a problem which faces everyone, for it is never easy to bring practice into line with ideals, let alone in the difficult circumstances which schools have faced in recent years.

At the same time, though, the issue has to be faced with openness if adjustments and further developments are to be soundly based. A reflective teacher will thus want to follow up official statements by enquiring into what actually happens in teaching and learning processes: an enquiry which may identify both expected and unintended outcomes and both overt and hidden aspects of the curriculum which is experienced by the children.

PRACTICAL ACTIVITY 11.7

Aim: To study, in practice, an area of the observed curriculum or an issue of policy across the school.

Method: The basic strategy here is to select one curriculum area, or a relatively discrete issue, to focus on and then to observe and document it through each class and in other school contexts. One relatively easy example would be to focus on the application of a handwriting policy. To study the application of an anti-racist or anti-sexist policy would be valuable but more difficult. The cooperation of teachers would be very important for the successful completion of this activity.

Follow-up: This activity will give an indication of the degree of continuity and coherence which exists in the application of the school policy which is studied. It will thus provide a basis for follow-up action and further review.

The third element in the cyclical model for curriculum development is evaluating: the process of monitoring and reviewing guidelines, policies and implementation on a whole-school basis. Clearly, this is absolutely crucial if the goal of continuous development and improvement is to be achieved. For this reason, it is worth focusing on in its own right.

PRACTICAL ACTIVITY 11.8

Aim: To describe and review the process for the whole-school evaluation of curriculum and practice in a school.

Method: In order to describe evaluation processes, one should study any available documents, attend meetings and talk to the people who are, or have been, involved. To form judgements about such processes, a set of clear criteria is required. One might include criteria such as:

1. Producing clear curriculum and policy guidelines.

2. Introducing socially and educationally worthwhile developments.

3. Acting as a means of individual staff-development.

4. Bring important issues into open discussion.

5. Leading to greater cohesion and a clearer sense of purpose among the staff.

Follow-up: This activity will facilitate judgements of the quality of school evaluation processes and may suggest areas in which they might be developed further.

---

3 STRATEGIES FOR INNOVATION

The notion of reflective teaching implies a willingness to adapt and a commitment to contribute towards social and educational developments. The basic stages advocated in this book begin with identifying, understanding and describing actual practice. We then move to judging the worth of that practice against specific criteria deriving from carefully identified educational aims and value-commitments. This should provide a basis for taking decisions about how best to improve practice where changes are called for.

This is a good deal more difficult to do in a school as a whole than it is in the context of our own classroom, and yet it is clearly the long-term responsibility of reflective teachers, with an awareness of issues beyond their classroom, to contribute towards whole-school developments. In this section, therefore, we discuss strategies and procedures by which such contributions might be made.

There are two main ways in which this issue can be approached. One common approach (e.g. Easen 1985, McMahon *et al.* 1984) suggests a logical procedure for identifying problems collectively as a staff team and for producing ways of resolving them. A less prominent, and perhaps more sceptical approach, considers ways of acting if such wholehearted collaboration is only partially forthcoming. We would suggest that both approaches are likely to be necessary in most situations.

There are several reasons for suggesting consideration of the best forms of strategic action, should review procedures falter. The first lies in the nature of evaluation itself. As Adelman and Alexander (1982) argue in their book on the 'self-evaluating institution', all evaluations or school reviews are 'political'. As they put it:

> an evaluation involves acts of valuing, of making judgements of worth or effectiveness, and this presupposes the existence of other . . . values and judgements. If some judgements prevail over others . . . [they] will have consequences for the distribution of resources and the status of individuals and groups. An evaluation . . . offers a critique of and a potential threat to [established] processes and interests and to the balance of institutional power.
>
> (1982, p. 146)

Change, review or evaluation is thus political, both substantively, in that particular values and judgements are given priority, and interpersonally, in that personal interests are likely to be affected.

As we have seen, an institutional bias represents normative conventions which are a negotiated product of the existing balance of power and influence in a school. It is exactly these conventions, policies and practices which are, implicitly, likely to come under review in a school evaluation.

If such issues are clearly recognized, then it is easier to understand the responses of an individual teacher who is involved in processes of change. Doyle and Ponder (1976) identified three typical responses:

- The 'rational adapter' who, by recognizing problems or issues and enacting logical procedures to tackle them, accepts innovation and helps to bring it about.

- The 'pragmatic sceptic' who assesses the consequences of change in a calculative way by considering the gains and losses from change in time, energy and personal development before deciding how to act.

- The 'Stone-Age obstructionist' who, by rejecting the value-position and judgements upon which a proposal for change is based and by refusing to become fully involved, attempts to retain the status quo.

Clearly, these are caricatures which simplify the complexity of people's motivations and involvements, but they do begin to describe the essence of three basic sorts of compliance (Etzioni 1961):

Moral: in which commitment is based on intrinsic acceptance of purposes and values.

Calculative: in which compliance is based on extrinsic judgements of personal interests.

Alienative: in which compliance is reluctant and is based on a powerlessness to resist.

The existence of such different types of perspectives and commitment clearly has serious implications for those who may wish to bring about changes in schools.

Having focused on the importance of the political context within a school, we now turn to consider a procedure for whole-school evaluation.

We start from the point of a reflective teacher having identified an issue or problem which is judged to require attention and which has implications for the whole school. The following stages might then be considered:

1. Focusing colleagues' attention on the issue and achieving agreement regarding its importance and the practicality of change.

2. Analysing the issue in detail.

3. Analysing factors constraining change and factors which will facilitate change.

4. Considering ideas for innovation and deciding collectively on a coherent programme of actions to introduce change.

5. Monitoring the change process—being prepared to amend plans and even to redefine the problem.

For each of these stages we could suggest some practical activities which might be engaged in as a staff group. However, it is the first stage which is likely to be most difficult and yet is also most important because it involves establishing the platform and rationale for change from which all else follows.

The key strategy which we would suggest here is that of forming alliances. This will not only make it more likely that others will take notice, but it also invites people to involve themselves openly in processes of change. For this to operate smoothly, it assumes an incorporative, democratic style of action.

Clearly, alliances will be relatively easy to form with those who share the same value-position, but it is usually also important to establish links with those who may have a more pragmatic, calculative view of suggested changes. With them, it is necessary to establish the potential gains from innovation, or indeed the losses from continuing with present practices, so that they join in the process. It is unlikely that it will be possible to form alliances with those who wish to obstruct and resist change from the status quo, but it may be important not to threaten their dignity and position overtly, in case this worsens the situation by causing them to become increasingly entrenched.

Alliances, however, can be formed with people both inside the school and with those beyond it. In this respect, it is vital to remember that schools are open systems and are influenced from outside. For instance, within a school the position of the head teacher is likely to be crucial and any reflective teacher in a relatively junior position is likely to want to enlist his or her support when suggesting any innovation. It is fortunate that, since head teachers occupy a difficult position and must act at the interface of internal and external pressures, they are likely to be exceptionally aware of events and concerns outside their school.

It is thus open to a reflective teacher, however junior in status, to make positive suggestions to a head teacher about innovations which would enable the school to contribute more fully to developments in the community and society generally. At the same time, and also constructively, the reflective teacher could seek the views of external groups who may be involved. The issues of parental involvement in reading and of school policies on multi-racial education provide examples where external participation of this sort has helped to bring about internal developments in many schools. Of course, alliances are possible with a whole range of other external groups, such as industrialists, trade unionists, advisers, academics, other teachers, community groups, politicians, governors, etc. A reflective teacher, acting strategically here, may consciously aim to affect the range of immediate influences on the school and thus set up conditions for new developments.

When it comes to action within a school, there are four basic strategic possibilities for a reflective teacher to consider:

Radical innovation. A strategy which is probably only possible with the strong support of those in very senior positions and is arguably only sensible with a solid measure of agreement among staff as a whole.

Reform. A gradualist strategy with the support of senior staff which, by phasing changes slowly, reduces the immediate threat to vested interests. The overall purposes of innovations can be subject to dilution in the process.

Subversion. A strategy where support from senior staff is lacking and in which individuals or groups, in alliance, seek to bring about change covertly.

Challenge. An overt strategy in which individuals or groups in alliance confront the status quo directly.

Consideration of the use of these strategies obviously requires careful thought, in particular by placing the importance of the issue under review in the context of other social and educational issues and by considering long-term, as well as short-term, consequences. Also, it is almost inevitable that one will have to take some hard, personal decisions about one's loyalties and responsibilities. After all, there is no reason why the views and interests of staff colleagues, head teacher, children, parents, etc. should overlap, so choices often become necessary. Having considered such issues, it is the responsibility of a reflective teacher, we would argue, to decide on a position and to act.

PRACTICAL ACTIVITY 11.9

Aim: To review strategies for action.

Method: The most profitable ways forward here are likely to come from discussions with sympathetic colleagues and other allies. It will be necessary to consider the people involved and features of the institutional bias, of policies and of practice, in relation to desired developments. Some may be constraining; others facilitating. There may even be contradictions which might provide initial ways forward.

Follow-up: Having reviewed such factors, a judgement about the best strategies to adopt should be easier to make. One has to consider not only which strategy might be most effective, but also what side-effects each might have.

Apart from negotiations within school, it is important to consider opportunities for encouraging participation from beyond the school. Practical Activity 11.10 suggests a way of beginning to encourage such external involvement.

PRACTICAL ACTIVITY 11.10

Aim: To review the possibility of encouraging external participation on an educational issue.

Method: We suggest that when a topical and locally relevant educational issue emerges, a meeting is held. Representatives of groups could be invited. Each representative could be asked to explain their perspective and concerns regarding the issue. Points of agreement could be identified and collectively confirmed. These might form a basis for future action together. Points of disagreement could be discussed further. The nature and range of such differences are likely to set parameters on the potential for future collective action.

Follow-up: Depending on what had happened at such a meeting, follow-up might involve a review of the whole approach, further negotiation, or a direct move to consider action.

CONCLUSION

In this chapter, we have looked at schools as a whole, at processes of development and at the part which reflective teachers might play. Having argued that reflective teachers should be active in whole-school development, we conclude with an important qualification. This is to point out that insensitive action or innovation can be counterproductive. It is relatively easy to force change in one area, only to find that so much goodwill has been lost that other areas have been adversely affected. School life is complex and if one can negotiate with colleagues to develop shared perspectives on issues and collective strategies for action, then many problems may be avoided.

NOTES FOR FURTHER READING

For good reviews of research on the influential concept of school climate, see:

Anderson, C. S. (1982) The search for school climate: a review of the research, *Review of Educational Research*, **52**, 368–420.

Strivens, J. (1985) School climate: a review of a problematic concept, in Reynolds, D. *Studying School Effectiveness*. London: Falmer Press.

An interpretive approach using the concept of institutional bias and focusing on staff relationships is:

Pollard, A. (1987) Primary school-teachers and their colleagues, in Delamont, S. *The Primary School Teacher*. London: Falmer Press.

A book which also looks at the internal politics of schools is:

Hoyle, E. (1986) *The Politics of School Management*. London: Hodder & Stoughton.

Four constructive and approachable books on the topic of school-based development are:

Day, C., Johnston D. and Whitaker, P. (1985) *Managing Primary Schools*. London: Harper & Row.

This is a clearly written and practical book for those in 'leadership positions'. It advocates that school innovation should be developed by increasing professional awareness.

Easen, P. (1985) *Making School-Centred INSET Work*. London: Croom Helm.

Designed as part of an Open University course, this book is intended to support teachers who are engaged in school development. It provides a particularly good range of activities for personal self-reflection.

McMahon, A. *et al.* (1984) *Guidelines for the Review and Internal Development of Schools: Primary School Handbook*. London: Schools Council/Longman.

This is a product of the so-called GRIDS project. It provides guidelines for whole-school review of policies and practice, drawn from work with fifteen primary schools.

Campbell, J. (1985) *Developing the Primary School Curriculum*. London: Holt, Rinehart & Winston.

A good book on the role of a curriculum post-holder in the context of school-based development. An interesting chapter on the idea of a 'collegial primary school'.

For a more international perspective on this topic, see:

Bolam, R. (1982) *Strategies for School Improvement*. Paris: OECD.

This report identified the major issues involved in the development of 'problem-solving schools' and has provided a basis for cooperative international research efforts.

Hopkins, D. and Wideen, M. (eds.) (1984) *Alternative Perspectives on School Improvement*. London: Falmer Press.

A collection of imaginative papers on school-based self-development. See, for instance, Schmuck on the 'Characteristics of the autonomous school'.

Chapter 12

Reflective Teaching and Society

INTRODUCTION

In many parts of this book, we have considered the internal workings of schools and classrooms with relatively few references to the social, economic, cultural and political contexts within which they are located. While this may be necessary for a book of this sort, it is not sufficient for a reflective teacher who is, hopefully, aware of the ways in which educational processes are influenced by, and contribute to, wider social forces, processes and relationships. In Chapter 2, we introduced the idea of social development being based on a dialectical process, as individuals respond to and act within the situations in which they find themselves. Actions in the present are thus influenced by the past, but also contribute to new social arrangements for the future. All teachers, as individuals, are members of society, but we would hope that reflective teachers would be particularly capable of acting in society to initiate and foster morally and ethically sound developments.

There are three sections in this chapter. The first discusses the relationship between education and society and reviews the theoretical framework which was first introduced in Chapter 2. The second considers the responsibilities of a socially aware reflective teacher in the classroom and discusses the formation of classroom policies. The final section focuses on the actions which a reflective teacher could take as a citizen in trying to influence the democratic processes of decision-making by local and national governments.

1 EDUCATION AND SOCIETY

Two major questions have to be faced with regard to the relationship between education and society. The first is, 'What should an education system be designed to do?'. The second is, 'What can actually be achieved through education?'. We will address these in turn and draw out the implications for reflective teachers.

Education has very often been seen as a means of influencing the development of society, and perhaps three central areas of purpose can be identified here. These are those of:

1. Wealth creation through preparation for economic production.
2. Cultural production and reproduction.
3. Developing social justice and individual rights.

Thus, one educational priority may be wealth creation. In the latter part of the Industrial Revolution in Great Britain, an important part of the argument for the establishment of an elementary school system was that it should provide a work-force which was more skilled and thus more economically productive. The idea became the linchpin of 'human capital' theory (Schultz 1961) in the 1960s, and many new nations, influenced by analyses such as Rostow's *The Stages of Economic Growth* (1962), put scarce resources into their education systems. In Britain in the 1980s, the supposed links between education and economic productivity are constantly being drawn by the Conservative government.

Alternatively, there are those who would highlight the 'function' of education in the production and reproduction of a national culture. Again, there were elements of the nineteenth-century British experience which illustrate this. For instance, the arguments and influence of Matthew Arnold helped to define the traditional classical curriculum which remains influential today. An even stronger example of cultural production is that of America in the twentieth century, where the education system was required to 'assimilate' and 'integrate' successive groups of new immigrants into an 'American culture'. The education system was seen as a vital part of the 'melting-pot'. Of course, a highly questionable assumption here was that there was an American culture, but the notion of the existence of a set of 'central values' was important in this formative period of the development of the USA. This use of an education system for the production of a sense of shared national identity is common in many parts of the world, particularly where independent states have been established relatively recently. Thus, another educational priority can be an integrative one, relating to the production or reproduction of 'culture'.

Contributing to social justice is a third central purpose which is often identified for educational systems. This concern was very much at the forefront of thinking in the production of the 1944 Education Act in Britain and also in the subsequent introduction of comprehensive schools. It has been an important element of policy in America and features prominently in the educational goals which are set by many developing countries. One critical point to make is that 'equality of opportunity' and the meritocratic ideal, which often lie behind policy and rhetoric on this issue, are concepts which need careful consideration. They can be used in ways which ignore the structural inequalities of wealth, status and power which exist. If such issues are glossed, then the promotion of social justice through education policy is very unlikely to be successful.

The concern for social justice through education can partly be seen as a desire to ensure that there is an acceptable and legitimated system for allocating jobs in society and for facilitating social mobility. However, there are more individualized and fundamental concerns which are perhaps more relevant to reflective teaching. A very clear exposition of such issues is contained in the Universal Declaration of Human Rights (United Nations 1948).

Article 1 of the Declaration states that:

All human beings are born free and equal in dignity and rights. They are endowed with reason and conscience.

These rights are to be enjoyed, according to Article 2:

> Without distinction of any kind, such as race, colour, sex, language, religion, political or other opinion, national or social origin, property, birth or other status.

There then follow many articles dealing with rights and fundamental freedoms of movement, thought, religion, assembly, political participation, work, leisure and an adequate standard of living. Article 26 deals with education and asserts that:

> Education shall be directed to the full development of the human personality and the strengthening of respect for human rights and fundamental freedoms. It shall promote understanding, tolerance and friendship among all nations, racial and religious groups.

Such inalienable rights are seen as 'the foundation of freedom, justice and peace in the world.'

Education is expected to have a crucial role in the dissemination of the UN Declaration across the world, for it was to be 'displayed, read and expanded principally in schools and other educational institutions' in all member-states.

Education policies and systems can thus be designed to emphasize economic production, cultural production or reproduction, social justice or individual rights. While such goals are not necessarily conflicting, there are various tensions and dilemmas which are often posed. One obvious dilemma concerns the rights of minority groups to maintain an independent culture and sense of identity within a majority culture. Another is the dilemma between the demands of individual development and those of economic production. We have raised these issues in Chapter 4 and argued that a reflective teacher should make informed and responsible judgements about them. The ways in which action might follow will be discussed further below, but we now move on to the second question: 'What can actually be achieved through education?'

There has been a long-running debate on this topic. Some people, such as Coleman, Coser and Powell (1966), Jencks *et al.* (1972) and Bowles and Gintis (1976), have argued that education can make little difference to social development. Although coming to the issue from different theoretical perspectives, they argue that educational processes reflect and reproduce major features of existing society. The suggestion is that relationships of power, wealth, status and ideology are such that education should be seen as a part of the dominant social system, rather than as an autonomous force within it.

Others, such as Berger and Luckman (1967), may be seen as taking a more idealistic theoretical position. They argue that, since our sense of reality is 'socially constructed' by people as they interact together, there is, therefore, scope for individuals to make an independent impact on the course of social developments. One could then argue that there is potential for education to influence change.

What we have here are the competing positions of those who believe in social determinism ranged against those who believe in individual voluntarism.

As we have already seen, education is often expected to bring about social and economic developments and it is an area which tends to attract idealists. However, we also have to recognize that the major structural features of societies are extremely resistant to change. What is needed, then, is a theoretical position which recognizes the importance of action and of constraint. Such a position would allow that education has a degree of relative autonomy and would thus guide and legitimate realistic and aware policies for action.

Such a theoretical framework is provided by what we have called the dialectic of the individual and society (see Chapter 2). As Berlak and Berlak (1981) put it:

> Conscious creative activity is limited by prevailing social arrangements, but human actions and institutional forms are not mere reflections of them.
>
> (1981, p. 121)

The clear implication is that people can make their own impact and history, but must do so in whatever circumstances they find themselves. If this theoretical framework is adopted, social developments can be seen as the product of processes of struggle and contest between different individuals and groups in society. Such processes are ones in which education must, inevitably, play a part.

Thus, our answer to the question of what education can actually achieve must be based on a guarded and realistic optimism. The dialectical model of the influence of individuals and social structures recognizes constraints, but asserts that action remains possible. This places a considerable responsibility on reflective teachers.

2 CLASSROOM TEACHING AND SOCIETY

One implication of the adoption of a dialectical model of the relationship between individuals and society is that it highlights the possible consequences for the 'macro' world of society, of actions, experiences and processes which take place in the 'micro' world of the classroom. In Chapter 1, we raised this issue with the assertion that 'reflective teaching implies an active concern with aims and consequences, as well as with technical efficiency' and we must pick up the themes again here. One of the most important issues concerns the influence of a reflective teacher's own value-commitments.

In Chapter 1, we argued that reflective teachers should recognize democratically determined decisions, but should act both as responsible professionals and as autonomous citizens to contribute to such decision-making processes. We also suggested that attitudes of 'openmindedness' and 'responsibility' are essential attributes. Openmindedness involves a willingness to consider evidence and argument from whatever source it comes. It is, thus, the antithesis of closure and of 'habituated' or narrow ideological thinking.

There are parallels here with the guidelines issued by the Politics Association about teaching politics in school (Jones 1986). Jones suggests that the aim should be to achieve a 'comprehensive awareness' and an 'overall understanding of political processes and issues'. On the basis of such awareness, children should be encouraged to form their own views and participate in the democratic process. An openminded tolerance to the exposition of a variety of views and opinions is obviously an initial necessity here, and we would say the same for reflective teaching.

However, the Politics Association also asserts the importance of a teacher's social responsibility with its guideline that 'the teacher cannot be neutral towards those values which underpin liberal democracy'. But what are such values? Clear guidance on this has been provided by the Council of Europe (1985). In a recommendation to all member-states of the EEC, the Council of Ministers reaffirmed the understandings embodied in the United Nations' Universal Declaration of Human Rights and the European Convention on Human Rights. The Council suggested that study in schools should 'lead to an understanding of, and sympathy for, the concepts of justice, equality, freedom, peace, dignity, rights, and democracy,' (Council of Europe 1985, Appendix). These are seen as being fundamental to democratic societies and all schools, including those for young children, are encouraged to introduce them to their pupils and to develop their understanding. Hugh Starkey (1986) claims that the United Nations'

Declaration is accepted as a world-wide moral standard and again suggests that fundamental freedoms are what make effective political democracies possible.

This brings us directly back to the issues of individual dignity, equality and freedom. It brings us back to issues such as sexism, racism and other forms of discrimination on the basis of social class or disability, and it focuses attention once more on the quality of relationships and the use of power in classrooms. These are issues on which, we would argue, children have rights on which socially responsible teachers should not compromise. We take this to constitute a 'bottom line', a value-commitment to the fundamental rights of citizens in a democratic society.

Such a value-commitment by reflective teachers might be manifested in two ways. First, classroom processes might be monitored with such specific issues in mind; indeed, we have made various suggestions of this sort with regard to race and gender. The second way of manifesting this value-commitment follows logically from such monitoring. It is to develop classroom social policies for the long term, so that actions, which are taken in the immediacy of classroom decision-making, support concerns with individual dignity, equality and freedom rather than undercut them. As we have suggested in Chapter 10, classroom social policies may, thus, be seen as attempts to anticipate, plan and pre-structure activities and procedures so that teacher actions reflect a consistent and socially responsible value-position.

We will illustrate these steps through the suggestion of practical activities. We begin with Practical Activity 12.1, designed to monitor the care of a child with a special educational need.

PRACTICAL ACTIVITY 12.1

Aim: To monitor the experience of a child with a physical disability in the classroom.

Method: We would suggest a form of focused child study here. Data-collection methods might include observation and field-notes, collecting examples of work, sociometry and discussions with the child. A colleague might also observe and provide comments on teacher–child interaction.

Follow-up: The criteria for analysis might ultimately be in terms of maximizing the child's dignity, equality and freedom, but more specific questions which could be used to interrogate the data might be:

1. To what extent is the child able to participate in class activities?

2. To what extent is tolerance and understanding of the child's disability shown by other children?

3. What is the quality of the relationship between the teacher and the child?

Having monitored an existing situation, it is then necessary to take action and to establish policy. The establishment of classroom policy in this area is by no means easy. It requires a sound analysis of the issues, both in terms of the specific situation and in the light of alternative approaches, experiences and research findings from elsewhere. Above all, it requires knowledge of oneself and personal commitment to implementation. In our view, it is very hard to develop such understanding without the insights of others and the opportunities to discuss the issues with colleagues and 'critical friends'. The establishment of a classroom policy might then take the form as suggested in Practical Activity 12.2. Again, we use the example of provision for children with special educational needs.

PRACTICAL ACTIVITY 12.2

Aim: To develop a classroom policy to maximize the participation of children with special educational needs.

Method: We would suggest the following stages:

1. Read some of the literature about provision for children with special educational needs in classrooms.

2. Discuss with colleagues how they make provision. Gather examples of practice elsewhere.

3. Consider your present provision. Are the physical resources, the learning activities and the quality of interactions in the classroom such that all children can participate, feel valued and maintain their dignity?

4. Discuss these issues with colleagues. Brainstorm on ways of providing support for children with particular needs. Sort out the ideas which seem to be both productive and practical.

5. Draw out the implications for practice, so that explicit policy decisions for one's actions are identified.

Follow-up: Attempt to develop classroom action which is guided by your policy. Monitor your degree of success.

Activities such as these should help in the development of socially aware teaching and can be applied to issues such as race, social class, beliefs, moral values and gender.

Classroom practice can never, following a dialectical model, fail to have some influence on the development of society at large; in particular, through the ways in which it influences the identity and life-chances of individuals. The development of classroom social policies thus enables a reflective teacher to take conscious control and to contribute productively to micro–macro linkages and to the future of both individual biographies and social history.

3 REFLECTIVE TEACHING AND THE DEMOCRATIC PROCESS

In Chapter 1, we suggested that, in addition to professional responsibilities to implement democratically determined decisions, teachers, as citizens, also have responsibilities to act to influence the nature of such decisions. Teachers have rights and it is perfectly reasonable that they should be active in contributing to the formation of public policy. This role, as White (1978) suggested, is close to that of the activist and the methods to be utilized are those which have been well developed in recent years by a variety of pressure groups.

There are five basic elements of successful pressure group activity:

1. Preparing the case.
2. Identifying decision-makers.
3. Forming alliances.
4. Managing publicity.
5. Lobbying decision-makers.

Such techniques have been evident in recent national debates about the curriculum in primary schools where lobbying of Members of Parliament has taken place. For instance, members of the National Association for Primary Education have been encouraged to write to MPs and the views of the Association were made clear to Education Ministers and to the House of Commons Select Committee on Primary Education. The techniques have also been deployed on more general educational issues such as cutbacks in educational expenditure, the growth of the private sector, corporal punishment in schools and even student grants.

Some national educational pressure groups are now well established. These include CASE (The Campaign for the Advancement of State Education), NCNE (The National Campaign for Nursery Education), NAPE (The National Association for Primary Education), NAME (The National Anti-racist Movement in Education) and NATE (The National Association for the Teaching of English).

At the more local level, pressure-group activity and lobbying by individuals of councillors and education officials also takes place regularly. As two specific examples, we can cite the 1986 NUT campaign in Avon to reduce class-sizes in primary schools and the very successful lobbying of Oxfordshire County Council by parents and the community around Barton First School, Oxford, which had been threatened with closure.

In the Avon case, statistical information and educational arguments were assembled with the help of union officials, colleagues and academics. The support of parents was enlisted and the campaign was publicized. Key political figures representing each of the major political parties were identified on the county council and were lobbied and invited to a seminar to discuss the issues. Continued lobbying led to a reappraisal of policies and a new ordering of priorities for expenditure by the council.

At Barton First School, on the outskirts of Oxford, the proposal to close the school met with the united opposition of the community. Parents, local councillors, clergymen and other community leaders developed a strong and determined campaign. This included letter writing, petitioning, lobbying education officials and councillors, providing publicity material for the Press and demonstrating outside the Council Chamber. The school remained open.

Pressure-group activity and collective action by individuals can thus both bring about new policy priorities and lead to a reappraisal of existing policies. This is an essential feature of democratic decision-making and we would suggest that reflective teachers have both the right and responsibility to contribute to such processes.

We are conscious, though, that this is a book which is primarily designed to support student teachers during periods of school-experience and that activities to influence wider policies may seem inappropriate. We include them because such activity is a logical consequence of taking reflective teaching seriously and because some preparation for such activity is perfectly possible before taking up a full-time teaching post. One of the most important aspects of this is to demystify the democratic process itself and we will make various suggestions on both this and the five elements of pressure-group activity which we have identified. These might be followed up by small groups of students or teachers, perhaps by taking an educational issue as a case study or, indeed, by facing a real current issue.

Demystifying the democratic process

There is a tendency to regard decision-making as something which is done by 'them', an ill-defined, distant and amorphous body. In fact, decisions in democracies are taken by people who are elected representatives and the connection between the ordinary citizen and decision-makers can be much more close, direct and specific. Some possible ways forward here are:

Visit a local council meeting or the House of Commons. Council committee meetings are normally open to the public and attendance at an education committee meeting is likely to be very interesting to reflective teachers.

Visit a local elected representative, MP, councillor or a candidate. Alternatively set up a meeting which they can attend. Discuss their views on educational issues and get them to explain the constraints and pressures within which they serve.

Preparing the case

It is essential to prepare a case well. This requires at least three things:

1. Appropriate factual information about the issue.
2. Good educational arguments in support of whatever is being advocated.
3. Some understanding and responses to the interests and concerns of those whom it is hoped to influence.

Information can be gathered from various statistical sources at a local or national level. For instance, the Statistics Branch of the Department of Science and Education publishes regular statistical information, and other important statistics on more general issues are available from Social Trends and Regional Trends. These are annual Government publications from the Central Statistical Office and should be available in good libraries.

Other sorts of information can be collected through discussion with those people who may be involved locally with the issue under consideration. Newspapers also offer a regular source of reports and comment on educational developments and can be monitored for relevant material.

For good educational arguments, one might want to consult the literature and certainly would wish to discuss the issues under consideration with colleagues.

Regarding the interests of those whom one wishes to influence, a good place to start is with any published policy statements. This could be followed up by discussion and judgements regarding the pressures and constraints which they face.

Identifying decision-makers

Lists of MPs and councillors are normally available in local libraries and from council offices. It is then necessary to identify those who have a particular interest in education and those who have a particular degree of influence over decisions.

A list of members of the education committee on a council or of members of the House of Commons with an interest in education will be helpful.

It is also often appropriate to identify the leaders of political groups and those who speak on educational issues. In addition, the chair of the finance committee on a local council or Treasury Ministers in the House of Commons are likely to be worth identifying—depending, of course, on the issue under consideration.

A further group to identify are the education officers and civil servants who advise decision-makers and implement many decisions. Chief education officers, for instance, can be extremely influential.

Forming alliances

Representative democracy is designed as a system which links decision-making with the views of a majority. It follows that the most successful type of campaigning is likely to be one which is broadly based: one which is produced by an alliance of interested parties bringing concerted pressure to bear on policy-makers.

Reflective teachers may thus wish to act with others if and when they wish to influence public policy. Obvious places to look for allies are:

- Other colleagues, perhaps through trade-union links. The fragmentation of the profession into different unions has been a considerable source of weakness on some issues in the past.

- Parents. The importance of parental support cannot be underestimated. It can help to establish the legitimacy of educational arguments and is a source of much energy and commitment to educational quality.

- Other workers in the public services, perhaps through trade-union links.

- Existing national pressure groups, such as those listed on page 194.

- Local community and interest groups who may be directly or indirectly affected by the issues under consideration.

Managing publicity

Possibilities here include:

- Carrying out a review of the types of media which might be interested in educational issues—press, radio, television, etc.

- Carrying out an analysis of the types of stories or news that each media outlet is likely to be interested in.

- Considering the timing constraints which media outlets face.

- Holding discussions with journalists to get first-hand knowledge of their concerns.

- Holding discussions with people who have had experience of managing publicity to learn from them.

- Preparing some press releases and considering suitable images for photographic purposes.

Lobbying decision-makers

There are any number of possibilities here and we provide a few examples:

- Discrete lobbying through discussion
- Letter-writing by individuals
- Delegations to put arguments
- Petitions
- Leafletting meetings
- Demonstrating with supporters
- Attending council or House of Commons debates to observe

One important strategy is to try to ensure, for as long as possible, that any policy changes can be introduced by politicians with dignity. Not many politicians enjoy being forced to change course, but most are open to persuasion if they have not previously taken up a hard, public position.

CONCLUSION

Education is inevitably concerned not just with 'what is', but also with what 'ought to be' (Kogan 1978). We hope that this book will help teachers and student teachers to develop not only the necessary skills of teaching, but also the reflectivity, awareness and commitment which will ensure the positive nature of their contribution to the education service in the future.

NOTES FOR FURTHER READING

Many of the books suggested as further reading for Chapters 1 and 2 will also be relevant here. Two of those books which we have found particularly challenging are:

Apple, M. (1982) *Education and Power*. London: Routledge & Kegan Paul.
Stenhouse, L. (1982) *Authority, Education and Emancipation*. London: Heinemann.

One more general way of following up many of these issues, particularly to gather information, would be through the use of textbooks in the sociology of education. For two of the most recent, see:

Burgess, R. G. (1986) *Sociology, Education and Schools*. London: Batsford.
Reid, I. (1986) *The Sociology of School and Education*. London: Fontana.

For optimistic assessments of the contribution to education which sociologists might make in collaboration with teachers, see:

Woods, P. and Pollard, A. (eds.) (1987) *Sociology and Teaching: A New Challenge for the Sociology of Education*. London: Croom Helm.

Human rights is an extremely important topic. The most important documents to consider are:

The Universal Declaration of Human Rights. New York: United Nations.

This Declaration was initially agreed in 1948 and is available through United Nations Associations.

The European Convention on Human Rights. Strasbourg: Council of Europe.

This Convention represents a collective guarantee of a number of the principles contained in the Universal Declaration. It came into force in 1953 and all of the twenty-one member states of the Council of Europe have ratified it. It is backed by the European Court of Human Rights. Copies of the Convention and further information is available from: Directorate of Human Rights, Council of Europe, F–67006 Strasbourg, France.

For specific guidance and ideas on classroom practice, see also:

Council of Europe, (1985) *Teaching and Learning about Human Rights in Schools*. Recommendation No. R (85)7 of the Committee of Ministers to Member States. Strasbourg: Council of Europe.
Fisher, S. and Hicks, D. (1985) *World Studies 8–13: A Teacher's Handbook*. Edinburgh: Oliver & Boyd.
Lyseight-Jones, P. (1985) *Human Rights Education in Primary Schools*, Report of Council of Europe Teachers' Seminar No. 28, Donaueschinger. Strasbourg: Council of Europe.
Starkey, H. (1987) *Practical Activities for Teaching and Learning about Human Rights in Schools: A Handbook to Accompany Recommendation R (85)7 of the Committee of Ministers of the Council of Europe*. Strasbourg: Council of Europe.

There is also a considerable amount of literature which is more specifically about children's rights. For an interesting collection of papers, see:

Franklin, B. (ed.) (1986) *The Rights of Children*. Oxford: Blackwell.

For consideration of some of the issues to do with political balance which may be raised, see:

Jones, B. (1986) Politics and the pupil, *Times Educational Supplement*, 30 May.
Wellington, J. J. (ed.) (1986) *Controversial Issues in the Curriculum*. Oxford: Blackwell.

Action by reflective teachers within the democratic process calls for some knowledge of political structures and processes. For excellent introductions, see:

Kogan, M. (1978) *The Politics of Educational Change*. London: Fontana.
Madgwick, P. J. (1976) *An Introduction to British Politics*. London: Hutchinson.

For analyses of recent conditions among local authority policy-makers, advisers and school governors respectively, see:

Hewton, E. (1986) *Education in Recession: Crisis in County Hall and Classroom*. London: Allen & Unwin.
Winkley, D. (1985) *Diplomats and Detectives: LEA Advisers at Work*. London: Robert Royce.
Kogan, M., Johnson, D., Packwood, T. and Whitaker, T. (1984) *School Governing Bodies*. London: Heinemann.

Bibliography

Adelman, C. (ed.) (1981) *Uttering, Muttering*. London: Grant McIntyre.

Adelman, C. and Alexander, R. (1982) *The Self-Evaluating Institution*. London: Methuen.

Adelman, C and Walker, R. (1975) *A Guide to Classroom Observation*. London: Methuen.

Adler, A. (1927) *The Practice and Theory of Individual Psychology*. New York: Harcourt.

Alexander, R. J. (1984) *Primary Teaching*. London: Holt, Rinehart & Winston.

Allen, I. *et al.* (1975) *Working an Integrated Day*. London: Ward Lock.

Althusser, L. (1971) Ideology and the ideological state apparatuses, in Cosin, B. R. (ed.) *Education, Structure and Society*. Harmondsworth: Penguin.

Anderson, C. S. (1982) The search for school climate: a review of the research, *Review of Educational Research*, **52**, 368–420.

Anning, A. (1983) The three year itch, *Times Educational Supplement*, 24 June.

Anthony, W. (1979) Progressive learning theories: the evidence, in Bernbaum, G. (ed.) *Schooling in Decline*. London: Macmillan.

Apple, M. W. (1979) The hidden curriculum and the nature of conflict, *Interchange*, **2** (4), 27–40.

Apple, M. W. (1982a) *Education and Power*. London: Routledge & Kegan Paul.

Apple, M. W. (1982b) Curricular form and the logic of technical control: building the possessive individual, in Apple, M. W. (ed.) *Cultural and Economic Reproduction in Education*. London: Routledge & Kegan Paul.

Archer, M. S. (1979) *The Social Origins of Educational Systems*. Beverley Hills, CA: Sage.

Armstrong, M. (1980) *Closely Observed Children*. London: Writers & Readers.

Ashton, P. M. (1981) Primary teachers' aims 1969–77, in Simon, B. and Willcocks, J. (eds.) *Research and Practice in the Primary Classroom*. London: Routledge & Kegan Paul.

Ashton, P. M. *et al.* (1975) *The Aims of Primary Education: A Study of Teacher Opinions*. London: Macmillan.

Avann, P. (ed.) (1985) *Teaching Information Skills in the Primary School*. London: Edward Arnold.

Ball, S. J. (1980) Initial encounters in the classroom and the process of establishment, in Woods, P. (ed.) *Pupil Strategies*. London: Croom Helm.

Ball, S. J. (1981) *Beachside Comprehensive*. Cambridge: Cambridge University Press.

Ball, S. J. and Goodson, I. F. (1985) *Teachers' Lives and Careers*. London: Falmer Press.

Bantock, G. H. (1965) *Education and Values, Essays in the Theory of Education*. London: Faber & Faber.

Bantock, G. H. (1980) *Dilemmas of the Curriculum*. Oxford: Martin Robinson.

Barker, R. G. (1978) *Habitats, Environments and Human Behavior*. San Francisco: Josey Bass.

Barnes, D. (1982) *Practical Curriculum Study*. London: Routledge & Kegan Paul.

Barnes, D., Britton, E. and Rosen, H. (1969) *Language, the Learner and the School*. Harmondsworth: Penguin.

Barr, M., D'Arcy, P. and Healy, M. K. (eds.) (1982) *What's Going On? Language/Learning Episodes in British and American Classrooms, Grades 4–13*. Montclair: Boynton/Cook.

Barrow, R. (1975) *Moral Philosophy for Education*. London: Allen & Unwin.

Barrow, R. (1984) *Giving Teaching back to Teachers*. Brighton: Wheatsheaf.

Barton, L. and Lawn, M. (1980/81) Back inside the whale: a curriculum case study, *Interchange*, **11** (4).

Bassey, M. (1978) *Practical Classroom Organisation in the Primary School*. London: Ward Lock.

Beech, J. (1985) *Learning to Read*. London: Croom Helm.

Bennett, N. (1979) Recent research on teaching: A dream, a belief and a model, in Bennett, N. and McNamara, R. (eds.) *Focus on Teaching*, London: Longman.

Bennett, N., Desforges, C., Cockburn, A. and Wilkinson, E. (1984) *The Quality of Pupil Learning Experiences*. London: Lawrence Erlbaum.
Berger, P. L. (1963) *Invitation to Sociology: A Humanistic Perspective*. New York: Doubleday.
Berger, P. L. and Luckman, T. (1967) *The Social Construction of Reality*. London: Allen Lane.
Berlak, H. and Berlak, A. (1981) *Dilemmas of Schooling*. London: Methuen.
Blenkin, G. M. and Kelly, A. V. (1981) *The Primary Curriculum*. London: Harper & Row.
Blenkin, G. M. and Kelly, A. V. (eds.) (1983) *The Primary Curriculum in Action*. London: Harper & Row.
Blishen, E. (1969) *The School That I'd Like*. Harmondsworth: Penguin.
Bloom, B. S. *et al.* (1956) *Taxonomy of Educational Objectives I: Cognitive Domain*. London: Longman.
Blyth, W. A. L. (1975) *Place, Time and Society, 8–11*. London: Collins.
Blyth, W. A. L. (1984) *Development, Experience and Curriculum in Primary Education*. London: Croom Helm.
Board of Education (1931) *The Primary School* (Hadow Report). London: HMSO.
Bolam, R. (1982) *Strategies for School Improvement*. Paris: OECD.
Bolster, A. (1983) Towards a more effective model of research on teaching, *Harvard Educational Review*, **53** (3), 294–308.
Borg, W. R. (1981) *Applying Educational Research: A Practical Guide for Teachers*. New York: Longman.
Bossert, S. T. (1979) *Tasks and Social Relationships in Classrooms*. Cambridge: Cambridge University Press.
Bourdieu, P. and Passeron, J. C. (1977) *Reproduction in Education, Society and Culture*. Beverley Hills: Sage.
Bowles, S. and Gintis, H. (1976) *Schooling in Capitalist America*. London: Routledge & Kegan Paul.
Boydell, D. (1978) *The Primary Teacher in Action*. London: Open Books.
Bronfenbrenner, U. (1979) *The Ecology of Human Development; Experiments in Nature and Design*. Cambridge, Mass.: Harvard University Press.
Brookover, W. P. and Thomas, P. (1965) *Self Concept and Academic Ability* (Research Project No. 8451636). Michigan: Michigan State University.
Brophy, J. E. and Good, T. L. (1974) *Teacher–Student Relationships*. New York: Holt, Rinehart & Winston.
Bruner, J. S. (1964) The course of cognitive growth, *Journal of American Psychology*, **18,** 1–15.
Bruner, J. S. (1968) *Towards a Theory of Instruction*. New York: Norton.
Bruner, J. S. (1977) *The Process of Instruction*. Cambridge, Mass.: Harvard University Press.
Bruner, J. S., Goodnow, J. J. and Austin, G. A. (1956) *A Study of Thinking*. New York: Wiley.
Burgess, R. G. (ed.) (1982) *Field Research: A Sourcebook and Field Manual*. London: Allen & Unwin.
Burgess, R. G. (1984) *In the Field: An Introduction to Field Research*. London: Allen & Unwin.
Burgess, R. G. (1986) *Sociology, Education and Schools*. London: Batsford.
Burgess, T. and Adams, E. (eds.) (1980) *Outcomes of Education*. Basingstoke: Macmillan.
Burns, R. B. (1982) *Self-concept Development and Education*. London: Holt, Rinehart & Winston.
Calderhead, J. and Miller, E. (1986) *The Integration of Subject Matter Knowledge in Student Teachers' Classroom Practice*. Lancaster: University of Lancaster.
Callaghan, J. (1976) Towards a national debate—the Prime Minister's Ruskin speech, *Education*, 22 Oct., 332–3.
Calvert, B. (1975) *The Role of the Pupil*. London: Routledge & Kegan Paul.
Campbell, R. J. (1985) *Developing the Primary School Curriculum*. London: Holt, Rinehart & Winston.
Cane, B. and Schroeder, C. (1970) *The Teacher and Research*. Slough: NFER.
Capra, F. (1982) Buddhist physics, in Kumar, S. (ed.) *The Schumacher Lectures*. London: Abacus.
Carnoy, M. and Levin, H. M. (1985) *Schooling and Work in the Democratic State*. Stanford: Stanford University Press.
Carr, W. and Kemmis, S. (1986) *Becoming Critical*. London: Falmer Press.
Cattell, R. B. and Kline, P. (1977) *The Scientific Analysis of Personality and Motivation*. London: Academic Press.

Central Advisory Council on Education (1967) *Children and Their Primary Schools* (The Plowden Report). London: HMSO.

Child, D. (1981) *Psychology and the Teacher*. London: Holt, Rinehart & Winston.

Clandinin, D. J. (1986) *Classroom Practice: Teacher Images in Action*. London: Falmer Press.

Clarricoates, K. (1978) Dinosaurs in the classroom—a re-examination of some aspects of the 'hidden' curriculum in primary schools, *Women's Studies International Quarterly*, **1**, 353–364.

Clarricoates, K. (1981) The experience of patriarchal schooling, *Interchange*, **12** (2–3), 185–205.

Clift, P., Weiner, G. and Wilson, E. (1981) *Record Keeping in the Primary School*. London: Macmillan.

Cohen, L. (1976) *Educational Research in Classrooms and Schools: A Manual of Materials and Methods*. London: Harper & Row.

Cohen, L. and Holliday, M. (1979) *Statistics for Education*. London: Harper & Row.

Cohen, L. and Manion, L. (1980) *Research Methods in Education*. London: Croom Helm.

Cohen, L. and Manion, L. (1981) *Perspectives on Classrooms and Schools*. London: Holt, Rinehart & Winston.

Cohen, L., Thomas, J. and Manion, L. (1982) *Educational Research and Development in Britain, 1970–1980*. Slough: NFER.

Coleman, J. S., Coser, L. A. and Powell, W. W. (1966) *Equality of Educational Opportunity*. Washington: US Government Printing Office.

Collett, P. (ed.) (1977) *Social Rules and Social Behaviour*. Oxford: Blackwell.

Collins, R. (1975) *Conflict Sociology*. London: Academic Press.

Collins, R. (1977) Some comparative principles of educational stratification, *Higher Education Review*, **47** (1).

Connell, R. W. (1985) *Teachers' Work*. London: Allen & Unwin.

Connell, R. W., Ashden, D. J., Kessler, S. and Dowsett, G. W. (1982) *Making the Difference; Schools, Families and Social Division*. Sydney: Allen & Unwin.

Corrie, M., Haystead, J. and Zaklukiewicz, S. (1982) *Classroom Management Strategies*. Edinburgh: Scottish Council for Research in Education.

Council of Europe (1985) *Recommendation No. R(85)7 of the Committee of Ministers to Member States on Teaching and Learning about Human Rights in Schools*. Strasbourg: Council of Europe.

Cox, C. B. and Dyson, A. E. (eds.) (1969) *Fight for Education: A Black Paper*. London: Critical Quarterly Society.

Cranfield, J. and Wells, H. (1976) *100 Ways to Enhance Self-concept in the Classroom*. New Jersey: Prentice Hall.

Croll, P. (1986) *Systematic Classroom Observation*. London: Falmer Press.

Croll, P. and Moses, D. (1985) *One in Five*. London: Routledge & Kegan Paul.

Cullingford, C. (1985) *Parents, Teachers and Schools*. London: Robert Royce.

Cyster, R., Clift, P. S. and Battle, S. (1980) *Parental Involvement in Primary Schools*. Slough: NFER.

Dale, R. (1977) Implications of the rediscovery of the hidden curriculum, in Gleedson, D. (ed.) *Identity and Structure*. Driffield: Nafferton.

Davey, A. (1983) *Learning to be Prejudiced*. London: Edward Arnold.

Davies, B. (1982) *Life in the Classroom and Playground*. London: Routledge & Kegan Paul.

Day, C., Johnston, D. and Whitaker, P. (1985) *Managing Primary Schools*. London: Harper & Row.

Dean, J. (1983) *Organising Learning in the Primary School Classroom*. London: Croom Helm.

Dearden, R. F. (1968) *The Philosophy of Primary Education*. London: Routledge & Kegan Paul.

Delamont, S. (1983) *Interaction in the Classroom*. 2nd edn. London: Methuen.

Denscombe, M. (1980) The work context of teaching: an analytical framework for the study of teachers in classrooms, *British Journal of Sociology of Education*, **1** (3), 279–292.

Department of Education and Science (1975) *A Language for Life* (The Bullock Report). London: HMSO.

Department of Education and Science (1977) *Education in Schools: a Consultative Document*, Green Paper, Cmd. 6869. London: HMSO.

Department of Education and Science (1978a) *Primary Education in England: A Survey by HM Inspectors of Schools*. London: HMSO.

Department of Education and Science (1978b) *Report of the Committee of Enquiry into the Education of Handicapped Children and Young People* (The Warnock Report). London: HMSO.

Department of Education and Science (1980) *A View of the Curriculum*. London: HMSO.
Department of Education and Science (1981) *The School Curriculum*. London: HMSO.
Department of Education and Science (1984) *English 5–16, Curriculum Matters 1*, an HMI series. London: HMSO.
Department of Education and Science (1985a) *The Curriculum from 5 to 16, Curriculum Matters 2*, an HMI series. London: HMSO.
Department of Education and Science (1985b) *The Effects of Local Authority Expenditure Policies on Education Provision in England*. London: HMSO.
de Vars, D. A. (1986) *Surveys in Social Research*. London: Allen & Unwin.
Dewey, J. (1916) *Democracy and Education*. New York: Free Press.
Dewey, J. (1933) *How We Think: A Restatement of the Relation of Reflective Thinking to the Educative Process*. Chicago: Henry Regnery.
Dickson, W. P. (ed.) (1981) *Children's Oral Communication Skills*. New York: Academic Press.
Dillon, J. (1983) Problem solving and findings, *Journal of Creative Behaviour*, **16** (2), 97–111.
Dixon, R. (1977) *Catching Them Young. 1. Sex, Race and Class in Children's Fiction*. London: Pluto Press.
Docking, J. W. (1980) *Control and Discipline in Schools*. London: Harper & Row.
Donaldson, M. (1978) *Children's Minds*. London: Fontana.
Donaldson, M., Grieve, R. and Pratt, C. (eds.) (1983) *Early Childhood Development and Education*. Oxford: Blackwell.
Doyle, N. (1977) Learning the classroom environment: an ecological analysis, *Journal of Teacher Education*, **28** (6), 51–5.
Doyle, W. and Ponder, C. A. (1976) The practicality ethic in teacher decision-making, *Interchange*, **8**.
Dreeben, R. (1968) *On What Is Learned in School*. Manchester: Addison-Wesley.
Easen, P. (1985) *Making School-Centred INSET Work*. London: Croom Helm.
Ebbutt, D. (1983) Educational action research: some general concerns and specific quibbles, *Mimeo*. Cambridge: Cambridge Institute of Education.
Ede, J. and Wilkinson, J. (1980) *Talking, Listening and Learning*. London: Longman.
Edwards, A. D. and Westgate, D. P. G. (1987) *Investigating Classroom Talk*. London: Falmer Press.
Edwards, V. (1983) *Language in the Multicultural Classroom*. London: Batsford.
Egan, K. (1983) *Educational Development*. Oxford: Oxford University Press.
Eisner, E. W. (1969) Instructional and expressive educational objectives, in Popham, W. J. *et al.* (eds.) *Instructions Objectives* (AERA Monograph No. 3). Chicago: Rand McNally.
Eisner, E. W. (1985) *The Art of Educational Evaluation: A Personal View*. London: Falmer Press.
Eisner, E. W. and Vallance, E. (eds.) (1974) *Competing Conceptions of the Curriculum*. Berkeley: McCutchan.
Elbaz, F. (1983) *Teacher Thinking—a Study of Practical Knowledge*. London: Croom Helm.
Elliott, J. (1980) Implications of classroom research for professional development, in Hoyle, E. and McGary, J. (eds.) *World Year Book of Education*. London: Kogan Page.
Elliott, J. (1981) 'Action research: a Framework for Self-Evaluation in Schools', Teacher–pupil Interaction and the Quality of Learning Project, Working Paper No. 1. Cambridge: Cambridge Institute of Education.
Elliott, J. and Adelman, C. (1973) Reflecting where the action is; the design of the Ford Teaching Project, *Education for Teaching*, **92**, 8–20.
Elliott, J. and Connolly, K. (1974) Hierarchical structure in skill development, in Connolly, K. and Bruner, J. S. (eds.) *The Growth of Competence*. London: Academic Press.
Ennever, L. (1972) *With Objectives in Mind: Guide to Science 5–13*. London: Macdonald Educational.
Entwistle, N. (1981) *Styles of Learning and Teaching*. Chichester: Wiley.
Entwistle, N. (ed.) (1985) *New Directions in Educational Psychology: Learning and Teaching*. London: Falmer Press.
Etzioni, A. (1961) *A Comparative Analysis of Complex Organisations*. New York: Free Press of Glencoe.
Evans, K. M. (1962) *Sociometry and Education*. London: Routledge & Kegan Paul.
Eysenck, H. J. and Cookson, D. (1969) Personality in primary school children, I: Ability and achievement, *British Journal of Educational Psychology*, **39**, 109–122.
Finch, J. (1986) *Research and Policy*. London: Falmer Press.

Fink, A. and Kosecoff, J. (1986) *How to Conduct Surveys: A Step by Step Guide*. London: Sage.

Finlayson, D. S. (1970) A follow up study of school achievement in relation to personality, *British Journal of Educational Psychology*, **40**, 344–347.

Fisher, S. and Hicks, D. (1985) *World Studies 8–13: A Teacher's Handbook*. Edinburgh: Oliver & Boyd.

Flanders, N. (1970) *Analysing Teaching Behavior*. Reading, Mass.: Addison-Wesley.

Fontana, D. (1981) *Psychology for Teachers*. London: Macmillan.

Fontana, D. (1986) *Classroom Control*. London: Methuen.

Franklin, B. (1986) *The Rights of Children*. Oxford: Blackwell.

Fransson, A. (1977) On qualitative differences in learning, IV: Effects of motivation and test anxiety on process and outcome, *British Journal of Educational Psychology*, **47**, 244–257.

Fraser, B. J. (1986) *Classroom Environment*. London: Croom Helm.

Fraser, B. J. and Fisher, D. L. (1984) *Assessment of Classroom Psychosocial Environment: Workshop Manual*. Bentley: Western Australia Institute of Technology.

Freeman, P. L. (1986) Don't talk to me about lexical meta-analysis of criterion-referenced clustering and lap-dissolve spatial transformations: a consideration of the role of practising teachers in educational research, *British Educational Research Journal*, **12** (2), 197–206.

French, P. and MacLure, M. (1983) Teachers' questions, pupils' answers: an investigation of questions and answers in the infant classroom, in Stubbs, M. and Hillier, H. (eds.) *Readings on Language, Schools and Classrooms*. London: Methuen.

Gagné, R. M. (1975) *Essentials of Learning for Instruction*. New York: Holt, Rinehart & Winston.

Galton, M. (1986) Attitudes and the infant teacher, *Child Education*, June.

Galton, M. J. (1978) *British Mirrors: A Collection of Classroom Observation Systems*. Leicester: School of Education, University of Leicester.

Galton, M., Simon, B. and Croll, P. (1980) *Inside the Primary Classroom*. London: Routledge & Kegan Paul.

Ghaye, A. L. (1984) Discovering classroom underlife: a prerequisite for assessing the match between what is taught and learned . . ., Paper presented at the Classroom Action Research Conference, Cambridge Institute of Education.

Giles, R. H. (1977) *The West Indian Experience in British Schools*. London: Heinemann.

Glaser, B. and Strauss, A. (1967) *The Discovery of Grounded Theory*. Chicago: Aldine.

Goffman, C. (1959) *The Presentation of Self in Everyday Life*. New York: Doubleday.

Golby, M., Greenwald, J. and West, R. (1975) *Curriculum Design*. London: Croom Helm.

Good, T. and Brophy, J. (1978) *Looking in Classrooms*. New York: Harper & Row.

Goodnow, J. and Burns, A. (1985) *Home and School: A Child's Eye View*. Sydney: Allen & Unwin.

Gorman, T. (1985) Language assessment and language teaching: innovation and interaction, in Wells, G. and Nicholls, J. (eds.) *Language and Learning: An Interactional Perspective*. London: Falmer Press.

Grace, G. (1978) *Teachers, Ideology and Control*. London: Routledge & Kegan Paul.

Grace, G. (1985) Judging teachers; the social and political contexts of teacher evaluation, *British Journal of Sociology of Education*, **6** (1), 3–16.

Grant, K. A. (ed.) (1984) *Preparing for Reflective Teaching*. Boston: Allyn & Bacon.

Gunning, D., Gunning, S. and Wilson, J. (1981) *Topic Teaching in the Primary School*. London: Croom Helm.

Halsey, A. H. (1986) *Change in British Society*. Oxford: Oxford University Press.

Halsey, A. H., Heath, A. F. and Ridge, J. M. (1980) *Origins and Destinations*. Oxford: Oxford University Press.

Hamilton, D. (1977) *In Search of Structure*. Edinburgh: Scottish Council for Research in Education.

Hammersley, M. (ed.) (1986) *Case Studies in Educational Research*. Milton Keynes: Open University Press.

Hammersley, M. (ed.) (1986) *Controversies in Classroom Research*. Milton Keynes: Open University Press.

Hammersley, M. and Atkinson, P. (1983) *Ethnography: Principles in Practice*. London: Tavistock.

Hargreaves, A. (1978) The significance of classroom coping strategies, in Barton, L. and Meighan, R. (eds.) *Sociological Interpretations of Schooling and Classrooms*. Driffield: Nafferton.

Hargreaves, D. H. (1967) *Social Relations in a Secondary School*. London: Routledge & Kegan Paul.

Hargreaves, D. H. (1972) *Interpersonal Relationships and Education*. London: Routledge & Kegan Paul.

Hargreaves, D. H., Hestor, S. K. and Mellor, F. J. (1975) *Deviance in Classrooms*. London: Routledge & Kegan Paul.

Harlen, W. (1975) *Science 5–13: A Formative Evaluation*. London: Macmillan.

Harlen, W. (1977) *Match and Mismatch. 1. Raising Questions, 2. Finding Answers*. London: Oliver & Boyd for the Schools Council.

Harlen, W. (1985) *Primary Science: Taking the Plunge*. London: Heinemann.

Harré, R. (1974) Rules as a scientific concept, in Mischel, T. (ed.) *Understanding Other Persons*. Oxford: Blackwell

Harré, R. (1979) *Personal Being*. Oxford: Blackwell

Harré, R. and Secord, P. F. (1971) *The Explanation of Social Behaviour*. Oxford: Blackwell

Hartley, D. (1985) *Understanding Primary Schools*. London: Croom Helm.

Hartnett, A. (ed.) (1982) *The Social Sciences in Educational Studies: A Selective Guide to the Literature*. London: Heinemann.

Hewton, E. (1986) *Education in Recession: Crisis in County Hall and Classroom*. London: Allen & Unwin.

Hillgate Group (1987) *Whose Schools? A Radical Manifesto*. London: Impact Mailing.

Hilsum, S. and Cane, B. S. (1971) *The Teacher's Day*. Slough: NFER.

Hirst, P. H. (1965) Liberal education and the nature of knowledge, in Archambault, R. (ed.) *Philosophical Analysis and Education*. London: Routledge & Kegan Paul.

Hirst, P. H. (1975) *The Curriculum and Its Objectives*. London: Doris Lee Lectures, London Institute of Education.

Hirst, P. H. and Peters, R. S. (1970) *The Logic of Education*. London: Routledge & Kegan Paul.

Hohmann, M., Banet, B. and Weikart, D. (1979) *Young Children in Action*. Ypsilanti, Mich.: High Scope Educational Research Foundation.

Holt, J. (1969) *How Children Fail*. Harmondsworth: Penguin.

Hook, C. (1981) *Studying Classrooms*. Victoria: Deakin University Press.

Hopkins, D. (1986) *A Teacher's Guide to Classroom Research*. Milton Keynes: Open University Press.

Hopkins, D. and Wideen, M. (eds.) (1984) *Alternative Perspectives on School Improvement*. London: Falmer Press.

Horton, T. and Raggit, P. (eds.) (1982) *Challenge and Change in the Curriculum*. London: Croom Helm.

House of Commons (1986) *Achievement in Primary Schools*, Third Report of the Education, Science and Arts Committee. London: HMSO.

Hoyle, E. (1986) *The Politics of School Management*. London: Hodder & Stoughton.

Hull, R. (1985) *The Language Gap*. London: Methuen.

Humphries, S. (1981) *Hooligans or Rebels?* Oxford: Blackwell

Hustler, D., Cassidy, T. and Cuff, T. (1986) *Action Research in Classrooms and Schools*. London: Allen & Unwin.

Jackson, P. W. (1968) *Life in Classrooms*. New York: Holt, Rinehart & Winston.

Jencks, C. *et al.* (1972) *Inequality: A Reassessment of the Effect of Family and Schooling in America*. New York: Basic Books.

Johnson, D. W. and Johnson, R. T. (1975) *Learning Together and Learning Alone*. New Jersey: Prentice Hall.

Jones, B. (1986) Politics and the pupil, *Times Educational Supplement*, 30 May.

Kagan, J. (1965) Reflection—impulsivity and reading ability in primary grade children, *Child Development*, **36**, 609–628.

Kagan, J. and Kogan, N. (1970) Individual variation in cognitive processes, in Mussel, P. (ed.) *Carmichael's Manual of Child Psychology*, 3rd ed., vol. 1. New York: Wiley.

Kagan, J. *et al.* (1964) Information processing in the child: significance and reflective attitudes, *Psychological Monographs*, **78**.

Kellmer-Pringle, M. (1974) *The Needs of Children*. London: Hutchinson.

Kelly, A. V. (1982) *The Curriculum: Theory and Practice*. London: Harper & Row.

Kelly, A. V. (1986) *Knowledge and the Curriculum*. London: Harper & Row.

Kemmis, S. and McTaggart, R. (1981) *The Action Research Planner*. Victoria: Deakin University Press.

Kerry, T. (1982) *Effective Questioning*. London: Macmillan.
Kerry, T. and Sands, M. K. (1982) *Handling Classroom Groups*. London: Macmillan.
King, R. (1978) *All Things Bright and Beautiful?* Chichester: Wiley.
Kirby, R. and Radford, J. (1976) *Individual Differences*. London: Methuen.
Kogan, J. (1965) Reflection-impulsivity and reading disability in primary children, *Child Development*, **36**, 609–28.
Kogan, M. (1978) *The Politics of Educational Change*. London: Fontana.
Kogan, M., Johnson, D., Packwood, T. and Whitaker, T. (1984) *School Governing Bodies*. London: Heinemann.
Kounin, J. S. (1970) *Discipline and Group Management in Classrooms*. New York: Holt, Rinehart & Winston.
Labov, W. (1973) The logic of non-standard English, in Keddie, N. (ed.) *Tinker, Tailor . . . the Myth of Cultural Deprivation*. Harmondsworth: Penguin.
Lacey, C. (1970) *Hightown Grammar*. Manchester: Manchester University Press.
Lang, R. (1986) *Developing Parental Involvement*. London: Macmillan.
Laslett, R. and Smith, C. (1984) *Effective Classroom Management*. London: Croom Helm.
Lawn, M. and Ozga, J. (1986) Unequal partners: teachers under indirect rule, *British Journal of Sociology of Education*, **7** (2), 225–238.
Lawrence, D. (1974) *Improved Reading Through Counselling*. London: Ward Lock.
Lawton, D. (1975) *Class, Culture and the Curriculum*. London: Routledge & Kegan Paul.
Lawton, D. (1977) *Education and Social Justice*. Beverley Hills: Sage.
Lawton, D. (1980) *The Politics of the School Curriculum*. London: Routledge & Kegan Paul.
Lewin, K. (1935) *A Dynamic Theory of Personality*. New York: McGraw.
Lewin, K. (1946) Action research and minority problems, *Journal of Social Issues*, **2**, 34–6.
Lobban, G. (1975) Sex roles in reading schemes, *Forum*, **16** (2), 57–60.
Lubeck, S. (1985) *Sandbox Society*. London: Falmer Press.
Lyseight-Jones, P. (1985) *Human Rights Education in Primary Schools*, Report of Council of Europe Teachers' Seminar No. 28, Donaueschingen, June. Strasbourg: Council of Europe.
McCall, G. and Simmons, J. (eds.) (1969) *Issues in Participant Observation*. London: Addison-Wesley.
McClelland (1963) The achievement motive in economic growth, in Hoselitz, B. F. and Moore, W. E. (eds.) *Industrialisation and Society*. The Hague: UNESCO.
McMahon *et al.* (1984) *Guidelines for the Review and Internal Development of Schools: Primary School Handbook*. London: Schools Council/Longman.
McNamara, D. and Desforges, C. (1978) The social sciences, teacher education and the objectification of craft knowledge, *British Journal of Teacher Education*, **4** (1), 17–36.
Madgwick, P. J. (1976) *An Introduction to British Politics*. London: Hutchinson.
Makins, V. (1969) Child's eye view of teachers, *Times Educational Supplement*, 19 and 26 September.
Marriott, S. (1985) *Primary Education and Society*. London: Falmer Press.
Maslow, A. H. (1954) *Motivation and Personality*. New York: Harper & Row.
Mead, G. H. (1934) *Mind, Self and Society*. Chicago: University of Chicago.
Meadows, S. (ed.) (1983) *Developing Thinking*. London: Methuen.
Mehan, H. (1974) Accomplishing classroom lessons, in Cicourel, A. *et al.* (eds.) *Language Use and School Performance*. New York: Academic Press.
Meighan, R. (1978) The learners' viewpoint, *Educational Review*, **30** (2).
Meighan, R. (1981) *A Sociology of Educating*. London: Holt, Rinehart & Winston.
Mills, C. W. (1959) *The Sociological Imagination*. New York: Oxford University Press.
Moos, R. H. (1979) *Evaluating Educational Environments: Procedures, Measures, Findings and Policy Implications*. San Francisco: Jossey-Bass.
Moran, P. R. (1971) The integrated day, *Educational Research*, **14**, 65–9.
Mortimore, P., Sammons, P., Stoll, L., Lewis, D. and Ecob, R. (1986) *The Junior School Project*. London: Inner London Education Authority.
Nash, R. (1976) *Teacher Expectations and Pupil Learning*. London: Routledge & Kegan Paul.
Nias, J. (1981) Commitment and motivation in primary school teachers, *Educational Review* (33), 181–190.
Nias, J. (1984a) The definition and maintenance of self in primary teaching, *British Journal of Sociology of Education*, **5** (3), 267–280.
Nias, J. (1984b) Learning and acting the role: in-school support for primary teachers, *Educational Review* (36), 1–15.

Nias, J. (forthcoming) *Becoming and Being a Primary School Teacher*. London: Methuen.

Nixon, J. (1981) *A Teachers' Guide to Action Research*. London: Grant McIntyre.

Open University (1979) *Research Methods in Education and the Social Sciences* (DE304). Milton Keynes: Open University Press.

Open University (1980) *Curriculum in Action: Practical Classroom Evaluation* (P533). Milton Keynes: Open University Press.

Open University (1982) *Curriculum Evaluation and Assessment in Educational Institutions* (E364). Milton Keynes: Open University Press.

Opie, I. and Opie, P. (1959) *Children's Games in Street and Playground*. Oxford: Oxford University Press.

Orlick, T. (1979) *Cooperative Sports and Games Book: Challenge Without Competition*. London: Writers & Readers.

Osborn, A. F., Butler, N. R. and Morris, A. C. (1984) *The Social Life of Britain's Five-Year-Olds*. London: Routledge & Kegan Paul.

Ozga, J. T. and Lawn, M. (1981) *Teachers, Professionalism and Class*. London: Falmer Press.

Parsons, T. (1951) *The Social System*. London: Routledge & Kegan Paul.

Parsons, T. (1959) The school class as a social system, *Harvard Educational Review*, **24** (4).

Pask, G. (1976) Styles and strategies of learning, *British Journal of Educational Psychology*, **46**, 128–148.

Peck, D. and Whitlow, D. (1975) *Approaches to Personality Theory*. London: Methuen.

Peters, R. S. (1966) *Ethics and Education*. London: Allen & Unwin.

Phelps, R. (1969) *Display in the Classroom*. Oxford: Blackwell.

Phillips, T. (1985) Beyond lip-service: discourse development after the age of nine, in Wells, G. and Nicholls, J. (eds.) *Language and Learning: An Interactional Perspective*. London: Falmer Press.

Piaget, J. (1926) *The Language and Thought of the Child*. New York: Basic Books.

Piaget, J. (1950) *The Psychology of Intelligence*. London: Routledge & Kegan Paul.

Pollard, A. (1979) Negotiating deviance and 'getting done' in primary school classrooms, in Barton, L. and Meighan, R. (eds.) *Schools, Pupils and Deviance*. Driffield: Nafferton.

Pollard, A. (1980) Teacher interests and changing situations of survival threat in primary school classrooms, in Woods, P. *Teacher Strategies*. London: Croom Helm.

Pollard, A. (1982) A model of coping strategies, *British Journal of Sociology of Education*, **3** (1), 19–37.

Pollard, A. (1985) *The Social World of the Primary School*. London: Holt, Rinehart & Winston.

Pollard, A. (1987) Primary school-teachers and their colleagues, in Delamont, S. (ed.) *The Primary School Teacher*. London: Falmer Press.

Pollard, A. (ed.) (1987) *Children and Their Primary Schools: A New Perspective*. London: Falmer Press.

Popper, K. R. (1968) *The Logic of Scientific Discovery*. London: Hutchinson.

Pring, R. (1976) Curriculum integration, in Hooper, R. (ed.) *The Curriculum; Context, Design and Development*. London: Oliver & Boyd.

Pring, R. (1984) *Personal and Social Education in the Curriculum*. London: Hodder & Stoughton.

Prisk, D. M. (1987) Letting them get on with it: a study of unsupervised group talk in an infant school, in Pollard, A. (ed.) *Children and Their Primary Schools: A New Perspective*. London: Falmer Press.

Prutzman, P., Burger, M. L., Bodenhamer, G. and Stern, L. (1978) *The Friendly Classroom for a Small Planet*. Wayne, New Jersey: Avery Publishing. (Available from Centre for Global Education, York University).

Radical Statistics Education Group (1982) *Reading Between the Numbers: A Critical Guide to Educational Research*. London: BSSRS Publications.

Reid, I. (1977) *Social Class Differences in Britain*. London: Open Books.

Reid, I. (1986) *The Sociology of School and Education*. London: Fontana.

Richards, J. (1979) *Classroom Language: What Sort?* London: Allen & Unwin.

Richards, M. and Light, P. (eds.) (1986) *Children of Social Worlds*. Oxford: Polity Press.

Rist, R. (1970) Student social class and teacher expectations, *Harvard Education Review*, **40**, 411–51.

Roberts, T. (1983) *Child Management in the Primary School*. London: Allen & Unwin.

Roberts, T. (1986) Reflection-impulsivity and lack of success in reading, *Support for Learning*, **1** (2), 8–13.

Rodger, I. A. and Richardson, J. A. S. (1985) *Self-Evaluation for Primary Schools*. London: Hodder & Stoughton.

Rogers, C. R. (1961) *On Becoming a Person*. London: Constable.

Rogers, C. R. (1969) *Freedom to Learn*. New York: Merrill.

Rogers, C. (1980) *A Way of Being*. Boston: Houghton Mifflin.

Rostow, W. W. (1962) *The Stages of Economic Growth*. Cambridge: Cambridge University Press.

Rowland, S. (1984) *The Enquiring Classroom*. London: Falmer Press.

Rowland, S. (1987) Child in control: towards an interpretive model of teaching and learning, in Pollard, A. (ed.) *Children and Their Primary Schools: A New Perspective*. London: Falmer Press.

Rowntree, D. (1977) *How Shall We Know Them*. London: Harper & Row.

Royal Society/Institute of Mathematics and Its Applications (1986) *Girls and Mathematics*. London: Royal Society/Institute of Mathematics and Its Applications.

Rubin, Z. (1980) *Children's Friendships*. London: Fontana.

Ruddock, J. (1970) *Learning to Talk Through Discussion*. Centre for Applied Research in Education, Occasional Publication No. 8, University of East Anglia.

Ruddock, J. and Hopkins, D. (1985) *Research as a Basis for Teaching*. London: Heinemann.

Ryle, G. (1967) *The Concept of Mind*. London: Hutchinson.

Sallis, J. (1987) *Schools, Parents and Governors: A New Approach to Accountability*. London: Croom Helm.

Salmon, P. and Claire, H. (1984) *Classroom Collaboration*. London: Routledge & Kegan Paul.

Saunders, M. (1979) *Class Control and Behaviour Problems*. Maidenhead: McGraw Hill.

Saunders, M. (1982) *Multicultural Teaching*. Maidenhead: McGraw Hill.

Schon, D. A. (1983) *The Reflective Practitioner*. London: Temple Smith.

Schools Council (1983) *Primary Practice, Working Paper 75*. London: Methuen Educational.

Schultz, T. (1961) Investment in human capital, *American Economic Review*, **51**, 1–17.

Secord, P. F. and Backman, C. W. (1964) *Social Psychology*. New York: McGraw Hill.

Serpell, R. (1976) *Culture's Influence on Behaviour*. London: Methuen.

Sharp, R. and Green, A. (1975) *Education and Social Control*. London: Routledge & Kegan Paul.

Shipman, M. (1981) *The Limitations of Social Research*. London: Longman.

Shipman, M. (1983) *Assessment in Primary and Middle Schools*. London: Croom Helm.

Shipman, M. (ed.) (1985) *Educational Research: Principles, Policies and Practice*. London: Falmer Press.

Sikes, P. J., Measor, L. and Woods, P. (1985) *Teacher Careers*. London: Falmer Press.

Silver, H. (1980) *Education and the Social Condition*. London: Methuen.

Simon, B. (1985) *Does Education Matter?* London: Lawrence & Wishart.

Sluckin, A. (1981) *Growing up in the Playground*. London: Routledge & Kegan Paul.

Snyder, B. R. (1971) *The Hidden Curriculum*. New York: Knopf.

South-West Herts. Teacher's Centre (1982) *Children Don't Listen*. Watford: Herts LEA.

Spender, D. and Sarah, E. (eds.) (1980) *Learning to Lose: Sexism and Education*. London: Women's Press.

Spradley, J. P. (1980) *Participant Observation*. New York: Holt, Rinehart & Winston.

Starkey, H. (1986) Human rights in action, *Times Educational Supplement*, 11 July.

Starkey, H. (1987) *Practical Activities for Teaching and Learning about Human Rights in Schools: A Handbook to Accompany Recommendation R(85)7 of the Committee of Ministers of the Council of Europe*. Strasbourg: Council of Europe.

Stenhouse, L. (1975) *An Introduction to Curriculum Research and Development*. London: Heinemann.

Stenhouse, L. (1983) *Authority, Education and Emancipation*. London: Heinemann.

Stewart, J. (1986) *The Making of the Primary School*. Milton Keynes: Open University Press.

Stierer, B. M. (1985) School reading volunteers; results of a postal survey of primary school heads, *Journal of Research in Reading*, **8** (1), 21–31.

Stinton, J. (1979) *Racism and Sexism in Children's Books*. London: Writers & Readers.

Strang, R. (1972) Observation in the classroom, in Melnik, A. and Merritt, J. (eds.) *The Reading Curriculum*. Milton Keynes: Open University Press.

Straughan, R. and Wilson, J. (1983) *Philosophising about Education*. London: Holt, Rinehart & Winston.

Strivens, J. (1985) School climate: a review of a problematic concept, in Reynolds, D. (ed.) *Studying School Effectiveness*. London: Falmer Press.

Stubbs, M. and Hillier, H. (eds.) (1983) *Readings on Language, Schools and Classrooms*. London: Methuen.

Sutton, C. (ed.) (1981) *Communicating in the Classroom*. London: Hodder & Stoughton.

Taba, H. (1962) *Curriculum Development, Theory and Practice*. New York: Harcourt, Brace & World.

Tann, C. S. (1981) Grouping and group work, in Simon, B. and Wilcocks, J. (eds.) *Research and Practice in the Primary Classroom*. London: Routledge & Kegan Paul.

Tann, C. S. and Armitage, M. (1986) Time for talk, *Reading*, **20** (3), 184–89.

Tattum, D. P. (ed.) (1986) *The Management of Disruptive Behaviour*. Chichester: Wiley.

Taylor, J. (1983) *Organisation and Integration in the First School*. London: Unwin.

Thomas, G. (1985) Room management in mainstream education, *Educational Research*, **27** (3), 186–193.

Tizard, B. and Hughes, M. (1984) *Young Children Learning*. London: Fontana.

Tizard, B., Mortimer, J. and Burchell, B. (1981) *Involving Parents in Nursery and Infants Schools*. London: Grant McIntyre.

Topping, K. and Wolfendale, S. (1985) *Parental Involvement in Children's Reading*. London: Croom Helm.

Torrance, E. P. (1962) *Guiding Creative Talent*. Englewood Cliffs, New Jersey: Prentice Hall.

Tough, J. (1976) *Listening to Children Talking*. London: Ward Lock.

Tough, J. (1981) *A Place for Talk*. London: Ward Lock.

Tough, J. (1985) *Talk Two: Children Using English as a Second Language*. London: Ward Lock.

Turner, J. (1975) *Cognitive Development*. London: Methuen.

Tyler, R. W. (1949) *Basic Principles of Curriculum and Instruction*. Chicago: University of Chicago Press.

United Nations (1948) *The Universal Declaration of Human Rights*. New York: United Nations.

Van Manen, M. (1977) Linking ways of knowing with ways of being practical, *Curriculum Inquiry*, **6**, 205–28.

Wadsworth, B. (1978) *Piaget for the Classroom Teacher*. New York: Longman.

Walberg, H. J. (ed.) (1979) *Educational Environments and Effects: Evaluation, Policy and Productivity*. Berkeley: McCutchan.

Walker, R. (1986) *Doing Research: A Handbook for Teachers*. London: Methuen.

Walker, R. and Adelman, C. (1975) *A Guide to Classroom Observation*. London: Methuen.

Walkerdine, V. (1983) It's only natural: rethinking child-centred pedagogy, in Wolpe, A. M. and Donald, J. (eds.) *Is There Anyone There from Education?* London: Pluto Press.

Walters, D. (1982) *Primary School Projects*. London: Heinemann.

Walton, J. (ed.) (1971) *The Integrated Day: Theory and Practice*. London: Ward Lock.

Waterhouse, P. (1983) *Managing the Learning Process*. London: McGraw Hill.

Wellington, J. J. (1986) *Controversial Issues in the Curriculum*. Oxford: Blackwell.

Werthman, C. (1963) Delinquents in school: a test for the legitimacy of authority, *Berkeley Journal of Sociology*, **8**, 39–60.

White, J. (1978) The primary teacher as servant of the state, *Education 3–13*, **7** (2), 18–23.

Whitehead, J. (ed.) (1975) *Personality and Learning*. Sevenoaks: Hodder & Stoughton.

Whitty, G. (1985) *Sociology and School Knowledge*. London: Methuen.

Willes, M. (1983) *Children into Pupils*. London: Routledge & Kegan Paul.

Willey, R. (1984) *Race, Equality and Education*. London: Methuen.

Winkley, D. (1985) *Diplomats and Detectives: LEA Advisers at Work*. London: Robert Royce.

Withall, P. H. (1949) The development of a technique for the measurement of social-emotional climate in classrooms, *Journal of Experimental Education*, **17**, 347–361.

Witkin, H. A., Moore, C. A., Goodenough, D. R. and Cox, P. W. (1977) Field-dependent cognitive styles and their educational implications, *Review of Educational Research*, 1–64.

Woods, P. (1977) Teaching for survival, in Woods, P. and Hammersley, M. (eds.) *School Experience*. London: Croom Helm.

Woods, P. (1983) *Sociology and the School: An Interactionist Viewpoint*. London: Routledge & Kegan Paul.

Woods, P. (1986) *Inside Schools*. London: Routledge & Kegan Paul.

Woods, P. (1987a) Managing the primary school teacher's role, in Delamont, S. (ed.) *The Primary School Teacher*. London: Falmer Press.

Woods, P. (1987b) Becoming a junior, in Pollard, A. (ed.) *Children and Their Primary Schools: A New Perspective*. London: Falmer Press.

Woods, P. and Pollard, A. (eds) (1987) *Sociology and Teaching: A New Challenge for the Sociology of Education*. London: Croom Helm.

Wragg, E. C. (1981) *Class Management and Control*. London: Macmillan.

Wragg, E. C. (ed.) (1984) *Classroom Teaching Skills*. London: Croom Helm.

Young, M. D. (ed.) (1971) *Knowledge and Control*. London: Collier–Macmillan.

Zeichner, K. (1981/2) Reflective teaching and field-based experience in pre-service teacher education, *Interchange*, **12**, 1–22.

Zeichner, K. M. (1986) Content and contexts: neglected elements in studies of student teaching as an occasion for learning to teach, *Journal of Education for Teaching*, **12** (1), 5–24.

Zimmet, S. G. and Hoffman, M. (1980) *Print and Prejudice*. London: Hodder & Stoughton.

Index